Mothers of PROMISE

Women *in the* Book of Genesis

TAMMI J. SCHNEIDER

Baker Academic
a division of Baker Publishing Group
Grand Rapids, Michigan

Published by Baker Academic
a division of Baker Publishing Group
P.O. Box 6287, Grand Rapids, MI 49516–6287
www.bakeracademic.com

Printed in the United States of America

Library of Congress Cataloging-in-Publication Data
Schneider, Tammi J. (Tammi Joy), 1962–
     Mothers of Promise : women in the book of Genesis / Tammi J. Schneider.
         p.   cm.
     Includes bibliographical references and index.
     ISBN 978-0-8010-2949-3 (pbk.)
     1. Matriarchs (Bible). 2. Bible. O.T. Genesis—Biography. 3. Bible. O.T. Genesis—Criticism, interpretation, etc. 4. Women in the Bible. I. Title.
BS575.S36 2008
222′.110922082—dc22   2008009542

In loving memory of my grandmother
Kate Braunstein Litwak

Contents

Acknowledgments

Many people deserve my sincere thanks for their help in the writing of this book.

I would like to thank all the people at Baker Academic who worked with me on this project. They have all been helpful and thorough. In particular I would like to single out Jim Kinney, who originally asked me what ideas I had and suggested I write the book.

There are too many students from my classes at Claremont Graduate University, Claremont School of Theology, and the Claremont Colleges to thank individually, but all the students in my classes have contributed to this work by asking the hard questions and working through many of these issues with me. In particular, I would like to single out Leah Rediger Schulte, my research assistant, for her help with all aspects of the manuscript. The women of the Orange County Jewish Feminist Institute are my students, friends, and mentors. I cannot thank them enough for what they have contributed to my research.

I am lucky to work with the two best colleagues in Hebrew Bible: Kristin De Troyer and Marvin A. Sweeney. Both are outstanding scholars who are extremely productive and yet they are always there to discuss anything from research to the personal.

Finally, my family deserves my sincerest thanks. I am lucky to have the love and support of my parents and siblings as well as a large array of cousins, some a bit removed genealogically but extremely close and loving personally. My children, Sarah and Kalilah, and husband, Farooq Hamid, bring me endless joy, ground me, and teach me what matters in the world.

Introduction

Eve got us kicked out of the garden, Sarah is mean to Hagar, Hagar runs away, Lot's wife does not listen and turns into a pillar of salt, her daughters sleep with their father, Rebekah tricks her old husband and firstborn son, Leah is a cow, her pretty sister Rachel is loved, Dinah deserves her rape, Tamar prostitutes herself, Potiphar's wife is a liar. Such is an overview of how religious leaders and scholars have described the women of Genesis.

Are these legitimate representations of female characters in Genesis? Many studies assume that women in Genesis are part of someone else's story. As secondary characters they have been treated as topics not worthy of their own category. Yet a careful reading of Genesis reveals that women function as determiners of who receives the Israelite Deity's promise.[1]

Recent studies show women's roles in the narrative are more than just footnotes to the men. Work on Sarah reveals that she is as important to the fulfillment of the Israelite Deity's promise as Abraham.[2] In Judges women are markers of how society is faring, culminating in the failure of a Levite to protect his woman, leading to her gang rape and death.[3] How women mark the life of David and the development of the royal line of Judah reveals women

---

1. Throughout the text I will refer to the entity written in Hebrew as *YHWH* as "the Deity" or "the Israelite Deity." This is not done to insult the Divine but to protect people's personal relationship with the Divine. *YHWH* is the only character in Genesis with whom most modern readers have a personal relationship. It is more difficult to gain an understanding of how this character functions in the book, especially in relationship to other characters, when using this particular character's modern name (God). Using "the Deity" distances that character from our personal relationships and places the character on a footing more similar to the others in the book.

2. Tammi J. Schneider, *Sarah: Mother of Nations* (New York: Continuum, 2004).

3. Tammi J. Schneider, *Judges*, Berit Olam (Collegeville, MN: Liturgical Press, 2000), 248.

functioning as more than secondary characters.[4] The recent dictionary of named and unnamed women edited by Meyers summarizes much of the new knowledge on women in the biblical text.[5]

At issue is how to consider the topic. Following the narrative from beginning to end does not allow for an analysis of the role and function of women, nor does it highlight those elements as part of the story. Inherent in approaching these women in categories is that they must be defined before they are investigated, something I tried to avoid in my initial research.

The data reveal that women in Genesis determine who receives the promise from the Israelite Deity. The designated heir is always male, yet the right mother is critical in that choice. The role of women as wives is significant, but their role as mothers is even more important. This thesis holds true even for Eve and for Adah and Zillah, who predate the divine promise.

The methodology for this book led me to this thesis. Women in the biblical text are seldom considered alone; instead, they are compared to others in the text, usually women.[6] The problem with this approach is that because their characters are already so connected to the actions of others, it is difficult to see what actions they carry out and how they are defined.

In this volume I examine each female character who is the singular subject of at least one verb by using a new approach, "verbing the character."[7] The goal is somehow to quantify qualitative data.[8] The approach examines each character from four perspectives: their description, their use as the subject of verbs, their use as the object of either verbs or prepositional phrases, and their relationships.

A few comments are necessary about how I employ this approach in the following study. What counts as a "description" is not just an adjective but

---

4. Elna K. Solvang, *A Woman's Place Is in the House: Royal Women of Judah and Their Involvement in the House of David*, Journal for the Study of the Old Testament Supplement 349 (London: Sheffield Academic Press, 2003).

5. Carol Meyers, preface to *Women in Scripture: A Dictionary of Named and Unnamed Women in the Hebrew Bible, the Apocryphal/Deuterocanonical Books, and the New Testament*, ed. Carol Meyers (Boston: Houghton Mifflin, 2000), ix–xv.

6. David Jobling, *1 Samuel*, Berit Olam (Collegeville, MN: Liturgical Press, 1998), 181–84. Note too Athalya Brenner, *The Israelite Woman: Social Role and Literary Type in Biblical Narrative*, Biblical Seminar 2 (Sheffield: JSOT Press, 1985), 93.

7. I would like to thank Leah Rediger Schulte for forcing me to come up with a "name" for this approach and for suggesting this title for it in her paper. If readers think the name is appropriate, the honor goes to Leah; for those who disagree with such a title for this approach, the fault lies with me.

8. Note that this approach can be applied to any of the characters of the Bible, male or female, or even divine. It is a great teaching approach in the classroom, using a white board with different colored markers to write down the terms of each category in a color-coded fashion. It can even be employed in analyzing secondary sources by doing what Rediger Schulte did in using this approach to unpack how modern scholars discuss, in her case, an ancient Egyptian pharaoh, though it could be used in any similar situation.

includes nouns applied to the character. Because the Hebrew language does not have a large class of adjectives, and nouns, especially kinship terms, define and describe characters, such nouns will be treated as "descriptions" of the characters. All the references are embedded in a literary text; thus, just because a character is the subject of a verb does not necessarily mean they are in charge of a situation. The Hebrew Bible was originally written in Hebrew (and Aramaic), and what appears in English translation as someone functioning as the subject may not be so in the original Hebrew. Because Hebrew grammar differs from English, there are places where the distinction between someone functioning as the subject is not as clear-cut as it may appear in a translation, and I will treat those cases that seem to best reflect the agency of that character.

A by-product of this method is that because many of the descriptions of women are in verses where they are subjects and objects, there is repetition. Other cases of duplication occur because many women are the object of another woman's actions and so the same situations will be repeated in different chapters. I have made every effort to minimize this repetition. Duplication is especially problematic where there is already a repetition in the Hebrew text. The problem is that each context reads differently depending on the angle from which it is viewed. I hope the reader will consider the redundancy useful for emphasizing how a different angle or lens reflects the biblical text more thoroughly.

The stress in this study is on the Hebrew and what the words mean or could mean. I use my own translations unless otherwise stated; I strive for a translation that best reflects the Hebrew text, unlike most translations, which try to make the text palatable to an English-speaking ear. As soon as one translates, one interprets, and in this examination I seek to excise some traditional interpretations that creep into the text already in the stage of translation.

This study progresses from some basic premises. There was a process by which the biblical text was constructed, but that process is either impossible or almost impossible to discern. In this analysis I treat the final result. I use the Masoretic Text as represented in *Biblia Hebraica Stuttgartensia* as the base text for my translations, though I use the versification of English versions. While employing the Masoretic Text in this volume I recognize that there is no "final" text.

The boundaries of a story govern a story. The breakdown of sections in this treatment highlights the thesis that the key function of the women in Genesis surrounds who inherits the Deity's promise.[9] In part 1 I address the matriarchs. Most traditions assume that there are four matriarchs, though the book of

9. Here the "promise" is defined as the Israelite Deity's promise of land to the offspring of Abraham in 12:7, reiterated and modified in 15:7–15 and 17:8, passed on to Isaac in 26:3–5, 23, and passed on to Jacob/Israel in 35:11.

Genesis never defines them as such. I question the concept of four matriarchs as rooted in the book of Genesis, as well as the concept that all of Jacob's children inherit the promise. Although I use the idea of four matriarchs as part of the structure of this volume, I have doubts about its veracity.

Part 2 concerns "Mothers of Potential Heirs," or "Slaves, Concubines, Daughters, and Daughters-in-Law." This section too seemed straightforward in my initial research design, since these characters are defined by their children not inheriting the promise. This situation suffers as well if the paradigm of four matriarchs with all the children of Jacob inheriting the promise is not sustained. In order to highlight and legitimate questioning the paradigm, I maintain the paradigm in the organization of the book.

Part 3 focuses on "Mothers Who Predate the Promise." This group includes mothers who predate the divine promise and whose children must therefore be categorized differently.

The final group, which we will consider in part 4, is "Women Who Do Not Bear." Prior to understanding the trend of women's roles in Genesis, most consider these women as side issues, especially since none are Israelite. Yet when the paradigm for the role of women in the text is clarified, these women tie in more neatly to the themes of the book.

I recognize that the volume of literature on Genesis, and on women in the book, is enormous. In the present study I do not refer to all of the available literature. Most of the available commentators pay little or no attention to the female characters, so I cite only a few examples.

The results of this study reveal and affect the image of women in modern scholarship and clarify that the primary role of women in the book of Genesis is to determine who will inherit the promise of the Israelite Deity.

The goal is not to answer all questions concerning women in Genesis but to present the data in such a way as to raise new questions and to answer some of those questions. This study highlights how attention to detail displayed in scholarship regarding issues of concern to male scholars has so shaped the field that the same attention to detail for female characters is only now beginning. Many details about the female characters shape the descriptions and actions of the male characters. In order to understand the role and function of the male characters, and of the Israelite Deity, we must pay attention to the fine details, role, and function of the female characters.

PART 1

Matriarchs

This section focuses on the wives of the patriarchs: Sarah, Rebekah, Leah, and Rachel. The Hebrew Bible focuses on the construction of the people Israel, and the people are formed in Genesis. The women who bear Israel must be central to the key concerns.[1] Scholarship regularly refers to "patriarchal narratives,"[2] "patriarchal stories,"[3] and "patriarchal history,"[4] clearly defining a category of "patriarchs"; thus "matriarchs" appears to be an appropriate category. "Patriarchs" is an ancient concept, with apocryphal books using the term in titles such as "Testaments of the Three Patriarchs" and "Testaments of the Twelve

1. Walter Brueggemann, *Genesis*, Interpretation: A Bible Commentary for Teaching and Preaching (Atlanta: John Knox, 1982), 2; Ronald S. Hendel, "Genesis, Book of," in *Anchor Bible Dictionary*, ed. D. N. Freedman, 6 vols. (New York: Doubleday, 1992), 2:935; Sharon Pace Jeansonne, *The Women of Genesis: From Sarah to Potiphar's Wife* (Minneapolis: Fortress, 1990), 1; Jon D. Levenson, "Genesis," in *The Jewish Study Bible*, ed. Adele Berlin and Marc Zvi Brettler (New York: Oxford University Press, 2004), 8.

2. Examples include A. R. Millard and D. J. Wiseman, eds., *Essays on the Patriarchal Narratives* (Winona Lake, IN: Eisenbrauns, 1980); most essays assume some historicity to the narratives; cf. Thomas L. Thompson, *The Historicity of the Patriarchal Narratives: The Quest for the Historical Abraham* (Harrisburg, PA: Trinity Press International, 2002), who questions the historicity of a recognized category of patriarchal narratives.

3. E. A. Speiser, *Genesis: A New Translation with Introduction and Commentary*, 3rd ed., Anchor Bible (Garden City, NY: Doubleday, 1985), liii, categorizes 12:1 as "The Story of the Patriarchs."

4. Gerhard von Rad, *Genesis*, rev. ed., Old Testament Library (Philadelphia: Westminster, 1972), 5, names 12:10 through the end of the book "The Biblical Patriarchal History."

15

Patriarchs."[5] All of the "patriarchs" have at least one female spouse who is the mother of the heir to the patriarch and the Deity's promise. The countergrouping and consideration of the matriarchs together follow this precedent.

The "matriarchs" are linked to one another through their actions, creating and maintaining descendants, devotion to the Israelite Deity, and the way the Israelite Deity rewards them. All are wives of patriarchs, stem from the right ethnic group,[6] and have a fair amount of text about them. These women are the most important for this volume because they form the basis of the thesis that the primary role of women in Genesis is to determine who will inherit the promise from the Israelite Deity. Furthermore, with the focus of Genesis on protecting the promised line, their roles in that process must be examined.

Despite solid reasons for treating these women as a group, modern scholarship does not consider this a relevant category. Commentators no longer subdivide Genesis using "patriarchy," but that does not result in usage of the term "matriarchy" or "matriarchs."[7] Even in approaches highlighting feminist concerns, the term does not appear frequently or with consistent meaning.[8] Scholars also seldom study these women in comparison to one another. When treating the patriarchs' wives, scholars usually compare the matriarchs to someone else, often a woman with whom the matriarch has a conflict or is a rival. Thus Sarah and Hagar are often paired,[9] as are Rachel and Leah.[10] Rebekah has no rival and is usually treated alone.[11]

5. E. P. Sanders, "Patriarchs, Testaments of the Three," in Freedman, *Anchor Bible Dictionary*, 5:180–81; and Marinus de Jonge, "Patriarchs, Testaments of the Twelve," in Freedman, *Anchor Bible Dictionary*, 5:181–86.

6. Rebekah, Leah, and Rachel are related to Abraham through Nahor and Milcah. Sarah will be discussed below.

7. David W. Cotter, *Genesis,* Berit Olam (Collegeville, MN: Liturgical Press, 2003), vii, refers to Gen. 12–50 as "Stories about the Troubled Family Chosen for Blessing: Genesis 12–50."

8. *Anchor Bible Dictionary* includes no entry on "matriarchs." Sarah, Rebekah, Rachel, and Leah are mothers of Israel but are not treated together or referred to as "matriarchs" in Tikva Frymer-Kensky, introduction to *Reading the Women of the Bible* (New York: Schocken, 2002), xv. They are treated as equal to patriarchs by Susan Niditch, "Genesis," in *The Women's Bible Commentary,* ed. Carol A. Newsom and Sharon H. Ringe (rev. ed. Louisville: Westminster/John Knox, 1998), 11. Athalya Brenner (*Israelite Woman,* 93) labels as matriarchs women who feature in the stories of Genesis as pairs and lists the following: Sarah and her maid, Lot's daughters, and Leah and Rachel.

9. Naomi Steinberg, "The Sarah-Hagar Cycle: Polycoity," in *Kinship and Marriage in Genesis: A Household Economics Perspective* (Minneapolis: Fortress, 1993), 35–86. Joyce Hollyday, "Sarah and Hagar: Trapped Rivals," in *Clothed with the Sun: Biblical Women, Social Justice, and Us* (Louisville: Westminster John Knox, 1994), 5–7. Katharine Doob Sakenfeld, "Sarah and Hagar: Power and Privileges," in *Just Wives? Stories of Power and Survival in the Old Testament and Today* (Louisville: Westminster John Knox, 2003), 7–26.

10. Steinberg, "The Rachel-Leah Cycle: Sororal Polygyny," in *Kinship and Marriage,* 115–34; Hollyday, "Rachel and Leah: Pawns in a Game of Love," in *Clothed with the Sun,* 8–12.

11. Steinberg, "The Rebekah Cycle: Monogamy," in *Kinship and Marriage,* 87–114; Frymer-Kensky, "The Hand that Rocks the Cradle: The Rivka Stories," in *Reading the Women,* 5–23.

Nowhere does the Masoretic Text group the matriarchs together, and no ancient text treats them as a group. I group "matriarchs" here because the role these women play is different from that of other women in Genesis and needs to be considered in parallel with the patriarchs. This section forms the basis to which other groups of women will be compared and thus will shy away from incorporating comparative discussions of the "matriarchs" with other women; I will focus on the comparative aspects when analyzing the other women.

1

Sarah

Sarah[1] is a complex figure; she is the first matriarch, married to the first patriarch, but she receives a negative evaluation by many scholars.[2] Sarah's negative reception by modern scholarship stems in part from her negative relationship with Hagar, the mother of Abraham's first son (16:16).[3]

The goal of this volume is to determine the role and function of the women in Genesis. Sarah, as the first matriarch and mother of the first heir to the Deity's promise, should hold a special place. As such, it is important to gain a clear

---

1. Sarah first appears as Sarai, and her name is not changed until Gen. 17, when Abram's name is changed to Abraham. In this volume I will refer to them as they are more commonly known: Sarah and Abraham. I will comment when the name change occurs and on the impact it has on the characters and their position in the story, but to avoid confusion I will not switch back and forth.

2. Phyllis Trible, "Hagar: The Desolation of Rejection," in *Texts of Terror: Literary-Feminist Readings of Biblical Narratives,* Overtures to Biblical Theology (Philadelphia: Fortress, 1984), 9–36, is one of the first and most influential studies to portray her in this manner, though she is defined as "cruel" as recently as Cotter, *Genesis,* 104. For some her passivity is problematic; see Esther Fuchs, "The Literary Characterization of Mothers and Sexual Politics in the Hebrew Bible," in *Feminist Perspectives on Biblical Scholarship,* ed. Adela Yarbro Collins (Atlanta: Scholars Press, 1985), 117–36. Trible argues that she is the one who needs to be tested since she is too overprotective; see Phyllis Trible, "Genesis 22: The Sacrifice of Sarah," in *Women in the Hebrew Bible: A Reader,* ed. Alice Bach (New York: Routledge, 1999), 271–92.

3. Her treatment in the New Testament may also be a factor. See Schneider, *Sarah,* 131–33.

understanding of how Sarah is described, how she acts, and how she is acted upon in the text; the nature of her relationships deserves special attention.

Sarah's Description

The Hebrew Bible does not describe its characters in much detail. When details are provided about a character they usually concern the plot surrounding them, as is the case with Sarah. The reader is introduced to Sarah early in Abraham's story,[4] though the beginning of Sarah's story is not the beginning of Abraham's. Abraham's beginning locates him in Ur of the Chaldeans as part of a family that continues into the generation following him, through the reference to Lot's birth (11:26–28). The beginning of Sarah's story does the direct opposite.

Sarah is introduced as the wife of Abraham at the same time that the reader meets Milcah, the wife of Nahor, Abraham's brother (11:29). The first issue is that the word in Hebrew for "woman" is the same as the word used for "wife," *'ishah*. While the Hebrew word for "woman" at first glance appears to be the feminized form of the word for "man," *'ish*, they actually come from different roots.[5] Thus the word "woman" is not simply the feminine form of "man." Furthermore, because the word in essence entails the sense of "female," the translator must determine when it means "woman" and when it means "wife."

In this introductory verse Sarah is named Abraham's wife, but Milcah, identified as Nahor's wife, receives the designation "daughter of Haran, the father of Milcah and Iscah" (11:29).[6] Both women are introduced as wives of Terah's sons, but Milcah has paternity; Sarah is not associated with anyone other than Abraham.[7] Some argue that this verse identifies Milcah as part of Terah's family since the previous verse just noted that Haran, Abraham's brother and son of Terah, dies. Is Milcah Nahor and Abraham's niece?[8] Note the contrast with Sarah. She has no family or city. She has no one but Abraham.

Sarah is again labeled a "wife" when the text notes that Terah takes his son Abraham; his grandson Lot, son of Haran; and his daughter-in-law Sarah, labeled the "wife" of his son Abraham, when they leave Ur of the Chaldeans

---

4. Ibid., 11–15.

5. Francis Brown, S. R. Driver, and Charles A. Briggs, *The Brown-Driver-Briggs Hebrew and English Lexicon* (repr. Peabody, MA: Hendrickson, 2000), 35 and 61.

6. Another possible translation would be "of the city of Haran" but would make the reference to Iscah more obscure.

7. For the *toledot* structure and the role Terah's line plays in the structure of the Hebrew Bible in Genesis, see Matthew A. Thomas, *These Are the Generations: Identity, Promise, and the Toledot Formula* (Ann Arbor, MI: University Microfilms, 2006).

8. Speiser, *Genesis*, 78. For more discussion of Milcah's parentage, see below in chapter 17 on Milcah.

for the land of Canaan (11:31). She is again a "wife" when Abraham takes her on a similar journey from Haran with Lot, along with the wealth they amass, and "all the souls they make" in Haran (12:4–5). She is at the bottom of Terah's list but at the top of Abraham's, though when the narrator first recounts that Abraham follows the Deity's instructions, only Lot is named as going with him (12:4).

Sarah is identified repeatedly as a "wife" when they are in Egypt. The first appearance of this title for her is when Abraham enters Egypt and says to his "wife" Sarah how beautiful she is (12:11). He continues: if the Egyptians see her and think she is his wife they will kill him and let her live (12:12). The implication is that as a wife she is a threat to Abraham. Abraham is correct about Sarah's beauty: when the courtiers see how beautiful the woman is, they praise her to Pharaoh and she is taken to his palace (12:15). Since 'ishah is the Hebrew word for both "woman" and "wife," this is a play on words: the courtiers see a "woman" even though the reader knows she is a "wife." Pharaoh is then plagued on account of Sarah, labeled "the wife of Abraham" (12:17). Pharaoh claims that he takes her for his "wife" (12:19), though he does not elaborate what that means. Finally, Pharaoh tells Abraham to take his "wife" and go.

Sarah is referred to as a "wife" twice in the Hagar episode: in the introduction (16:1) and again when Sarah takes Hagar and gives her to Abraham (16:3). Sarah is not called a "wife" when she and Abraham argue over the outcome of his encounter with Hagar.

Sarah is a "wife" when the Deity changes her name. Elohim labels Sarah "your [Abraham's] wife" when informing him that her name is Sarah (17:15).[9] Elohim again refers to her after Abraham suggests that Ishmael might live by Elohim's favor (17:19). Sarah is called Abraham's "wife" in the following chapter when the Deity's messengers tell Abraham that Sarah will have a son (18:10).

The narrator is careful to label Sarah a "wife" when Abraham tells another foreign king she is his sister (20:2). In Abimelech's dream the Deity tells Abimelech to return the "man's wife," referring to Sarah (20:7). When Abraham is asked why he said that Sarah was his sister, he admits he thought he would be killed if they knew she was his "wife" (20:11). Abimelech restores Sarah, Abraham's "wife," along with wealth (20:14). Finally, Abraham prays for Abimelech, his wives, and his slave girls, because the Deity had closed every

9. There is great speculation about the meaning behind the different terms the Hebrew Bible uses to refer to the Israelite Deity. One common explanation is that different names reveal different "authors" for the text. There are many scholarly discussions about why and how this approach does and does not work. Since I am treating the text as a unified whole, and the presentation of the characters is consistent throughout the text, I will separate the use of the Tetragrammaton from that of Elohim by referring to the first as the Deity or Israelite Deity and the second as Elohim.

womb of the household of Abimelech on account of Sarah, again labeled "the wife of Abraham" (20:17–18).

The next and final time Sarah is labeled "wife" is when Abraham buries her in Machpelah (23:19). Sarah is not labeled a "wife" when she bears Isaac, banishes and frees Hagar, or dies, but only after Abraham finishes negotiations for her burial place.

The only times Abraham refers to Sarah as a wife are when he thinks being married to her will get him killed. The Deity, the messengers of the Deity, and the narrator are the ones reminding Abraham that she is his wife and that she plays a role in Abraham's life and in naming this child who inherits the promise.

Another description of Sarah appears in the verse following her introduction as Abraham's wife (11:30) and magnifies the impact of Sarah's attachment to Abraham. Genesis 11:30 focuses only on Sarah, noting that she "is barren and she has no child." A number of problems are inherent in this verse. If Sarah is barren, what is the need to also state that she has no child? One answer may lie in the translation of the *waw* consecutive that begins the verse. Should it be translated "now" or "and"? The difference affects how the verse relates to the previous verse, which focuses on paternity, the generation before Sarah and Milcah. The second half of the verse includes a *hapax legomenon*, meaning it is the only place in the Masoretic Text where *walad*, "offspring, child," occurs.[10] Genesis 11:29 implies that Sarah has no past, and it seems unlikely, according to 11:30, that she will have a future. Trible notes, "Unique and barren Sarai . . . has neither pedigree nor fertility, neither past nor future."[11]

Abraham's next description could be considered complimentary when he tells Sarah, "Please, I know you are a woman beautiful of appearance" (12:11). Sarah's beauty is reconfirmed by the Egyptians a few verses later when the narrator notes, "the Egyptians saw the woman, that she was very beautiful" (12:14). The result of her beauty, and apparently Abraham's comment to them that she is not his wife but his sister, is that she is taken into Pharaoh's palace (12:15).

According to Bar-Efrat, "In biblical narrative information about someone's outward aspect serves solely as a means of advancing the plot or explaining its course."[12] Introducing Sarah's beauty should be connected to the plot. Since the narrator uses no other qualifiers of Sarah's physical appearance, but twice in a few verses mentions her beauty, the reference must be important.[13]

---

10. Brown, Driver, and Briggs, *Lexicon*, 409. Some manuscripts of 2 Sam. 6:23 contain a similar Kethib: *waled* (the same consonantal form, though vocalized differently).

11. Trible, "Genesis 22," 281.

12. Shimon Bar-Efrat, *Narrative Art in the Bible*, Journal for the Study of the Old Testament Supplement 70 (Sheffield: Almond, 1989), 48.

13. When Sarah is in a similar situation with Abimelech, her beauty is not mentioned (20:1–18).

There are a number of problems with the reference to beauty in this context and in the biblical text in general. In the modern world beauty is highly prized. The media would lead us to believe it is the only thing that matters.[14] Despite Frymer-Kensky's claim that beauty is always a desirable trait in a wife and, in the Bible, a mark of divine favor,[15] beauty, especially in women, often leads to trouble. The case here is one example: Sarah's beauty is raised as a threat to Abraham's life, and Sarah pays the price. Some argue that Bathsheba's beauty is what makes her attractive to David and leads to their adulterous sexual encounter (2 Sam. 11:2).[16] Tamar, daughter of David, is raped by her brother because of her beauty (2 Sam. 13:1).

What this brief review of the beauty of some women in the Hebrew Bible reveals is that beauty can be dangerous: Abraham insinuates that his life is at risk because of his wife's beauty. The way Abraham expresses his acknowledgment of her beauty is not complimentary. Van Dijk-Hemmes notes, "The expressions 'behold now/please' and 'say now/please' indicate that Abraham's speech to Sarah can be characterized as an urgent request."[17] Abraham begins the verse with an entreaty suggesting that he fears for his life.[18] Van Dijk-Hemmes also notes, "In this situation Abraham's praise of Sarah's beauty is, however, not an utterance of joy which might evoke a similar reaction from Sarah . . . but a statement of a potential risk."[19]

The ramification of Abraham's presentation of Sarah's beauty leads to Sarah being taken to Pharaoh's house (12:15). Pharaoh and his household are then afflicted with plagues because of Sarah (12:17). Pharaoh identifies the presence of Sarah in his house as the source of the plagues and says to Abraham, "Why did you not tell me she is your wife? Why did you say 'she is my sister' so that I took her as my wife?" (12:19). Nowhere does the text reveal a plan by which Abraham will retrieve Sarah from Pharaoh's house. Thus far the Israelite Deity has promised the land to Abraham's descendants, not to him (12:7). One way of understanding Sarah's beauty is that Abraham uses it to rid himself of her, his barren wife, in Egypt.[20]

Sarah's beauty leads to her description as a sister, though the veracity of that description is questionable. The first time the term "sister" appears in

---

14. For a few examples describing this for the modern world, see Naomi Wolf, *The Beauty Myth: How Images of Beauty Are Used Against Women* (New York: W. Morrow, 1991).

15. Frymer-Kensky, *Reading the Women,* 9.

16. Bar-Efrat, *Narrative Art,* 49; he refers to the sexual encounter as "licentious behaviour."

17. Fokkelien van Dijk-Hemmes, "Sarai's Exile: A Gender-Motivated Reading of Genesis 12.10–13.2," in *A Feminist Companion to Genesis,* ed. Athalya Brenner, The Feminist Companion to the Bible 1st ser., 2 (Sheffield: Sheffield Academic Press, 1993), 227.

18. There is uncertainty as to whether he is sincere in his fear. See Frymer-Kensky, *Reading the Women,* 94; and Schneider, *Sarah,* 32–34.

19. Van Dijk-Hemmes, "Sarai's Exile," 227.

20. The Israelite Deity sends plagues to inform Pharaoh of Abraham and Sarah's relationship (12:17). The Deity steps in intentionally on behalf of Sarah when Abraham does not.

connection with Sarah is in 12:13, where Abraham asks her to say she is his sister. He does not confirm the relationship nor does the genealogy (11:26–31). After he and his household are plagued because of her, Pharaoh questions why Abraham said she was his sister, thus leading Pharaoh to take her as a wife (12:19). Abraham's response is not included, and the text never verifies Abraham's suggestion that she is his sister.

Such is not the case when Abraham again claims Sarah as his sister in Gerar. Here Abraham says that Sarah his wife is his sister (20:1), leading the king, Abimelech, to have Sarah brought to him. In Abimelech's dream, he tells Elohim that he himself (referring to Abraham) says she (Sarah) is his sister (20:5). Later, Abimelech asks Abraham what his purpose was in doing this (20:10). Abraham notes that he thought they would kill him because of his wife but also claims she is his sister since she is the daughter of his father, though not of his mother (20:12). If this statement were true, it would elevate the importance of the mother in a character's background. But there is no evidence in the genealogy of Abraham or Sarah that Sarah is Terah's daughter. Thus, despite being named a sister, it is nowhere documented that Sarah is a sister to anyone. In this case, the term "sister" does not show connection of a woman to a family or to people who may be interested in protecting her but highlights how alone she is.

Another description of Sarah appears in 18:11, where she and Abraham are described as old. As with Sarah's beauty, this information is critical at this juncture of the story because Abraham has one son (Ishmael) and has just been told he will have a son through Sarah (17:16). His reaction: "he fell on his face laughing" (not the traditional translation but a fair translation of the Hebrew), commenting to himself on the unlikelihood of a child being born to a man one hundred years old or to a woman at ninety (17:17).[21] He does not describe himself or Sarah as old but does list their ages. In 18:10 Sarah hears the messengers of the Deity claim that she will have a son. In 18:11 the narrator explains Sarah's next actions, then labels the couple "old" and goes further by noting that Sarah has stopped having her period, which makes the news of the impending birth of a child extraordinary.

The narrator emphasizes her age prior to conceiving Isaac, but Abraham's servant is the only one to comment on it again. It is not referred to when she is taken by Abimelech (Gen. 20), who intends to approach her sexually (20:3–5), or when she finally conceives and bears Isaac (21:1–8). Both the narrator (21:2) and Sarah (21:7) refer to Abraham's old age at this time but not to hers. Only when Abraham's servant searches for a wife for Isaac following Sarah's death is there mention that Sarah bore his master a son in her old age (24:35). Despite Sarah's description as old only once by the narrator,

21. For more details and a discussion of commentaries on this see Schneider, *Sarah*, 58–59.

in most artistic representations of Sarah, she is pictured as old rather than beautiful.[22]

Sarah is described with five main characteristics in the Hebrew Bible: no family, married, barren, beautiful, and old. The impact of Abraham's apparent attempt to rid himself of Sarah in Egypt is magnified by what the text revealed earlier about Sarah. Sarah has no one but Abraham, and Abraham uses Sarah's beauty to rid himself of her. The Deity overturns Sarah's first descriptor, "barren," when she receives her final description, "old." Once Sarah's first description is overturned and she is no longer barren, she is also no longer alone.

Sarah carries out no action until her descriptions, with the exception of being old, are made. The narrator establishes who she is to explain why she carries out the actions she does.

Sarah as a Subject

Sarah's story begins in 11:29. She journeys with Abraham to Haran (11:31), to the land of Canaan (12:5), to Egypt (12:11–20), and stays with him when he and Lot separate (Gen. 13) and through the wars involving Lot (Gen. 14). Yet she does not act until Genesis 16! While it takes time for her to act, her actions are tied to her experiences up to that point.

Since the bulk of the narrative focuses on Abraham, a review of his actions is necessary. Abraham moves with his father, Terah, to Haran, and his new Deity tells him to move to an unknown country (12:1), where land is offered to his offspring (12:7). Famine strikes his offspring's new land and he moves temporarily to Egypt (12:10), where he lets Pharaoh take his barren wife (12:15). When Pharaoh discovers that Sarah and Abraham are married (12:17), he returns Abraham's barren wife to him (12:19). Abraham is now rich because of her (12:16; 13:2).

Abraham meets up with his nephew Lot (13:1; it is unclear if he is in Egypt with them),[23] and they have too much livestock (13:5–8), so Abraham offers Lot whatever land he wants (13:9). Lot chooses "the whole plain of the Jordan" (13:11), apparently not the original land offered to Abraham's offspring, and the Deity decides that Abraham too shall receive the land (13:15). Lot becomes caught in a battle between nations and is kidnapped (14:1–12). When Abraham learns of this (14:13) he attacks this international unified force (14:14–15), saves Lot (14:16), and gains the thanks of the kings of the plain (14:17–24). When the Deity reminds Abraham that the Deity is his shield and that his

---

22. Phyllis Silverman Kramer, "The Dismissal of Hagar in Five Art Works of the Sixteenth and Seventeenth Centuries," in *Genesis,* ed. Athalya Brenner, The Feminist Companion to the Bible 1st ser., 2 (Sheffield: Sheffield Academic Press, 1998), 195–216.

23. Schneider, *Sarah,* 36–37.

reward will be great (15:1), Abraham reminds the Deity he has been promised offspring and the Deity has not come through with them (15:2–3). The two negotiate and Abraham seals the deal with a sacrifice (15:5–21).

Sarah's story thus far is very different. There is no information about Sarah's parents—she appears as Abraham's wife (11:29). The family moves from Ur to Haran (11:31). Abraham takes her with him to the land his Deity tells him to go to (12:5). Abraham takes Sarah to Egypt during the famine and asks her to lie for him and say they are brother and sister (12:11).[24] She is given away to live in Pharaoh's house (12:15). Abraham becomes wealthy through her (12:16). Pharaoh claims to treat her as a wife (12:19), suggesting a sexual union. After Pharaoh and his people are plagued because of Sarah (12:17), Pharaoh confronts Abraham (12:18) and returns her to Abraham (12:19), though Abraham makes no such request. Sarah and Abraham are banished from Egypt (12:20).

Sarah does not appear in the narrative of chapters 13 through 15, and yet she must be affected by all that her husband goes through and accomplishes. Her husband gives away land (13:8), potentially that promised to his descendants, to Lot. Her husband forms a band to fight an international coalition of warriors to recover his nephew Lot (14:13–15), in contrast to his doing nothing to rescue her in Egypt. Sarah's husband is now an internationally recognized warrior who negotiates with the Israelite Deity (14:17–15:21). With all the wealth Abraham now has, the one reward he requests from the Deity is offspring (15:2–3). It is also the one thing Sarah cannot provide (11:20). Sarah knows that her husband considers her a liability. He has given her away once before when he considered her a threat. The reference to Pharaoh treating her as a wife implies that Abraham is not concerned about guarding sexual access to Sarah. Sarah cannot bear children, which is apparently the one thing her husband wants.

With this in mind Sarah's first actions make sense in terms of protecting herself, possibly from her husband, and fulfilling the Deity's promise. Sarah's first action is speech. Genesis 16 begins by providing two important pieces of information: Sarah has not borne Abraham any children,[25] and she has an Egyptian servant named Hagar. With this background, Sarah speaks to Abraham: "Behold please, the Deity has stopped me from bearing. Please come to my maid and maybe I will be built up through her" (16:2).

This verse has numerous issues even from the perspective of translation. Most English translations do not include a "please" in the verse. The problem

24. In the second episode in which Abraham offers Sarah to a foreign ruler, he claims they are half siblings, with the same father but different mothers. No attempt is made in Gen. 12 to pretend they are brother and sister.

25. The text states categorically that Sarah had not borne to him (Abraham) children (16:1), whereas in the earlier reference the text simply notes she had no offspring (11:30). Is this intentionally opening up the possibility that while in Pharaoh's house she bore children to someone else?

concerns how and whether to translate the Hebrew word *na'*. In the first sentence *na'* is coupled with the term *hinneh*, a word usually translated as a demonstrative particle, "Lo!" or "Behold!" which generally introduces clauses involving prediction.[26] When a proposal is a request, or entreaty, *hinneh-na'* is used.[27] In English the standard form of entreaty is "please," hence the above translation.[28] The point of an entreaty is either to be polite or to indicate that the person making the request recognizes that the other person has power to make the decision. Abraham too uses this precise phrase when asking Sarah to say she is his sister and not his wife upon their entry into Egypt (12:11), and there too it is seldom translated.

This word transforms the translation of the other verbs in the sentence. If one translates "please do . . . ," one is making a request. Without translating the entreaty, the speaker is giving a command. This difference changes the power dynamics. Without any form of entreaty, Sarah, in her first action in the narrative, is commanding Abraham to impregnate Hagar. With the entreaty Sarah is seeking his help as she explains the situation and suggests a resolution.

The second translation problem is in precisely what Sarah is asking Abraham to do. The term *'ibbaneh* literally translates as "I will be built up" and means the same as to become the mother of a son/child.[29] She is asking to have a child through Hagar, and through this process she will attain status. The verb is also a play on words because the word for "son," *ben*, sounds like the verb. Thus Sarah's first action is to suggest a plan whereby Abraham receives the son he wants, the Deity fulfills the promise, and she too benefits. Sarah's suggestion does not differ from what Abraham asks Sarah to do earlier in Egypt.[30]

Sarah brings the Israelite Deity into the conversation by stating that it is the Deity who has kept her from bearing. Thus far in the narrative there is nothing to indicate any attitude Sarah should or should not exhibit toward the Deity. Since the idea of worshiping the Israelite Deity is somewhat new with Abraham, and the Deity has spoken only to Abraham thus far, why should Sarah mention the Deity at all? The text contains no indication that Sarah knows of the Deity's role in freeing her from Egypt, and yet she is the one to bring the Deity into the conversation. Since the chapter follows immediately upon the Deity's promise to Abraham for children, not including the name of the mother in that promise, Sarah's actions are in full compliance with the

26. Brown, Driver, and Briggs, *Lexicon*, 243–44.

27. Ibid.

28. Many do not agree with the translation. Gender issues are involved because there is a pattern of the term not being translated specifically in cases involving female characters.

29. Brown, Driver, and Briggs, *Lexicon*, 125. Note that the Deity uses the same verb to "build" the woman in the garden (2:22).

30. J. Cheryl Exum, "Who's Afraid of 'The Endangered Ancestress'?" in Bach, *Women in the Hebrew Bible*, 142.

Deity's promise, and "Sarai's plan will meet with divine sanction."[31] Sarah's first words—her first action—suggest her acknowledgment of the Israelite Deity as the one who controls her destiny.

The next time Sarah speaks she again invokes the Deity, this time in anger against Abraham. Sarah's plan for Abraham to impregnate Hagar is successful. Hagar's reaction to pregnancy provokes a reaction, and Sarah continues to act through speech, saying, "My wrong is upon you! I gave my slave to your bosom and now that she sees she is pregnant I am lowered in her esteem. Let the Deity judge between you and me" (16:5). These are strong words from Sarah, who prior to this speaks only with entreaty. Clearly she is unsettled and deeply angered by Hagar's reproach and considers Abraham at fault. She is so certain she is correct that she calls upon Abraham's Deity, this time to adjudicate the situation.

Sarah's use of legal language may relate to legal precedents in the ancient Near East. According to the Code of Hammurabi: "If a man marries a *nadītu*, and she gives a slave woman to her husband, and she (the slave) then bears children, after which that slave woman aspires to equal status with her mistress—because she bore children, her mistress will not sell her; she shall place upon her the slave-hairlock, and she shall reckon her with the slave women."[32] Hammurabi's law addresses a woman in a specific status, a *nadītu*; there is no evidence in the Hebrew Bible that Sarah has this status.[33] This is an example of how severely Old Babylonian society considered the actions of a slave.

There is no record of Sarah saying anything again until after she bears Isaac. Here she says, "Elohim has made me laughter. All the ones who hear will laugh with me" (21:6). Sarah continues, "Who would have said to Abraham, Sarah will suckle children? Yet I have borne a son in his old age" (21:7). This time her speech expresses nothing but joy.

Abraham heeds Sarah's first spoken suggestion (16:3), leading to Sarah's next actions as she carries out the plan she suggested earlier. To do this she

---

31. Steinberg, *Kinship and Marriage*, 61.

32. Martha T. Roth, *Law Collections from Mesopotamia and Asia Minor*, Society of Biblical Literature Writings from the Ancient World 6 (Atlanta: Scholars Press, 1995), 109. The Code of Hammurabi (§46) is used here as an example of how the role and relationship of slaves and their owners was adjudicated in certain circumstances. This is not to say that this form of law was used when the stories of Sarah and Abraham were written, but it is one example, dating to the 18th century BCE, well known in both the ancient and modern worlds, of how someone thought such an issue should be resolved. For discussion surrounding the role and function of the Code of Hammurabi, see Jean Bottéro, "The Code of Hammurabi," in *Mesopotamia: Writing, Reasoning, and the Gods*, trans. Zainab Bahrani and Marc Van De Mieroop (Chicago: University of Chicago Press, 1992), 156–84. For an introduction to general law in the ancient Near East, see Samuel Greengus, "Legal and Social Institutions of Ancient Mesopotamia," in *Civilizations of the Ancient Near East*, ed. Jack M. Sasson, 4 vols. (New York: Charles Scribner's Sons, 1995), 1:469–84.

33. For more on the *nadītu* see Norman Yoffee, "The Economy of Ancient Western Asia," in Sasson, *Civilizations of the Ancient Near East*, 3:1395–96.

"takes" (*laqach*) her maid, Hagar the Egyptian, and gives her to her husband, Abraham, "a woman for a wife." The last phrase, "a woman for a wife," has generated a wide range of translations and meanings.

The Hebrew *'ishah lo le'ishah* could be translated a number of ways, including: "as a concubine" (NJPS), "to be his wife" (KJV), and "as a wife" (NRSV). The issue is whether she becomes a concubine, "like" a wife, or an actual wife.

The translation "concubine" stems from Speiser's treatment of the phrase connecting it to the Akkadian cognate *ashshatum*,[34] which he argues may signify either "wife" or "concubine." Since Akkadian uses the term *hirtum* for "wife" in nonlegal contexts, meaning "chosen woman," he translates "concubine" here.[35] He is influenced by the situation at Nuzi, where a childless wife is required to provide a concubine to her husband to procure children.[36] Scholars' dependence on the Nuzi archive as an explanation for what is happening in the Hebrew Bible is used less often more recently because of the publication of more Nuzi material.[37] Despite this, biblical translators have followed Speiser's understanding, even into the recent *Jewish Study Bible*, which follows the NJPS translation.[38] What this translation offers is a way for Sarah to give Hagar to Abraham without including marriage rights.

The translation "as a wife" skirts the issue whether Hagar is promoted to wife. Translating "to be his wife" implies that Abraham is taking her as an official wife. There is much discussion about the role of second wives and concubines in the Hebrew Bible.[39] Despite all this discussion, the Hebrew Bible primarily legislates monogamy.[40]

Genesis 16:3 is not the first time that the phrase *le'ishah* appears in Sarah's story. Pharaoh asks, when referring to what happens to Sarah, "Why did you say 'she is my sister' so that I took her to me for a wife (*le'ishah*)?" (12:19). Regardless of Hagar's status, the text states that Sarah is giving Hagar to Abraham exactly as Abraham gives Sarah to Pharaoh.

34. Speiser, *Genesis*, 117.
35. Ibid.
36. Ibid., 121.
37. For the change in how Nuzi material relates to the Hebrew Bible, see Barry L. Eichler, "Nuzi and the Bible: A Retrospective," in *DUMU-E2-DUB-BA-A: Studies in Honor of Ake W. Sjoberg*, ed. Erle Leichty, Occasional Publications of the Samuel Noah Kramer Fund 11 (Philadelphia: University Museum, 1989), 107–20.
38. Levenson, "Genesis," 36.
39. Peggy L. Day's definition of "concubine" highlights the problems involved: "A female whose status to her sole legitimate sexual partner, a nonslave male, is something other than primary wife" (Peggy L. Day, "Concubine," *Eerdmans Dictionary of the Bible,* ed. David Noel Freedman [Grand Rapids: Eerdmans, 2000], 273).
40. Victor P. Hamilton, "Marriage (OT and ANE)," in Freedman, *Anchor Bible Dictionary*, 4:559–69. To some extent the only legislation of polygamy is Deut. 21:15, which deals with the inheritance of the son of an unloved wife.

Sarah's next action concerns Hagar's reaction to pregnancy. Sarah's plan works, Hagar conceives, and the text notes that Sarah does something in Hagar's eyes (16:4), usually translated along the lines of, "was lowered in her esteem" (NJPS). The form of the verb describing Sarah first appears as a stative in the narrator's description of Hagar's actions, where it is in a "neutral" voice (16:4), whereas in the next verse Sarah is the subject when she states, "I am lowered in her esteem" (16:5). The Hebrew verb is *qalal*, and its base meaning is "to be slight," and here "to be despised, counted as trifling."[41]

How one translates the verb here relates to how people view both Hagar and Sarah. Most English translations treat what happens to Sarah as a personal slight, yet an evaluation of the term reveals that its meaning is harsher than a personal insult. According to Exodus 21:17 one who "insults" one's parents should be killed. When Shimei does this to David, it is argued that he should be killed (2 Sam. 19:22). In Genesis 12:3 the Deity claims, "I will bless those who bless you and curse those who curse you." The Hebrew uses two different verbs for "to curse" here. The first, those who do this to Abraham, is the Piel (intensive form) of *qalal*, the Qal form of which occurs in 16:5. The Israelite Deity's response uses *'arar*, an action more severe and reserved for what the Deity does to the serpent and the ground as a result of the fruit episode (3:14, 17). Thus Sarah is treated and made to feel a way that would draw a severe curse from the Deity (12:3) if it were done to Abraham.

Abraham acquiesces to Sarah and she carries out her next action: she "abuses" Hagar (16:6). The verb is *'anah*, which has a base meaning of "be bowed down, afflicted," and in transitive use means "to afflict."[42] Sarah is not distressed that Hagar is pregnant; she is upset that she has been "lowered in her esteem," and so she does to Hagar what Hagar has done to her, using a slightly different verb. This verb is from the same root used for what the Egyptians later do to the Israelites (Exod. 1:11–12). There the more the Egyptians "oppress" (*'anah*) the Israelites, the more they increase and spread (Exod. 1:12), precisely what Hagar is about to do, increase. This term reminds the reader of what happens to Sarah earlier at the hands of Hagar and what will happen to the Israelites when they go to Egypt.

While more happens in Genesis 16, Sarah does not appear, though Sarah's actions from 16:2 have the desired outcome: Abraham has a child.

Sarah does not act again until 18:10, where she listens at the tent to the word of the Deity's messengers (18:10). When changing Sarai's name to Sarah (17:15), the Deity decrees that Sarah will have a child (17:16), and it is Sarah's child who will inherit the Deity's covenant (17:19). The Deity will bless Ishmael and he will be fertile, and the Deity will make him a great nation (17:20); but the

41. Cf. Brown, Driver, and Briggs, *Lexicon*, 886.
42. Ibid., 776. The form here is the Piel of *'anah*, thus meaning, "humble, mishandle, afflict."

Deity stresses that the covenant will be maintained with Isaac (17:21). Prior to Sarah's listening at the tent door, the Deity had promised Abraham that Sarah would have a child who would inherit the covenant with the Deity. Her reaction indicates that Abraham has neglected to inform her of this promise.

What Abraham does not share with Sarah is likely the point of the messengers' visit.[43] Gunn and Fewell argue that the Deity must send a messenger because Abraham never agrees to the Deity's plan for Sarah to become the mother of the heir to the covenant.[44]

Sarah's response confirms that this is her first hearing of her impending pregnancy.[45] Sarah's reaction is to laugh to herself, adding, "Now that I am withered, am I to have pleasure, and with my husband so old?" (18:12). This follows the narrator's note that Sarah and Abraham are both old and that Sarah has stopped having her period. Her laughter and comment are to herself.

The rest of Sarah's comment has received a range of interpretation. The first element, "now that I am withered," is Sarah reconfirming what the narrator notes in the previous verse: she is old and has stopped having her period (18:11). The continuation, "am I to have pleasure?" indicates that this is an act she views positively. The term, often translated as "joy," is 'ednah; it has the sense of "delight" and carries a sexual connotation.[46]

The final element of the verse, "and with my husband so old?" is directed toward Abraham's abilities. According to Darr, the rabbis noticed this and commented, "Abraham might have taken amiss what his wife had said about his advanced years."[47] This is the only place in the Hebrew Bible where Sarah refers to her husband as 'adoni, meaning "my husband," but the term 'adon also means "lord."[48] This verse is the prooftext for the New Testament reference in 1 Peter 3:6 where Sarah is an example of holy women who trust in God by subjecting themselves to their husbands because Sarah obeys Abraham and calls him "lord." The New Testament uses this verse to emphasize how docile Sarah is, obeying her husband, though the original context denotes Sarah's surprise that he will perform the necessary function to impregnate her. Sarah's response to the news is positive. She laughs (usually indicating happiness), refers to the sexual encounter she is expecting as joy, and is surprised about her husband's abilities.

Sarah's next action is to lie, though an intervening verse modifies her actions. Following her expression to herself, the Deity asks Abraham why Sarah

43. Schneider, *Sarah*, 71.

44. Dana Nolan Fewell and David F. Gunn, *Gender, Power, and Promise: The Subject of the Bible's First Story* (Nashville: Abingdon, 1993), 103.

45. Jeansonne, *Women of Genesis,* 24.

46. Brown, Driver, and Briggs, *Lexicon*, 726.

47. Katheryn Pfisterer Darr, "More than the Stars of the Heavens: Critical, Rabbinical, and Feminist Perspectives on Sarah," in *Far More Precious than Jewels: Perspectives on Biblical Women*, Gender and the Biblical Tradition 1 (Louisville: Westminster John Knox, 1991), 103.

48. Brown, Driver, and Briggs, *Lexicon*, 10–11.

laughs, implying that Sarah says, "Is it true that I will bear?" The Deity has not been in any of the scenes thus far, but the Deity and the Deity's messengers are somewhat interchangeable in this episode. What the Deity tells Abraham that Sarah says is not what the narrator informs the reader that Sarah says. According to the text, Sarah laughs in joy about having a sexual encounter with her aged husband; she is excited he will be able to perform. The Deity asks Abraham why Sarah laughs, though he is not there; she is in a tent, by herself, laughing. When Abraham hears the news that Sarah will bear a child, he falls down on his face laughing (17:17). His comments directly pertain to the Deity's question about Sarah because Abraham's comments to himself question whether a child can be born to a man one hundred years old or to Sarah, who is ninety (17:17).

Abraham has no answer, and someone (it is not clear who) asks if anything is too wondrous for the Deity and reiterates that he (presumably the messenger of the Deity) will return next year and Sarah will have a son (18:14). The text shifts and is traditionally translated, "Sarah lied, saying, 'I did not laugh,' for she was frightened. But He replied, 'You did laugh'" (18:15 NJPS). This verse is translated and treated as Sarah lying to the Deity, who then asserts that she laughed. The text confirms that Sarah laughs earlier but not who she fears or who uses her laughter as proof. Most translations assume that the Deity is the speaker, though the text does not state this explicitly.

Sarah fears Abraham. She has no reason to fear the Deity, who repeatedly comes to her aid, saving her from Pharaoh's house (12:17), blessing her and promising her a son (17:16), and in this chapter sending messengers to inform her. Sarah has reason to fear Abraham. Abraham gives her to Pharaoh in Egypt, allows Hagar to treat her with disrespect, and does not inform her of the Deity's promise of a child. Thus it is likely Abraham who charges her with laughing.

The grammar supports the interpretation that Abraham speaks to Sarah. The narrator does not name the male speaker. The subject of the verb "lie" is Sarah, and the subject of the next verb is a third masculine singular person. The last male speaker is the messenger of the Deity, though there is some confusion in this text as to the difference between the Deity and the messenger of the Deity. Another reason for doubting that the Deity speaks here is that the Deity never speaks with Sarah before or after this verse. Throughout this chapter the messengers do not speak to her directly; she is hidden from everyone's sight—everyone but Abraham (18:6).

Who would speak to Sarah? Abraham laughs when he hears the news that Sarah and he will have a child together, yet when the Deity accuses Sarah of doing so, Abraham says nothing (18:13). The purpose of the messengers' visit is to inform Sarah of Isaac's birth, news only Abraham and the Deity have (17:16). Sarah's private response (18:12) does not question the Deity's plans, as does the later account of her inner speech (18:13). The Israelite Deity conveys the interpretation to Abraham (18:13), and the Deity may know about Abraham's doubting laughter when he originally receives the news (17:17). The one whom Sarah fears is most likely her husband. He has not protected her in the past, though he has protected others (such as Lot in 14:13–16). Thus it is likely Abraham who says, "No, you did laugh," and whom Sarah fears. Her fear of Abraham could explain why she might lie to him.

Sarah's next action is a direct result of the announcement in Genesis 18, though it takes a few chapters until she has her child. Sarah appears in the text, and many things happen to her family in the interim, but she does not say or do anything.[49] Despite the text's claims in both chapters 17 and 18 that Abraham and Sarah will have a child, that reality seems suspect because of the Abimelech episode. As in Egypt, Abraham claims that Sarah is his sister and not his wife, so she is taken by Abimelech, king of Gerar (20:2). There are significant differences between the two stories, such as: no reason for going there is mentioned; Elohim comes to Abimelech in a dream, so he does not touch Sarah (20:3); Abraham claims that they are siblings, sharing the same father but not mother (20:12); and Abimelech pays something to Abraham to protect her image (20:16). The timing of the two episodes also differs considerably: in Gerar the Deity has just announced that Abraham and Sarah will have a child together. A final difference is that Abraham prays for the Deity to open the wombs of the women under Abimelech's control since the Deity had closed them on account of Sarah (20:17). Only after Abraham prays to Elohim do Abimelech's wife and slave girls bear children (20:18), and so does Sarah.

Despite all the buildup to the birth of Sarah's child, she conceives and bears a son in one verse (21:2). Her advanced age is not mentioned.

When Isaac is weaned, Abraham holds a celebration. The text is vague about the relationship of this event to Sarah's subsequent actions. Either at that event or shortly thereafter Sarah sees the son whom Hagar the Egyptian bears to Abraham "playing" (*metsacheq*) with Isaac (21:9). Precisely what Sarah sees is debated, ranging from the two boys playing to Ishmael sexually molesting Isaac.[50] Many scholars focus on what Sarah sees and on assumptions about her personality and the motivation that leads to her actions.[51] Since her next action leads to banishing Hagar and Ishmael, presumably what she sees is the issue. But it is possible that it is not what she sees but when she sees it.

49. Abimelech claims "she," presumably Sarah, said to him, independently of Abraham, "He is my brother" (20:5). Because it is in the words of Abimelech, it will not count here as a direct action by Sarah.

50. For the former see NRSV, which follows both the Septuagint and Vulgate in including "with her son Isaac" in the text. For a discussion of the latter see Robert Alter, *Genesis: Translation and Commentary* (New York: Norton, 1996), 98. For a detailed discussion see Schneider, *Sarah*, 93–94.

51. Cotter, *Genesis*, 141; Speiser, *Genesis*, 155; von Rad, *Genesis*, 232.

Some scholars discuss weaning in the ancient world and when it happens, but they seldom consider the emotional impact. Since a high infant mortality rate is assumed and weaning is an event indicating that the child lived through infancy, then the event marking weaning must have an emotional impact on the mother: her child has survived. The text emphasizes this in Sarah's earlier comments about suckling a child. There she does not comment upon the unlikelihood she would bear a child and survive the birth but that she would have the ability to suckle the child. Thus the narrator hints that the event celebrating that she no longer needs to suckle him and that she manages to bring her child through that period has great meaning for her.

The emphasis is not on Ishmael but on his mother, Hagar the Egyptian. Sarah never utters either's name. The verse recounting Isaac and his brother "playing" is in the narrator's voice, and the reader is reminded that Hagar is Egyptian. The narrator does not indicate Hagar's status.

The next verse is in Sarah's voice, and here her words are a command: "Banish this slave and her son because the son of this slave will not inherit with my son, with Isaac" (21:10).[52] Sarah focuses on Hagar's status, twice referring to her as an *'amah* (female slave).[53] Relevant here is that Sarah refers to Hagar with a title Hagar has not yet had.

Sarah focuses on the fact that Hagar is a slave and that her son will not inherit with Isaac. Harsh as this may seem, it is in line with the Deity's promise to Abraham, as early as 17:19. Despite the Deity's clarity, Abraham's actions are not straightforward. The text refers to Ishmael as Abraham's son (16:15; 17:23, 25–26), but Abraham never labels Ishmael his son. Yet, Abraham pleads for Ishmael to the Deity (17:18), circumcises him as soon as he learns of that command (17:25), never asks for a son by Sarah, and does not encourage the probability of such an event (Gen. 20). Abraham has shown no intention of carrying out the Deity's wish for Isaac to inherit.

Ancient Near Eastern law and custom may explain why Sarah fears for her son's inheritance. Regulations in the Laws of Lipit-Ishtar stipulate:

> If the second wife whom he marries bears him a child, the dowry which she brought from her paternal home shall belong only to her children: the children of the first-ranking wife and the children of the second wife shall divide the property of their father equally. (Lipit-Ishtar 24)

> If a man marries a wife and she bears him a child and the child lives and a slave woman also bears a child to her master, the father shall free the slave woman and her children; the children of the slave woman will not divide the estate with the children of the master. (Lipit-Ishtar 25)

52. This frees Hagar, to be discussed below in chapter 6 on Hagar.
53. Brown, Driver, and Briggs, *Lexicon*, 51, defines as "handmaid" or "maid." For more discussion see chapters 6, 8, and 9 on Hagar, Zilpah, and Bilhah, respectively.

If his first-ranking wife dies and after his wife's death he marries the slave woman (who had borne him children), the child of his first-ranking wife shall be his (primary) heir; the child whom the slave woman bore to her master is considered equal to a native free-born son, and they shall make good his (share of the) estate. (Lipit-Ishtar 26)[54]

According to the Laws of Lipit-Ishtar, much depends on Hagar's status: is she a wife or is Abraham planning to marry her, possibly after Sarah's death?

Ishmael's status would be cause for alarm according to the Code of Hammurabi:

If a man's first-ranking wife bears him children and his slave woman bears him children, and the father during his lifetime then declares to (or: concerning) the children whom the slave woman bore to him, "My children," and he reckons them with the children of the first-ranking wife—after the father goes to his fate, the children of the first-ranking wife and the children of the slave woman shall equally divide the property of the paternal estate; the preferred heir is a son of the first-ranking wife, he shall select and take a share first. (§170)[55]

The children of Zilpah and Bilhah inherit land and are counted as legitimate sons of Jacob, and their sons seem to inherit with the sons of Rachel and Leah. Even internal biblical material indicates that Sarah has reason to worry about the inheritance status of her son and Ishmael. But the Deity notes that Isaac will inherit the promise, not Ishmael (17:19).

Sarah's command to banish Hagar and Ishmael is her penultimate action. Sarah does not send them off herself; she commands Abraham to do it, and he does.

Following Isaac's survival of his trip with his father and after the announcement that Milcah too has borne children (Gen. 22), Sarah carries out her last action: she dies (23:2).

A summary of Sarah's actions reveals some interesting issues. All of her actions, except two, center on procuring a child for Abraham and ensuring that her child inherits. The two exceptions concern how she is treated in her efforts to do the others. In the first case, she is "lowered" in Hagar's eyes, immediately after giving Hagar to Abraham so he could have a child. The term used for this could also be understood a "weakened curse," the kind that could draw a more severe curse from the Deity.[56] The second action is her lie about laughing. The narrator notes that she lies about laughing; her reasons for lying and her fear are directed toward Abraham.

54. These laws show that at some point in time, for the Laws of Lipit-Ishtar, in the southern Mesopotamian city of Isin ca. 1930 BCE, this is how these issues were adjudicated. For more about Lipit-Ishtar and the translation used here, see Roth, *Law Collections,* 23–24, 30–31.

55. Ibid., 113–14.

56. See the earlier discussion on p. 30.

Sarah as an Object

One of the most common actions done to Sarah is that she is "taken." Terah takes her, along with Abraham and Lot, to Canaan (11:31). When Abraham is told to go forth from the house of his father, he takes Sarah and Lot (12:5). Sarah is taken by Pharaoh's courtiers into his house (12:15), where he takes her for a wife (12:18). She is taken because she is beautiful (12:15). After the Deity's intercession on Sarah's behalf, Pharaoh tells Abraham, "Take her and go." (12:19).

The next action taken against her is by Hagar, in whose eyes she is lowered (16:4). This follows Sarah's act of giving Hagar to Abraham, though that action is one already carried out against her.

Only in Genesis 17 are positive actions taken toward Sarah, and all are carried out by the Israelite Deity. Sarah's name is changed from Sarai to Sarah. Scholars refer to this as a name change, though the way the Hebrew presents it is not as a change, since the text does not use that terminology, as it does with Abraham (17:5). Instead the Deity states, "Sarai, your wife, you will no longer call her name Sarai because Sarah is her name" (17:15). This is worded as though the Deity is not changing her name but correcting Abraham, as if he has been calling her the wrong name all along. It is also here that the Deity blesses her and reveals to Abraham he will have a son by her and that she will give rise to nations and that rulers of peoples shall issue from her (17:16).

In the following chapter Abraham commands Sarah to make cakes (18:6). It is not clear why she is charged with this task (Hagar does not appear in this episode) or if she does it, since the text does not note that she does and no cakes are served (18:8). Someone replies to her that she did laugh, and she fears that entity, though the text does not state who it is (18:15). Despite the impending pregnancy Sarah is again brought to another man (20:2). To rectify the relationship misunderstanding, Abimelech says to Sarah that he is giving "her brother" one thousand pieces of silver, apparently to clear his good name (20:16).

Again positive things happen to Sarah through the actions of the Deity. The Deity takes note of Sarah and does for her as the Deity had said (21:1), resulting in her conceiving and bearing a son to Abraham precisely at the time when the Deity had said she would (21:2). The Deity also tells Abraham to listen to her voice (21:12).

The last actions carried out on Sarah's behalf concern her death. Abraham comes to her (23:3), mourns for her (23:2), buys a burial plot for her (23:3–18), and buries her in the cave of Machpelah (23:19). Following her death, her son Isaac brings his new wife to Sarah's tent and finds comfort in Rebekah, which is tangentially an action concerning her (24:66).

This section highlights how Sarah is "taken" by most men in her life, even in her old age. Few actions carried out concerning her are positive. The main positive actions carried out toward her are by the Deity and her son.

Sarah's Relationships

Marriage in the Hebrew Bible is difficult to define, especially when viewing it from a modern vantage point. The reality is that the Hebrew Bible has examples of the full range of marital relationships, from multiple wives to loving husbands. A norm would be difficult to determine. Rather than assume that any ancient relationship was one way or another, in this volume I will evaluate the relationships of the couples based only on the interactions described in the data provided in Genesis.

There is little interaction between Sarah and Abraham. Whatever vestiges of a relationship there may be are qualified by the fact that the narrator does not view the nature of their relationship as a central issue but raises it only to move the story forward, in much the same way that description is used to advance the plot.

The text reveals nothing about why or how the marriage is arranged. Abraham claims to Abimelech that they are truly brother and sister, of the same father but different mothers (20:12), but there is no evidence of this in the genealogy of Sarah or Abraham (11:26, 29). The narrator hints that Milcah might be related to Abraham through his brother, Haran, who is also listed as Milcah's father (11:29). Sarah, who has no paternity, is contrasted with Milcah, who has clear paternity. Furthermore, the Deity commands Abraham to leave his father's house (12:1), and he takes Sarah with him (12:5); she would be part of his house if they were siblings through his father (he also takes Lot with him, a possible violation of the Deity's command).

When they approach Egypt Abraham asks her to say that she is his sister, another case where if they were related the narrator could have noted it. While Abraham's treatment of Sarah has not been categorized traditionally as selling his wife, to some extent that is what happens. Abraham has no strategy to retrieve her, so the Deity frees her from Pharaoh's house (12:17). This episode contrasts with the following story of Lot in which, because their flocks are too great, they must separate (13:8). Sarah is given away, supposedly to protect Abraham's life, whereas Lot is given land. The contrast between what Abraham will do for Lot versus what he will or will not do for Sarah is highlighted in Genesis 14, where Abraham fights an international army to protect Lot.

When Sarah gives Hagar to Abraham and trouble ensues, Sarah blames Abraham for the problem (16:5). When the messengers of the Deity visit Abraham, Sarah's comments about her impending sexual encounter with Abraham hint that they have ceased having sexual relations (18:11). If the person Sarah fears is Abraham, this would be a clear indication of a lack of harmony between them.

In Genesis 20 Abraham again gives away his wife. This time Abimelech claims that Sarah too says they are siblings (20:5), so the onus is not only on Abraham this time. Clearly some union must take place between Sarah and

Abraham subsequent to Genesis 18 since Isaac is born to Sarah and Abraham is the father (21:2). Sarah is pleased that she is suckling her son in Abraham's old age (21:7), but the text reveals nothing about their relationship.

The final encounter between Sarah and Abraham has an angry Sarah banishing Hagar and Ishmael. The narrator states, "The matter distressed Abraham very much" (21:11), but does not focus on what the matter is other than, "because it concerned a son of his" (21:11). A number of issues are raised by Sarah's demand and all concern his sons, so the verse is vague. It is not clear what Abraham intends to do about Sarah's command until Elohim intercedes (21:12).

There is no record of the two interacting again. After the incident with Isaac, Abraham departs for Beer-sheba and, according to the text, stays there (22:18). When Sarah dies she is in Kiriath-arba/Hebron (21:2). It is not clear whether Abraham is with her when she dies, since according to the Hebrew text Abraham has to come to her (23:2). At best one could say the data reveal that they had a long marriage that was fraught with difficult situations. One could also say that each of them makes difficult decisions that the other one agrees to, with more or less consent. Anything else is conjecture.

Such is not the case with Sarah's son, Isaac. The debate about what makes a good mother is complex and often politicized.[57] What is clear is that Sarah takes action to procure a son for Abraham (16:2). The Deity decrees that she will have a son (17:16). She is joyful when she learns the news (18:12). She is happy when her son is born (21:6) and she can nurse him (21:7). When she fears that her son's place in Abraham's family is at risk, she acts (21:10). To some this is a woman who wants a child and takes seriously her responsibility to protect her child, and those are positive traits. For others, like Trible, these traits demand that "she find liberation from possessiveness and that she free Isaac from maternal ties."[58]

The analysis of Sarah as a mother is rooted in what various religious traditions believe should be one's approach to the Divine and what the goal of a life is. Trible's full quotation reveals one approach toward the Divine by claiming, "The dynamic of the entire saga, from its genealogical preface on, requires that Sarah be featured in the climactic scene [i.e., sacrifice of Isaac, Gen. 22], that she learn the meaning of obedience to God, that she find liberation from possessiveness, that she free Isaac from maternal ties, and that she emerge a solitary individual, nonattached, the model of faithfulness."[59] Trible has applied New Testament and Christian ideas of faith in God to what the Hebrew Bible character of Sarah "should" and "should not" do. Her comments demand something of a figure in the Hebrew Bible that is never

57. Susan J. Douglas and Meredith W. Michaels, *The Mommy Myth: The Idealization of Motherhood and How It Has Undermined All Women* (New York: Free Press, 2004).

58. Trible, "Genesis 22," 286.

59. Ibid., 285.

intended by the narrator. Nowhere in the Hebrew Bible is being "attached" identified as a problem.

There is little material on Isaac himself, and less on his relationship to his mother, though the biblical text reveals that Isaac appreciates his mother or at least her actions. Abraham's servant finds Rebekah as a wife for Isaac and brings her to him (24:66). In the following verse he brings her to the tent of his mother Sarah as his wife (24:67). The verse notes that Isaac loves her, and "he finds comfort" after his mother's death.

Little is known about women's tents, how they receive them, who is allowed into them, and what is done inside the tent versus outside the tent. Despite this, the reference to Isaac still having Sarah's tent is striking, especially since he is the only son to do so. The Hebrew Bible does not state Isaac's age explicitly when this event happens, but Sarah is one hundred and twenty-seven years old when she dies (23:1), she is ninety or ninety-one years old when she bears Isaac (17:17), and Isaac is forty years old when he marries Rebekah (25:19). Therefore, Isaac mourns his mother for three or four years after her death.

One who probably does not mourn Sarah's death is Hagar. Sarah's relationship with Hagar, and by extension with her son Ishmael, is fraught with problems and, for many scholars, defines Sarah's character. Despite the impact the two have on each other, there is no recorded conversation between them. All their interactions are in the words of the narrator recording what happens, or Sarah's remarks to Abraham about what has happened or should happen.

The narrator does not explain how Hagar comes into Sarah's possession but does state that Sarah has an Egyptian servant (16:1). The reference to Hagar as Egyptian follows Sarah's experience in Egypt when Pharaoh takes her as a wife (12:15–19). Thus Sarah does to Hagar as Abraham does to Sarah.

Sarah reacts to the way Hagar treats her when she learns she is pregnant (16:4). It is uncertain if it is this action that makes clear to Sarah that any son Hagar bears will not be counted as Sarah's (apparently, according to 16:2, Sarah's original intention), or if Sarah would not accept a son of Hagar as her own, but in either case the original plan is no longer functioning. Sarah's response is to take it out on Hagar, severely (16:6). Hagar follows the Deity's messenger's command to return to Sarah and submit to her harsh treatment (16:10), but the text does not recount what happens when she returns. Hagar is absent until after the birth of Isaac. There is no hint as to where Hagar is when the angels or the messengers arrive to tell Sarah the news that she will have a child, nor do we know Hagar's whereabouts when the couple visits Abimelech of Gerar and Sarah is again given to another foreign ruler (Gen. 20).

Sarah and Hagar's relationship is revisited only when Sarah's son is weaned. Based on the few references to weaning, von Rad determines that children were weaned around three to four years of age (citing 1 Sam. 1:23; 2 Macc. 7:27).[60]

60. Von Rad, *Genesis*, 232.

Thus there is some period of time when Isaac is born and Ishmael and Hagar are living with them in some configuration in which there is no turmoil, or at least none that is reported. It is only when Isaac is weaned or only when Sarah sees Ishmael "playing" with Isaac that trouble erupts.

The above discussion clarifies that while Sarah focuses her remarks on Hagar (Gen. 21:10), she emphasizes inheritance. Sarah's attention to the status of Ishmael's mother emphasizes elements about her that deal with inheritance: Hagar is a slave. This situation is not a personality clash but concerns inheritance issues. Thus, as with all of Sarah's actions, the key points in her relationship with Hagar concern who is Sarah's child and heir of the promise.

Though some of the actions Sarah carries out against Hagar are not "nice," Sarah has the support of Abraham or the Israelite Deity, or both. When Sarah asks Abraham to lay with her maid, Abraham does not need encouragement (16:3). When Sarah is distressed about Hagar's treatment of her, Abraham hands Hagar back to Sarah (16:6). When Sarah commands Abraham to banish Hagar, the Deity commands him to listen to her voice (21:12) and Abraham carries out her commands (21:14).

The Deity's support for Sarah highlights their relationship, which is positive. Despite never having a conversation with the Deity, Sarah brings the Deity into the conflict she has with Abraham (16:5). She is prepared not to be the birth mother of a child so the Deity can fulfill Abraham's wish for a child (16:2), and she protects Isaac, who the Deity states will inherit the promise (17:19).

Sarah's relationship with the Israelite Deity seems mutual. The Deity saves Sarah in Egypt (12:17), blesses her and promises to make her a mother of nations (17:16), sends messengers to her to let her know she will have a child (18:10),[61] and grants her the child she desires (21:1–2), thereby bringing her laughter (21:6). Finally, the Deity supports her decision to banish Hagar (21:12). Thus it is clear that Sarah is chosen by the Deity and they support each other.

Conclusion

Sarah's character evolves, something not all the other female characters do. She is silent until the Deity stresses that Abraham will have a child, and then she moves into action. Most of her actions are focused on having a child, responding to news of having a child, having the child, and protecting her child's position, which is ordained by the Deity.

---

61. Though the messengers never see Sarah, they impart information Abraham already has and that Sarah needs to know: they will have a child. Since they report this intentionally within Sarah's hearing, she appears to be the primary target of this information.

2

Rebekah

Rebekah is often described as a trickster because of her later actions and the role her favored son, Jacob, plays.[1] Other treatments suggest that she cares about only one of her children and that she is an obedient vessel or a scheming wife.[2] More recently, scholars focus on her role in carrying out the Deity's prophetic statement to her about her children (25:23) and her prominence and activity compared to her husband and patriarch, Isaac.[3]

The issues surrounding Rebekah are similar to and different from those around Sarah. Both are attractive, have fertility problems, move to Canaan from elsewhere, are named sisters to their husbands rather than wives at least once in the story, and bear heirs to the Deity's promise. Differences concern their family of origin, the number of children they have, and the role of other women around them. Jeansonne notes that Rebekah is not just part of Isaac's story, since not all of the narratives about Rebekah concern Isaac.[4] These unique variations within Rebekah's story are carried over into the list of relationships she has, which is more extensive than the lists of other women and includes

1. Niditch, "Genesis," in Newsom and Ringe, *Women's Bible Commentary*, 19–20. She claims of Rebekah, "the woman herself is the trickster who formulates the plan and succeeds, moving the men around her like chess pieces."
2. Jeansonne, *Women of Genesis*, 53.
3. Carol Meyers, "Rebekah," in Meyers, *Women in Scripture*, 143–44.
4. Jeansonne, *Women of Genesis*, 54.

Abraham's servant, her brother Laban, her husband Isaac, her sons Jacob and Esau, and the Israelite Deity.

Rebekah's Description

Rebekah's first description is repeated numerous times: she is the daughter of Bethuel, the son of Milcah and Nahor, brother of Abraham, or some variation (22:23; 24:5, 24, 47; 25:20; 28:2, 5). The data contained in the description, the numerous times it is repeated, and the placement of many of these references highlight the importance of her lineage.

The first time she is described appears immediately after the messenger of the Deity keeps Abraham from sacrificing Isaac. After they leave the mountain, Abraham and his servants depart together and stay in Beer-sheba (22:19). The next verse claims that sometime later Abraham is told that Milcah has borne children to his brother, Nahor (22:20). Milcah's name is the subject of the verb and appears more prominently in the verse even though Nahor is Abraham's brother. After the children are listed in 22:21–22, along with one grandchild, the narrator repeats that these are the eight whom Milcah bears to Nahor, Abraham's brother, again highlighting Milcah (22:23).

Of the eight sons Milcah bears, the last named is Bethuel, and the narrator adds that he is the father of Rebekah. Frymer-Kensky notes that Rebekah is the only female with a birth story in the Hebrew Bible.[5] In this genealogy only Rebekah and Aram are named from their generation. Although her introduction may not be dramatically presented, "Genealogies call for special attention, however, as they indicate important links between peoples."[6] Despite the prominence of Rebekah's grandmother, Milcah, her mother is never named.

Rebekah's introduction is significant. A major theme of the story has been which child of Abraham shall inherit. The story begins with difficulty having children, and then having too many. When he is left with one child,[7] he is about to sacrifice him before the Deity stops him. Milcah and Nahor's children appear only when Isaac's survival is secure (22:20–24).

The timing is relevant to what follows. In the next verse the narrator summarizes Sarah's lifetime (23:1) and her death (23:2). The paragraph about Nahor's children is transitional, preparing the reader for the next generation, that of Isaac and Rebekah. It does so by stressing Nahor, and Nahor and Milcah's granddaughter. The focus on the next generation prepares the reader

5. Frymer-Kensky, *Reading the Women*, 5.

6. Jeansonne, *Women of Genesis*, 54.

7. After he banishes Ishmael, there is no reference in the text addressing whether Abraham knows that Ishmael survives. There are no other encounters between Abraham and either of his sons following 22:13 except at his burial. Isaac is identified as Abraham's "only" son in 22:2, though the reader knows such is not the case.

for what will happen to the next patriarch and also establishes that, as with Sarah, the matriarch is as important as the man she will marry.

The reference to Milcah and Nahor returns the reader to Terah and the family's origins. The last the reader knew of them they were in Haran (11:31–32). Neither Nahor nor Milcah is on the list of those who go to Haran with Terah.

Abraham's story begins as part of a line of Terah (11:26–27). Abraham is listed as just one of Terah's children. Terah's other children and their lives are discussed in this chapter as much as Abraham, since the death of Haran is noted (11:28), as is the existence of his son, Lot (11:27). Lot plays an important role in Abraham's story, and, according to some scholars, for much of the story he appears as a potential heir.[8] It is possible that Milcah is both his niece and the wife of Abraham's brother Nahor, since she is identified as the daughter of Haran (11:29). Regardless of her relationship to Terah, the text provides her ancestry (11:29). There the question is which line of Terah will survive. Does 22:23 relate Rebekah to Abraham through Nahor, or through Terah, through both Nahor and Milcah? In either case, Rebekah has both the correct father and grandmother.

Rebekah's parentage is repeated often as part of the story, which reinforces her lineage. In 24:15, Rebekah's first appearance, the narrator describes her as Rebekah, who is born to Bethuel, the son of Milcah, the wife of Abraham's brother Nahor. This is relevant information since Abraham's servant is seeking someone like her. There is a great deal of repetition in this chapter, so it is not surprising that she then identifies herself as "the daughter of Bethuel, the son of Milcah whom she bore to Nahor" (24:24), in response to the servant's question concerning who she is. Since the servant repeats everything that happens to him, one expects that when he recounts his conversation with her he repeats her self-identification almost verbatim.

Rebekah continues to be identified as the daughter of Bethuel, but following her marriage to Isaac her connection to Milcah and Nahor disappears and stress is placed on where she is from and who her brother is. This begins when the narrator summarizes Isaac's story (25:19), noting that he takes her as a wife when he is forty years old, where she is identified as "Rebekah, daughter of Bethuel the Aramean of Paddan-aram, sister of Laban the Aramean" (25:20). Rebekah's association with Paddan-aram and Laban is noted again in 28:2. When Isaac instructs Jacob to go to Paddan-aram to find a wife, he is told to go to the house of Bethuel, his mother's father. A few verses later these elements are raised when the narrator notes that Isaac sends Jacob off to Paddan-aram, to Laban, the son of Bethuel the Aramean, the brother of Rebekah, mother

---

8. Steinberg, "Sarah-Hagar Cycle," 45. The opposite notion is expressed by R. Christopher Heard, *Dynamics of Diselection: Ambiguity in Genesis 12–36 and Ethnic Boundaries in Post-Exilic Judah*, Semeia Studies (Atlanta: Society of Biblical Literature, 2001), 25–30.

of Jacob and Esau (28:5). Rebekah's parents and grandparents are significant before she marries Isaac, but her brother and her place of origin become key markers for her later life. This is a function of the changing story line; most of the later occurrences concern finding a wife for Jacob, but they are still descriptors of Rebekah showing how her role in the story line changes.

Rebekah's second description is that she has a jar on her shoulder (24:15). This describes her at one moment, but because the style of this chapter records the servant thinking something, it happening, and his repeating it, this detail is repeated in 24:45 when he recounts his story to Rebekah's family. The servant mentions the jar even before he describes her looks.

Many elements of this story are repeated to highlight for the servant and reader that Rebekah is the wife, picked by Abraham's Deity, for Isaac. The servant is nervous about accomplishing his task correctly and so creates a scenario whereby he will know that the woman is picked by Abraham's Deity (24:12). Even as part of the story this first repeated detail is significant in that it reinforces, at least for the servant if not the reader, that Rebekah has all the necessary qualities.

The question is, what quality does having a jar on her shoulder represent? Most fundamental for the story is that the servant asks Abraham's Deity to let the maiden whom he asks to lower her jar that he may drink be the one. Having a jar on her shoulder is the necessary first step for that process.[9]

Rebekah's next description (24:16) notes that she is "very nice of appearance" (*tobat mar'eh me'od*). Later, Rebekah and Isaac are in Gerar, and Isaac fears that they might kill him on account of Rebekah, for she is "good of appearance" (26:7). For the former some translations have she is "very beautiful," and the latter simply "beautiful." Neither is precise.[10] Sarah is labeled "beautiful," *yaphah* (12:11, 17), as is Rachel, who is both *yaphat to'ar* and *yaphat mar'eh* ("beautiful of shape" and "beautiful of appearance," 29:17). The thrust of the different terms may be the same but they are not identical. The adjective "beautiful" is not ascribed to Rebekah; instead, the text uses the word *tob*, "good." The Hebrew term *tob* carries a different range of meanings than "beautiful," with its primary meaning being "pleasing, good,"[11] and it is used for a far wider range of situations than *yaphah*, "fair, beautiful."[12]

Most assume that the reference is to Rebekah's beauty. Von Rad notes, "in addition to all of her excellent qualities she would also be beautiful!"[13] The second reference to Rebekah as "good of appearance" seems to refer to her

9. Jeansonne, *Women of Genesis,* 58.

10. NJPS and Speiser (*Genesis,* 175, 198) translate in both places "beautiful." In 24:16 KJV has "very fair" and "fair" for 26:7. NRSV translates "very fair" for 24:16 but "attractive in appearance" for 26:7.

11. Brown, Driver, and Briggs, *Lexicon,* 373.

12. Ibid., 421.

13. Von Rad, *Genesis,* 256. Note that the Scripture translation used in his commentary is RSV, which uses "fair" here.

looks thereby endangering Isaac, and appears in Isaac's thoughts. The first use of the term is less clearly referring to Rebekah's beauty. The description appears immediately following the notification of her parentage and that she has a jar on her shoulder. Labeling her appearance "good" could be like the description of Moses (Exod. 2:2), or even the Deity identifying recent acts of creation as "good" (Gen. 1:4, 10, 12, 18, 21, 25). Are all those things beautiful, or are they good? The same can be asked of Rebekah, especially since the servant is not charged with finding a beautiful wife for Isaac, and in light of the trouble Sarah's "beauty" causes, it may not be defined as important or even desirable.

Rebekah is also named a "young woman," *na'arah*. When Abraham's servant originally concocts his scenario, he asks that a *na'arah* be the one to offer him a drink (24:14). Rebekah is again labeled a *na'arah* when she runs to tell the news to her mother's household (24:28). When Abraham's servant wants to leave immediately and take Rebekah with him, her mother and brother refer to her as a *na'arah* when they ask that she remain a few more days (24:55). To resolve the dilemma they call the *na'arah*, Rebekah, and ask her (24:57).

Precisely what this term means and what it says about Rebekah is uncertain. In general, the term is translated as "girl, damsel, maid," suggesting a stage of life.[14] Leeb argues that a close reading of the Hebrew texts where the term appears suggests that it connotes a girl or young woman who is away from home, perhaps in danger or at risk in some way.[15] A large number of the persons referred to as *na'arah* in the Hebrew Bible are maids or serving girls.[16] Leeb argues that in Rebekah's case she is named a *na'arah* because she is out and about, talking to a stranger at the well, and may be fatherless.[17]

If so, the text is making a number of points about Rebekah. Abraham's servant seeks a *na'arah*, rather than any other term to refer to a young woman (24:14). The term is usually applied to a servant girl, and in this scene Rebekah serves the servant.[18]

This term is used to reiterate the servant's ideal scenario, so applying the term to Rebekah reinforces that she is the one picked by Abraham's Deity. The servant requests a woman whose status is ambiguous and who has more autonomy than one might expect from a young woman under her father's control.[19] Her status changes, since following Rebekah's marriage she is no longer characterized with this term.[20]

14. Carolyn S. Leeb, *Away from the Father's House: The Social Location of na'ar and na'arah in Ancient Israel*, Journal for the Study of the Old Testament Supplement 301 (Sheffield: Sheffield Academic Press, 2000), 125. For the definition see Brown, Driver, and Briggs, *Lexicon*, 655.

15. Leeb, *Away from the Father's House*, 125.

16. Ibid., 126.

17. Ibid., 136.

18. Ibid., 126.

19. Ibid., 136.

20. Ibid.

This same verse notes that Rebekah is a "virgin whom no man has known" (24:16). There are numerous problems with the phrase, which appears in a number of places in the Hebrew Bible and is redundant, if we understand a virgin to be a woman who has not had sexual intercourse with a man.[21] The Akkadian cognate means "young (unmarried) girl."[22] Many scholars now suggest that the first term, Hebrew *betulah*, does not refer to virginity but designates a young woman who has not yet married, though in Joel 1:8 it appears to refer to a woman who already has a husband.[23] Bal suggests that when the term is used with Jephthah's daughter (also noting that she had not known a man) it identifies her as a pubescent woman (Judg. 11:37), meaning she is of an age when she could be married and is no longer a girl.[24] If so, then Hebrew has no real word for virginity, suggesting that such a state did not carry the importance in Israel that it does in other cultures and societies.[25] The verse identifies Rebekah as a young woman of ambiguous status, of marriageable age, and who has not known a man, precisely what Abraham's servant seeks.

Rebekah's ambiguous status is highlighted by the prominent role of her brother, who is used to describe her. In 24:29 Rebekah has a brother, Laban. This verse follows the reference that Rebekah, named a *na'arah*, runs to tell all of this to her mother's household (24:28). Thus in two verses the narrator emphasizes that Rebekah is a *na'arah*, that she views her household (or her important location) as related to her mother, and that she has a brother.

A number of scholars remark on the important role Laban, Rebekah's brother, plays in contrast to her father, Bethuel, who almost never appears in the text. The reference to being the daughter of Bethuel is cited a number of times, usually in the context of identifying Rebekah as a descendant of both Milcah and Nahor. Speiser argues that the reference to Rebekah's mother's house "can only mean that Bethuel was no longer alive; hence the immediate reference to Rebekah's brother (29), whose authority in such circumstances would be an overriding factor."[26] When gifts are presented, they are given to Rebekah's mother and brother, not to her father (24:53), as one would expect.[27] The reference to her having a brother reinforces why she is a *na'arah* and explains why her brother is so prominent and her father is not.

Another description of Rebekah appears in the following line when Laban sees the nose ring and bands on his sister's arms (24:30). This functions as a

---

21. John J. Schmitt, "Virgin," in Freedman, *Anchor Bible Dictionary*, 6:853.

22. Ibid.

23. Ibid.

24. Mieke Bal, *Death and Dissymmetry: The Politics of Coherence in the Book of Judges* (Chicago: University of Chicago Press, 1988), 46–52.

25. Schmitt, "Virgin," 853.

26. Speiser, *Genesis*, 180–81.

27. Leeb, *Away from the Father's House*, 135.

description because the articles describe how she appears, especially to her brother. Laban is often treated as motivated by personal gain, something the later stories can be read as reinforcing (Gen. 29–30).[28] Here Rebekah is described as suddenly appearing with signs of wealth. This wealth is not lost upon her brother and is likely a contributing factor in both his and Bethuel's decision (if Bethuel is still alive) to allow Rebekah to marry Isaac, an unnamed stranger to them.

Though Abraham's servant asks Abraham's Deity to reveal a *na'arah* to him, when he recounts the story to Rebekah's family he tells them it is a "young woman," Hebrew *'almah*, he seeks (24:43). An *'almah* is also defined as a young woman who is ripe sexually or newly married.[29] When Abraham's servant recounts what he is looking for in a wife for Isaac, he highlights to the family that he is interested in a woman who is the right age, one ready to be married, whereas to himself he seeks one who could be more easily influenced, especially by wealth. Speiser notes a number of instances where the story the servant recounts is not completely in line with what the text notes earlier.[30] In 24:41 Abraham's servant uses stronger terminology to refer to the oath he makes to Abraham and neglects to mention Abraham's categorical injunction not to take Isaac out of Canaan.[31] He also claims that he gives the jewelry to Rebekah after asking about her family, though he actually inquires after giving her the gifts.[32] Using different terminology to refer to Rebekah's status reinforces the use of *na'arah* as referring to a more unprotected woman earlier in the story.

Laban's response to Abraham's servant is a description: "let her be a wife to your master's son" (24:51). He is not describing what she is at that moment but what she will become. Her role as somewhat unprotected previously is slightly emphasized by the reference to "your master's son." Laban cannot name Isaac because he does not know his name. Up to this point in the narrative the entire focus has been on Abraham, whom the servant serves. In Abraham's servant's account of the story not once is Isaac identified by name (24:34–49). Thus Laban, influenced either by the servant's wealth or by the story of Abraham's Deity's role in it, sends his sister to be the wife of a man whose name he does not even know.

The next description of Rebekah is as a sister. When she is sent to marry Isaac the narrator notes, "They sent off their sister Rebekah" (24:59). It is not clear who "their" refers to since the text has defined only one sibling for Rebekah. Clearly Rebekah is Laban's sister but she is not named as such until this point.

28. Claude F. Mariottini, "Laban," in Freedman, *Anchor Bible Dictionary*, 4:113–14.
29. Brown, Driver, and Briggs, *Lexicon*, 751.
30. Speiser, *Genesis*, 181.
31. Ibid.
32. Jeansonne, *Women of Genesis*, 61.

Rebekah is again called a sister by her husband when they meet a foreign ruler (25:67), just as Abraham said of Sarah (12:13; 20:1). There are significant differences between this case and those with Sarah and Abraham, especially the last episode in Gerar, where this scene also occurs. With Isaac, only the men of the place ask him about his wife, and he answers that she is his sister (26:7). It seems unlikely that Rebekah is ever handed over to anyone, because Abimelech looks out the window to see Isaac "playing" (*metsacheq*) with his wife, Rebekah (26:8). The word *metsacheq* used here is the same word used when Sarah sees Ishmael "playing" with Isaac that leads her to banish Ishmael and his mother, Hagar (21:9). This may be more proof that Abraham's statement that he and Sarah are really siblings (20:12) is untrue, because Isaac never argues that he and Rebekah are brother and sister and the reader knows they are not.

Rebekah is first labeled a "wife" when Isaac brings her to the tent of his mother and takes her as a wife (24:67). The narrator notes that he loves her, which may be why the next time she is called a wife he is pleading on her behalf (25:21). She appears as his wife in Gerar, where he tells the men she is his sister because he fears saying that she is his wife (26:7). She is also referred to as a wife when Abimelech catches Isaac "playing" with her, indicating that she is truly his wife (26:8). Based on this incident Abimelech is distressed because one of his people might have lain with her (26:10). He further charges that anyone who molests either Isaac or his wife will be put to death (26:11).

Rebekah's next description is that she is barren (25:21). The text has just recounted the genealogy of the son not chosen to bear the promise.[33] The text moves immediately from the certainty of Ishmael's line to the uncertainty of Isaac's lineage continuing.[34] Rebekah is married and has been for quite a while. Isaac is forty years old when he marries Rebekah (25:20) and is sixty years old when she gives birth (25:26). Isaac prays for her to the Deity because she is barren. The matriarchs are not a fertile group, highlighting how important the role of the Deity is to them to ensure they have children to carry on the promise. Contrary to Sarah's situation, the Deity responds much sooner in this situation; Isaac's role may have helped. The timely resolution of this situation raises the issue that becomes the defining one for this second generation of patriarchs: there are twins in her womb (25:22).

The final description of Rebekah is as a mother. Most women in Genesis are mothers because they bear children, but few are labeled this way. She is identified as a mother only when she helps Jacob prepare a dish that Isaac is expecting from Esau. The narrator informs the reader that Jacob answers his mother Rebekah when she makes her original suggestion (27:11). The narrator describes Rebekah as his mother when she gives her response, telling Jacob

33. Steinberg, *Kinship and Marriage*, 88.
34. Ibid.

Isaac's curse will be upon her and he should just do what she says (27:13). She is described as his (Jacob's) mother when he brings the things to her and she prepares a dish that his father (Isaac) likes (27:14). Isaac refers to her obliquely in the middle of his blessing to Jacob, who he thinks is Esau, when he claims: "let your mother's sons bow to you" (27:29). She is Jacob's mother when Isaac instructs Jacob to go to Paddan-aram to the house of Bethuel, "your mother's father," defining Laban as his "mother's brother" (28:2). Only in the final reference to Rebekah as a mother is she mother to Esau and Jacob. The last time Isaac sends Jacob off to Paddan-aram to Laban, the latter is qualified as "the brother of Rebekah, mother of Jacob and Esau" (28:5).

The text never recounts Rebekah's death, and in the rest of her story she acts. Rebekah's descriptions focus on her family. Her family tree is full of the right people; she may embody the two other lines of Terah, through Nahor her great-grandfather, and her grandmother Milcah. Her brother allows her to be married off fairly easily and sets up the story for the next generation when Jacob, Rebekah's son, must return to Paddan-aram. She is described as chosen by the Israelite Deity. The servant's scenario comes true and highlights how Rebekah is the correct one for Isaac. Her description intimates that she is attractive or more than just attractive, maybe even somehow innately good. After being barren she is a mother of two sons.

Rebekah as a Subject

Many of Rebekah's actions support the portrait of Rebekah drawn by her description. Rebekah is one of the more active women in Genesis, and her actions contribute almost as much to her character as her description does.

In Rebekah's first actions she goes down to the spring, fills up her jar, and returns from the well (24:16). The scenario that Abraham's servant builds as the test case for the right woman for Isaac determines who and what Rebekah should do and be. Rebekah exceeds his expectations, emphasizing that she is the one picked by Abraham's Deity for Isaac. Her first actions, with the jar on her shoulder, reveal to the servant that she could be the one. The reader, who knows her family tree, has more information than Abraham's servant. Her actions will be the test.

Rebekah's next action is a direct response to Abraham's servant, who asks her if he could have a sip of water from her jar. She says, "Drink, my lord," and quickly lowers her jar and lets him drink (24:17). Rebekah fulfills the servant's dream scenario when, with her next action, she tells him she will draw for his camels until they finish drinking (24:19). Her offer is what he wants a woman to say upon his request for water, and he receives his answer.

Rebekah speaks again when she tells the servant she is the daughter of Bethuel, the son of Milcah, whom she bore to Nahor (24:24), and there is plenty of feed for his animals and room for him to spend the night with her family (24:25). She also tells all this to her family, identified as her mother's household. The reader is reminded that this happens only after Laban sees the nose ring and bands on his sister's arms and hears her say, "Thus the man said to me" (24:30). Rebekah's side of the story is generalized to "Thus said the man," without unpacking precisely what pieces of the situation she understands as key elements. This fits with the image of Rebekah moving quickly. Yet this generalization of Rebekah's story emphasizes the servant's story and how many variations and modifications lie in its numerous retellings.

The servant tells his story and requests Rebekah as a wife for Isaac (24:49), to which her brother and father agree (24:50); objects of gold and silver are given to Rebekah, her brother, and mother (24:53); the men eat, drink, and spend the night (24:54); and when the servant wants to leave immediately, the family asks Rebekah if she wants to go. In another story this might not stand out since so few women carry out many actions, but in light of the prominent role Rebekah has played thus far it is odd that she is not included earlier. Rebekah answers immediately and decisively, "I will go" (24:58). This too appears definitive of Rebekah's character: she is willing to leave everything she knows without a moment's hesitation.

Rebekah last speaks to the servant when she asks, upon seeing Isaac, "Who is the man for that one, the one who is walking in the field to greet us?" (24:65).[35] Unclear speech from Rebekah also appears during pregnancy, complicated because the children struggle in her womb, leading her to say, "If so why this, I . . ." (25:22). The difficulty translating here is because the Hebrew is not complete. Most translate, "why do I live?" following the Syriac with an eye on 27:46, though Speiser notes that the two passages are not analogous.[36] Alter suggests she is so uncomfortable that her cry of anguish is unintelligible because it is a broken-off sentence.[37] Jeansonne's recognition is useful: "Translators have attempted to explain this statement, but ultimately it proves to be elusive," leading her to conclude that whatever the meaning of the verse is, it leaves Rebekah distraught enough to inquire of the Israelite Deity.[38]

Rebekah's inquiry of the Israelite Deity is the first by a woman in the Hebrew Bible. Sarah suggests that the Deity intervene between Abraham and herself, but Abraham does not take up the offer (16:5). Twice Hagar has a conversation with the Deity's messenger, both instigated by the Deity (16:9–13; 21:17–19). Rebekah acts decisively.

What Rebekah's relationship is with the Israelite Deity prior to this occasion is unclear. In the city of Nahor, Abraham's servant invokes the Israelite

35. This translation conveys the problems translating the Hebrew. For more about this scene see below.
36. Speiser, *Genesis*, 194.
37. Alter, *Genesis*, 127.
38. Jeansonne, *Women of Genesis*, 63.

Deity, naming the Deity the *'elohim* of his master Abraham when he reveals himself and his mission to Rebekah at the well (24:27). Since the text summarizes Rebekah's account of the scene, it is not clear if she recounts which deity the servant invokes (24:28). When Laban invites the servant into their home, invoking the Israelite Deity (24:31), and later, after listening to the story saying the matter is decreed by the Israelite Deity (24:50), it is not clear if he has already been told that the servant invokes Abraham's Deity. Isaac pleads with his Deity for Rebekah to conceive (25:21), so this verse is the first time Rebekah recognizes the Israelite Deity.

Rebekah's next speech indicates that she understands Isaac's intended blessing of Esau as connected to the Deity's blessing. She tells Jacob that she heard his father speaking to his brother Esau (27:6), telling him he should bring him game and make a meal for him to eat so he may bless Esau before the Israelite Deity, before he dies (27:7). Rebekah is not the only one to understand Isaac's actions this way, since Brueggemann too notes, "The first scene begins with the resolve of the father to give his blessing, transmit the promise, and settle the inheritance."[39] He continues that both "assume that it is their proper business to engage in a regular transmission to the elder son."[40] Rebekah's actions are motivated on an understanding that Isaac's actions conflict with the words that the Israelite Deity gives her prior to their children's birth.

Rebekah tells Jacob what he should do: go to the flock, fetch two choice kids so she can make a dish that his father likes (27:9), and take it to his father (27:10). Her reasoning is clear; he should do all of this so Isaac may bless Jacob before he dies (27:11). Scholars describe Rebekah as "shrewd" and "strong-willed" and describe her actions as a "scheme."[41] Similar to Sarah's actions (21:10), Rebekah's actions could be motivated by her desire to ensure that the promise goes to the one identified by the Israelite Deity (27:7).

Jacob is skeptical about Rebekah's plan. First he raises the issue that his brother is hairy and he is smooth-skinned (27:11), and he is nervous that if his father touches him he shall appear as a trickster and bring upon himself a curse rather than a blessing (27:12). Rebekah's response is immediate and decisive, "Upon me your curse, my son." She follows this by telling him, "Listen to my voice, go and take for me" (27:13).

Rebekah's statements resonate with the first patriarch and matriarch. Rebekah begins by telling him she will accept the "curse" (*qll*) upon him; she uses the same term that the Deity uses when the Deity tells Abraham that if anyone curses (*qll*) him that person would receive a more severe curse (12:3), and it is the same root used when Hagar "despises" Sarah and Sarah feels "cursed" (16:4–5; see discussion of Sarah and Hagar in chapters 1 and 6). The

39. Brueggemann, *Genesis*, 231.

40. Ibid.

41. For the first see ibid.; for the second see Speiser, *Genesis*, 211; and for the third see both Speiser, *Genesis*, 211; and Brueggemann, *Genesis*, 231.

Deity tells Abraham to "listen to her [Sarah's] voice" (21:12) when Sarah tells Abraham to banish Hagar and her son. There the Deity informs Abraham he must listen to Sarah's voice because it is through Isaac's seed that offspring will be called (21:12). The narrative reinforces the legitimacy of Rebekah's actions through Sarah's earlier actions justified by the Deity.

Rebekah must again say to Jacob, "listen to my voice," and flee to Haran, to her brother Laban (27:43), following the switched blessing. She suggests that Jacob stay with Laban until Esau's anger subsides (27:44) and he forgets what Jacob has done to him (27:44). Her final speech reveals her concern as a mother of two, "Let me not lose you both in one day" (27:45).

Rebekah's last speech is when she tells Isaac that she is disgusted with life because of the Hittite women (Esau's wives), and she does not know what good life will be if Jacob marries a Hittite woman like them (27:46). She does not say what about these women bothers her.[42]

Returning to the initial scene with the servant, Rebekah's next actions highlight her quickness. After suggesting she water the camels, Rebekah quickly empties her jar into the trough and runs back for more water and draws for all his camels (24:20). This reaffirms to the reader that Rebekah is the one as she does more than what is requested by doing it quickly. The amount of work involved is impressive. The use of a camel highlights how much work is required, how much of an offer Rebekah makes, and how much Abraham's servant expects. His expectation is that some local woman will offer to water his camels, highlighting how his dream scenario seeks unique qualities.

While Rebekah is doing this backbreaking work, the man is gazing at her wondering whether the Deity has made his errand successful (24:21). He requests a daunting task that some young woman, possibly unprotected, would spend a great deal of time and effort watering his camels, and he still has not figured it out! Despite his unease as to whether she is the correct one, he gives her a gold nose ring and two gold bands for her arms (24:22) and only then asks her whose daughter she is and whether there is room for him at her father's house to spend the night (24:23).[43] Jeansonne notes that the servant later stresses "loyalty, service, and trust in his God."[44] In the original cycle, however, the servant seems more interested in finding a woman to do his work for him and whose situation would make it easy to convince her to leave, especially with the right amount of wealth.

After replying to him who she is, she runs to tell her family. When the servant originally asks her for water, she lowers her jar quickly (24:17). Moving quickly is a family trait since Laban also runs out to the man at the spring (24:29).

42. Heard, *Dynamics of Diselection*, 109.
43. Jeansonne, *Women of Genesis*, 59.
44. Ibid., 61.

Rebekah's next action is, with her maids, to arise, mount the camels, and follow the servant (24:61). Isaac comes out to the fields, lifts up his eyes, and sees the camels approaching (24:63). Rebekah too lifts up her eyes and sees Isaac (24:64). The expression "to lift up the eyes" conveys seeing and yet carries with it slightly greater connotations. Abraham lifts up his eyes on the third day after leaving with Isaac to sacrifice him to the Deity (22:4), and again on the mountain after being told not to touch Isaac when he sees a ram to sacrifice instead (22:13).

Seeing Isaac leads Rebekah to alight from the camel (24:64). Upon hearing the servant's response that the person she sees is the servant's master, she takes her veil and covers herself (24:65). Thus far the servant belongs to Abraham. His mission is so devoted to Abraham's wish that when recounting his whole story to Rebekah's family the servant never mentions Isaac or his name. Speiser argues that the reference to the servant belonging to Isaac means that Abraham has died.[45] Speiser explains why the death notice follows this but not how the servant knows of Abraham's death when they are only now arriving. Here the servant considers Isaac his master and informs Rebekah that this is the man she has come to marry (24:65).

Rebekah's action is immediate, decisive, and another hint that she is the right one: she veils herself. Her gesture is unique. Presumably reference to her dress is meaningful. Yet "any description of dress and its importance in the biblical tradition is complicated by the long period involved (ca. 2000 B.C.E.–125 C.E.), the diversity of peoples and nations depicted, the distinctive dress worn by various classes and groups, the extensive geographic areas with which the texts deal, the paucity of sculptural or physical evidence in Palestine, and the fluid meaning of terms used for dress in literary texts."[46]

The veil is rarely referred to in the Bible; hence, it was either rarely used or it was so common it did not need comment. In Tamar's story when she puts on a veil she is perceived to be a prostitute (38:14, 15, 19), which many take to mean that prostitutes wore veils.[47] The Priestly tradition states that when a woman is accused of adultery by her husband, the priest unbinds or uncovers her hair as part of a ritual proving her guilt or innocence (Num. 5:11–28; cf. Sus. 32).

The Middle Assyrian Laws address who veils and when. These laws are represented only by one source per tablet, which date to the eleventh century BCE and are copies of fourteenth-century originals, excavated in the Assyrian capital Ashur, though there is one later Neo-Assyrian fragment from Nineveh that duplicates some of the first paragraphs of Middle Assyrian Law A.[48] The

45. Speiser, *Genesis*, 183.
46. Douglas R. Edwards, "Dress and Ornamentation," in Freedman, *Anchor Bible Dictionary*, 2:232.
47. Ibid. See the discussion of Tamar in chapter 12 below.
48. See Roth, *Law Collections*, 153–54.

laws suggest one way someone thought people should deal with certain issues (and maybe imposed it on them)—in this case, who should be veiled, when and where. The somewhat broken laws state,

Wives of a man, or [widows], or any [Assyrian] women who go out into the main thoroughfare [shall not have] their heads [bare]. Daughters of a man [. . . with] either a . . . -cloth or garments of [. . .] shall be veiled, [. . .] their heads [. . . (gap of ca. 6 lines) . . .] When they go about [. . .] in the main thoroughfare during the daytime, they shall be veiled. A concubine who goes about in the main thoroughfare with her mistress is to be veiled. A married *qadiltu*-woman is to be veiled (when she goes about) in the main thoroughfare, but an unmarried one is to leave her head bare in the main thoroughfare, she shall not be veiled. A prostitute shall not be veiled, her head shall be bare. (v. 68) Whoever sees a veiled prostitute shall seize her, secure witnesses, and bring her to the palace entrance. They shall not take away her jewelry, but he who has seized her takes her clothing; they shall strike her 50 blows with rods; they shall pour hot pitch over her head. (v. 77) And if a man should see a veiled prostitute and release her, and does not bring her to the palace entrance, they shall strike that man 50 blows with rods; the one who informs against him shall take his clothing; they shall pierce his ears, thread them on a cord, tie it at his back; he shall perform the king's service for one full month. (v. 88) Slave women shall not be veiled, and he who should see a veiled slave woman shall seize her and bring her to the palace entrance; they shall cut off her ears; he who seizes her shall take her clothing. (v. 94) If a man should see a veiled slave woman but release her and not seize her, and does not bring her to the palace entrance, and they then prove the charges against him and find him guilty, they shall strike him 50 blows with rods; they shall pierce his ears, thread them on a cord, tie it at his back; the one who informs against him shall take his garments; he shall perform the king's service for one full month.

If a man intends to veil his concubine, he shall assemble five or six of his comrades, and he shall veil her in their presence, he shall declare, "She is my *aššutu*-wife"; she is his *aššutu*-wife. A concubine who is not veiled in the presence of people, whose husband did not declare, "She is my *aššutu*-wife," she is not an *aššutu*-wife, she is indeed a concubine. If a man is dead and there are no sons of his veiled wife, the sons of the concubines are indeed sons; they shall (each) take an inheritance share.[49]

The Middle Assyrian Laws have harsh rules, particularly concerning women. These laws take veiling seriously, addressing who can and cannot be veiled, meting out severe punishments for those who falsely veil or for those who know of someone falsely veiled and do not act. The main differences about who veils concern marriage status. Married women are veiled, concubines are veiled only when awarded special status, prostitutes are not allowed to veil, and unmarried women are not veiled. The Middle Assyrian Laws address

49. Ibid., 167–69, Law A 40–41.

major thoroughfares, which would be public situations. It is unlikely that these laws governed anyone in the biblical text, but they stand as an example of harsh laws about veiling.

Some scholars use the verse referring to Rebekah to contend that women used a veil or part of their outer garment to cover their faces on wedding days.[50] The problem concerns Rebekah's status in connection to the Middle Assyrian Laws and within the text. It is not clear that Rebekah veils herself because it is her wedding day, since it is the day she arrives and first meets Isaac, and the text's chronology is uncertain as to whether he marries her as soon as she arrives or if some period of time intervenes. Does she veil herself because it is mandated by some law (although according to the Middle Assyrian Laws she is exempt, being unmarried), because it is her marriage day, because she wants to portray modesty, or because she wants to observe Isaac without being observed? It could be something as simple and vain as Rebekah not wanting Isaac to see her after she has journeyed. Rebekah is not veiled during the journey, no one tells her to veil herself, and it is unlikely that as an unmarried woman, even under the strictest laws, she would have to veil. She decides to veil after learning that Isaac could soon see her. Again Rebekah carries out a unique and decisive action.

Next, Rebekah "conceives," an action that is not uncommon but not easy for the matriarchs (25:21). The narrator notes that this is a direct response to Isaac's plea for her (25:21), but nonetheless she is the one who conceives.

Rebekah's next action as a subject is to love Jacob. It is not clear if this is a reaction to receiving the Deity's answer to her inquiry that Jacob will be the one to inherit the promise. The reference follows the note that Isaac loves Esau (25:28). The text indicates that Isaac loves Esau because "game was in his mouth" (25:28), while no explanation is given for Rebekah's love. The text does not say that Isaac does not love Jacob, or that Rebekah does not love Esau. Since the surrounding verses highlight the differences between the two boys, differences that lead to conflict between them, referencing which parent loves which child appears significant.

After loving Jacob, Rebekah is next the subject in the context of her manipulating Isaac so Jacob receives his blessing. In between, Esau sells his birthright to Jacob (25:33–34), Isaac receives the Deity's blessing, Isaac and Rebekah go down to Gerar (26:6) where Isaac presents Rebekah as his sister (26:7), they become rich through sowing the land (26:12), and Esau marries two Hittite women (26:34).

Rebekah first listens while Isaac speaks to his son Esau (27:5). Scholars chastise Rebekah for this, just as they condemn Sarah for listening to the messengers there to tell Abraham something he already knows (see discussion of 18:10 above). The question concerns whether her listening is negative and is

---

50. Edwards, "Dress and Ornamentation," 234.

rooted in issues surrounding sources of power. When people are part of the power structure, listening when not being addressed is a negative action. The literature on patriarchy shows that women outside the traditional circles of power must resort to other means to make things happen. Rebekah's action appears differently depending on whether one considers that working within the realms of power is always appropriate or possible.

Evaluation of Rebekah's actions depends on what Isaac is going to do. The length of time between Esau's marriage to the Hittite women (26:34) and Isaac's old age is not noted. Since Isaac is already sixty (25:26) when the twins are born and Esau is forty years old in the previous episode, Isaac is old, yet the thrust of the verse is not on his age but on unfinished business as he thinks he is near death. Isaac decides he is going to "bless you [Esau] with my soul" before he dies (27:4). Speiser notes that the blessing must carry some "technical nuance" since it is used four times in this narrative (27:4, 19, 25, 31), but the connotation "is difficult to decide."[51] Most scholars, including von Rad, assume that Isaac's action is legitimate: "The blind old man feels himself near death; therefore he wants to give his favorite son the paternal blessing, according to the context of the patriarchal blessings."[52] Should Isaac give Esau a special blessing, especially since the Deity indicates to Rebekah that Jacob will receive the Deity's promise (25:23)?[53]

Jacob listens to his mother and brings her the things she requested (27:14). Rebekah prepares a dish his father likes (27:4). She takes the best clothes of her older son Esau (to which she has access) and has Jacob put them on (27:15). She covers Jacob's hands and the hairless parts of his neck with skins of the kids (27:16) and puts the dish and the meal she prepared in Jacob's hands (27:17). She enables the scenario where Jacob receives Esau's blessing.

Rebekah's actions are often considered manipulative and conniving. Von Rad claims that her plan has a "comic aspect" to it and is "rather ridiculous."[54] Even he admits that Rebekah's actions are not negative, according to the narrator. While Isaac questions Jacob disguised as Esau, one could argue that either he wants to be fooled, or he, like Esau, is not smart enough or does not care enough about the responsibility inherent in the promise to deserve it and pass it on to the next generation.

Rebekah's actions are geared to making the Deity's promise happen. Thus far Rebekah has been a perfect Israelite woman. Genesis 24, the longest chapter in Genesis, focuses almost entirely on how she is identified by the Deity as the correct wife for Isaac. She has the right pedigree, is hardworking, acts decisively, and is modest. She herself, either before her marriage or afterward,

51. Speiser, *Genesis*, 208–9.
52. Von Rad, *Genesis*, 276.
53. Adrien Janis Bledstein, "Binder, Trickster, Heel and Hairy-Man: Rereading Genesis 27 as a Trickster Tale Told by a Woman," in Brenner, *Feminist Companion to Genesis*, 282–95.
54. Von Rad, *Genesis*, 277.

becomes a devotee of the Israelite Deity, inquiring of the Deity when in difficulty. Suddenly commentators heap terms upon her that ignore her previous positive attributes.

Her last actions are colored by her involvement in getting Jacob the promise. Rebekah sets up the scenario whereby Jacob receives the blessing, but she does not appear in the narrative again until the end of the episode. It is reported to Rebekah that Esau will kill his brother when the mourning period for his father is over.[55] Rebekah sends for Jacob and tells him his brother Esau is consoling himself by planning to kill him (27:42) and asks that she not lose them both in one day (27:45).

Speiser notes that the reason Rebekah would be bereft of both of them is, "Killing Jacob would expose Esau to the death penalty, through blood vengeance or otherwise."[56] While his comment is correct and explicates the verse, it generates no sympathy for Rebekah.

Does Rebekah deserve contempt? Her husband, for reasons never expressed in the text, decides that one of his sons will get his blessing, despite his Deity telling his wife that the other son will receive the blessing. Rebekah acts to keep the Deity's plan on track, and she is labeled contemptuous. In 27:45 Rebekah expresses her concern for both her sons. While Rebekah does not know this, Jacob will be gone a long time, and the text never records them seeing each other again. To save the lives of both of her sons, she sends one away, never to see him again.

Isaac instructs Jacob to go to Paddan-aram, to the house of Bethuel, his mother's father, to take a wife there from among the daughters of Laban (28:1), his mother's brother. Isaac then asks that El Shaddai bless him and make him fertile and numerous so he becomes an assembly of people (28:3). He also asks that he receive the blessing of Abraham for his offspring so he will possess the land where he is sojourning, land that Elohim assigns to Abraham (28:4). This is in line with the blessing Rebekah fears that Isaac will give to Esau and is more in line with what happens than Isaac's blessing for Jacob when Isaac thinks Jacob is Esau. This transitional verse also reminds the reader of Rebekah's lineage. Rebekah's last action is somewhat out of keeping with her previous behavior because it is a complaint rather than a decisive action; it leads Isaac to take the decisive action accompanied by the blessing only he can give.

Rebekah as an Object

Comparing what actions are carried out to or for Rebekah illustrates how active she is. Contrary to Sarah, few actions are taken toward or for Rebekah.

55. This is a problem since Isaac has not yet died.
56. Speiser, *Genesis,* 210.

Contrasting again with Sarah, most actions where Rebekah is the object are positive for her or result from her previous actions.

The first action carried out toward Rebekah is that they (her family) "call" Rebekah, named a *na'arah* for the last time, to ask if she is willing to leave immediately (24:57), to which she agrees (24:58). The next action taken toward her, to send her off (24:59), is in direct response to her previous action. These actions appear at the end of Genesis 24 after Rebekah has shown that she is the correct wife for Isaac and is picked by the Israelite Deity.

Rebekah's family blesses her as they send her off (24:59). Her blessing highlights her status as ordained by the Deity because it is connected to that of Abraham.[57] After the binding of Isaac the Israelite Deity calls to Abraham a second time, and one of the Deity's blessings is that his descendants shall seize the gates of their foes (22:17). These words are repeated, almost verbatim, by Rebekah's family to her as she leaves (24:60). In Abraham's context the Deity so blesses him, and thus Rebekah's family repeating the same blessing can only be treated as the narrator's final confirmation that Rebekah is the correct wife for Isaac, chosen by the Israelite Deity.

After the blessing, Rebekah rises, mounts the camel, follows the man, and the narrator notes that he takes Rebekah and leaves (24:61). When he "takes" her it is different than the "taking" experienced by Sarah. Rebekah carries out a series of actions that indicate she is ready to go, she makes the decision, and action is only taken toward her once she has initiated the situation.

After they arrive Rebekah sees Isaac, veils herself (24:65), and the servant tells Isaac all the things he did (24:66). Only then does Isaac bring her into the tent of his mother, where he "takes" her as his wife (24:66). The next action is one rarely recorded for married couples in the biblical text: Isaac loves her (24:67).[58] Isaac "takes" her only when he learns the Deity chooses her for him, and Rebekah herself agrees to go with the servant to become Isaac's wife. It is possible that Rebekah's actions predicate his love.

Isaac's response to Rebekah's barren state is to "pray" to the Deity on her behalf (25:21). The verb used is *'atar*, meaning "pray, supplicate."[59] The narrator states that he carries out this action "on behalf" of his wife, implying that she wants children. In contrast, Abraham never prays for Sarah or pleads with the Deity for her.

Rebekah's children are the next to carry out actions toward Rebekah when they are still in utero (25:22). The narrator notes that the children "struggled"

57. Frymer-Kensky, *Reading the Women*, 6.

58. In the Hebrew Bible it is usually the man who loves the woman, and not all of those situations end well. Samson loves Delilah, leading to his death (Judg. 16:4–30); Amnon loves Tamar (2 Sam. 13:4), a disaster for Tamar. Michal is the only example given of a woman loving a man, David (2 Sam. 18:20), and that relationship is a disaster for her. See chapter 4 for discussion of Rachel. Isaac's love for Rebekah is one of the rare cases where love appears to be positive.

59. Brown, Driver, and Briggs, *Lexicon*, 801.

in her womb, causing her much distress. The verb *ratsats* means "crush."[60] This is the only case where it appears in the Hithpoel in the Hebrew Bible; its reciprocal sense should be something like "they crushed one another" within her. This prebirth situation foreshadows what Rebekah understands, leading her to inquire of the Deity. Here too someone does something to her, but it is something she commits to by asking to be pregnant.

Rebekah's uncomfortable pregnancy leads her to inquire of the Deity, who responds. Cotter argues that there is no indication Isaac hears back from the Deity after his prayer, but Rebekah does because she is the one who ensures that the Deity's plan for the family is carried out.[61] The difficult pregnancy leads Rebekah to action. The Deity's answer highlights the importance of Rebekah to the Deity and lays the foundation for Rebekah's later actions. Like Sarah, the matriarch ensures that the Deity's plan is followed.

Following in the footsteps of his father, Isaac too passes his wife off as his sister. There are significant differences between the two stories, though the similarities demand comparison. As with Abraham, there is a famine in the land (26:1). Here the Deity explicitly tells Isaac not to go down to Egypt (26:2). Instead, like his father, he goes to Abimelech in Gerar (26:6). This time some men of the place ask him about his woman. Like his father, he says she is his sister, because he is afraid they might kill him on account of her (26:7). The difference is that this time the woman is not handed over to the man; the only action carried out against Rebekah is that the king sees Isaac "fondling" her (26:8), something legitimate for a man who loves his wife (24:67). This is one event no action of Rebekah seems to cause. It is unusual since it is the one incident where Isaac endangers Rebekah. The implication is that the two are not separated since their actions together reveal the truth about their relationship.

The one episode where Rebekah is the object of something that distresses her concerns Esau's marriage, and this sets the stage for the transition to the next generation. When Esau is forty years old, the age his father married (Gen. 20), he marries Judith, daughter of Beeri the Hittite, and Basemath, daughter of Elon the Hittite (26:34). The narrator claims that these wives are a source of bitter spirit for both Isaac and Rebekah. This action leads her later to send Jacob back to her home so he will not marry local women (27:46). That a wife from her hometown would solve the daughter-in-law situation implies that where the Hittite women are from is the problem.

In 27:14 Jacob brings to Rebekah the items she told him to bring her, so Jacob could receive Isaac's blessing. Here too she is an object in reaction to her actions.

Rebekah's death is not recorded, nor is where or how she is buried. When Jacob is dying he wants to be interred in Machpelah and refers to Rebekah as

---

60. Brown, Driver, and Briggs, *Lexicon*, 954.
61. Cotter, *Genesis*, 188.

buried there (49:31). This reference is in the context of Jacob wanting to be buried in the cave of his ancestors, with his parents. Reference to Rebekah is a sign that she is accorded the status of other important ancestors.

Rebekah's Relationships

Rebekah has relationships with more individuals than Sarah does. In contrast to Sarah and Abraham, there is more material about Rebekah's relationship with Isaac. The narrator states that Isaac loves Rebekah (24:67). When she is barren he prays for her (25:21). Surrogacy is never raised. Positive feelings for Rebekah are reflected in the "fondling" in Gerar (26:8).

Rebekah's feelings toward Isaac are never stated, but there are signs she has positive feelings for him. She keeps Isaac interested in her to the extent that he would still consider her "good of appearance" and worth "fondling" more than twenty years into their marriage and after giving birth to twin boys (26:7–8). They agree regarding Esau's marriage to the Hittite women (26:35). She knows what dishes he likes, a sign of fondness or at least that she knows him well (27:9). One cannot confirm that she loves Isaac, but there is nothing in the text to suggest otherwise.

The text implies that Rebekah does not just love Jacob but favors him over his brother (25:28). The reference to her love of Jacob follows the reference that Jacob will be mightier, and the two may be connected (25:23), but it immediately follows the reference that Isaac loves Esau (25:28). Rebekah's actions to ensure the blessing for Jacob follow the notification that Esau marries the Hittite women (26:35). It is tempting to claim that her actions are because of her love of Jacob, but the reality is that it is difficult to discern whether Rebekah's actions stem from her greater love of Jacob, her concern that Isaac give the right son the blessing, or even her belief that Esau does not deserve the blessing because of the Hittite women. She is prepared to take the blame for her child (27:13), but her reasons are not stated. She loves Jacob (25:28) and is prepared to fight for him, even to the extent of sending him away to save his life, probably never to see him again (27:44).

At issue is whether Rebekah's love for Jacob means that she does not love her other son. The text only claims that Rebekah loves Jacob after the reader learns that Isaac loves Esau (25:28), but it never says each son is not loved by the other parent.

The conflict between the brothers concerns their relationship to each other. Does the parents' differing relationship with each son play a role in this? The role of Jacob's interest in some of his children over the others is made explicit in the stories of his children (33:1–2; 37:3–4; 44:27) but such is not the case here. Both Rebekah and Isaac are upset about Esau's Hittite wives. Rebekah is possibly more so since she repeats the complaint later, though that instance follows the reference to Esau's intent to kill Jacob and may be part of her plan to save her sons (27:46).

Rebekah carries out actions designed to ensure that Jacob, rather than Esau, receives the blessing from Isaac (27:5–17). She may be acting not out of love for Jacob but out of devotion to the Israelite Deity. Her willingness to take on any potential curse could be proof of that just as easily as it is proof that she loves Jacob more (27:13). The narrator does not consider it relevant for the reader to understand the living arrangements of the family, even after Esau's marriage, but Rebekah knows the men in her family well, as she is able to take "the clothes of Esau, her bigger son, the best that were with her in the house" (27:15). Either Esau still dwells with them or he keeps clothes at his mother's house. Both are signs of motherly closeness.

Rebekah is distressed that Esau may kill Jacob, so she sends Jacob away as she claims, "Why should I be bereaved of both of you in one day?" (27:45). It is hard to imagine she would fear losing a son for whom she did not care. Her actions mean that Jacob remains alive, but there is no recorded meeting of Rebekah and Jacob in the text after this point so she appears to spend the rest of her days with Esau. The family dynamics are complex, but the data do not prove that Rebekah does not care for Esau, and there is just as much data indicating that she does.

Sibling rivalry is far from Isaac's mind when he first meets Rebekah and the Deity chooses her to be his bride. The servant is unique in the text because he has a great deal of contact with Rebekah, something not usually depicted in the biblical text as happening between a man and a woman who are not related. Abraham's servant originally asks that a *na'arah* appear, and may have intentionally sought a woman who would not be excessively protected. Rebekah, in her relationship with the servant, is honest, hardworking, and polite. She must have trusted him because she quickly assents to go with him immediately, traveling some distance in order to marry Isaac, a man whose name is not even mentioned in the marriage arrangement.

Her relationship with her brother may cause her to trust men or to want to leave home quickly. Laban is not portrayed negatively in the chapter with Rebekah, but because his later actions are considered manipulative, most scholars treat him as such already in his relationship with Rebekah. Speiser notes that Laban "is greedy and insincere, the sort of person the reader will find easy to resent later on."[62] The narrator notes that he moves into action when he sees the nose ring and bands on Rebekah's arms—and hears what Rebekah says (24:30). He does not agree to marry his sister to the unknown Isaac until after Abraham's servant finishes his story, which reveals the Israelite Deity's role in the servant's mission (24:50).

What Laban's relationship is with his sister is unclear. When Rebekah learns the servant's story, she runs to the house of her mother to tell Laban or anyone

62. Speiser, *Genesis*, 184.

who is there (24:28). Laban is the one who acts as the person with control over her life, though the text does not state why this is. When the servant wants to take Rebekah immediately, her brother and mother (the presumed "they") do not want to send her (24:55), and they ask Rebekah if she wants to leave immediately (24:57), showing her respect.[63] Laban later raises the issue that he did not have a chance to say good-bye to his daughters because Jacob took them when Laban was gone (31:28). Many question Laban's motivation there, but his words in both places suggest that he regards saying good-bye as significant.

The final key to their relationship is that Rebekah sends her son to Laban. Whether she acts out of desperation since she has nowhere else to send him or whether she assumes that Laban's home is a safe place for Jacob because Laban is her brother is not stated. Since the point of sending Jacob away is to protect him, then Rebekah seems to regard her brother positively.

Rebekah's relationship with the Deity is good. She is chosen by the Deity, emphasized by having such a long chapter devoted to finding her. Whether or not she is an adherent of the Israelite Deity before marrying Isaac, by the time she becomes pregnant she is (25:22). The Deity responds to her and gives her insight into the twin sons in her womb and the roles they will play in the future. This information drives many of Rebekah's actions to ensure that her husband does not cause the Deity's plans to unravel.

Conclusion

The descriptions of Rebekah and her actions show that she is a strong, decisive individual chosen by the Israelite Deity to bear and ensure that the correct child inherits the Deity's promise. Rebekah has a positive relationship with her husband and her son Jacob, and probably even with her son Esau, her brother Laban, and the Israelite Deity.

63. Speiser argues that Laban is following Nuzi law (*Genesis*, 185).

3

Leah

Leah, wife of Jacob, sister of Rachel, and mother of Judah, is seldom treated as her own topic in modern scholarship because Rachel is the pretty one, the one with the love affair, who steals the idols, dies in childbirth, and weeps over her exiled children. Leah's story is not as glamorous.

It is difficult to discuss one woman without comparing or contrasting her with another.[1] There are a few exceptions to this rule, but Leah is not one of them. The narrator wants us to compare them: they are sisters, married to the same man, they are seldom depicted with anyone but each other, and their children become the focus of the Hebrew Bible. Because of the love story, most assume that Rachel and her sons are the correct ones to inherit the promise, or that all the sons do.[2]

Here I will challenge the idea that all of the sons inherit and that Rachel's sons are more important than Leah's.[3] To see Leah more clearly, we will examine her before Rachel. There is support for this in the Hebrew Bible: Jacob initially meets Rachel but marries Leah first and his first children are hers. With a slightly different picture of Leah, Rachel's picture is altered.

---

1. Brenner, *Israelite Woman*, 93.

2. Tikva Frymer-Kensky, "Leah," in Meyers, *Women in Scripture*, 109; Steinberg, *Kinship and Marriage*, 116.

3. Timothy Finlay concludes similarly based on birth reports (*The Birth Report Genre in the Hebrew Bible*, Forschungen zum Alten Testament 2/12 [Tübingen: Mohr Siebeck, 2005], 160).

Leah's Description

How Leah is described is a major component in her evaluation because she is so often compared to her pretty sister.[4] The first comment about Leah directly relates to her sister: Leah is literally Laban's "greater" daughter (29:16). Most texts translate *gedolah* with something signifying their comparative ages, therefore identifying Leah as "older." The Hebrew *gedolah* covers a wide range, including number and things.[5] Since later Laban claims that he gives Leah to Jacob rather than Rachel because of their age difference (29:16), the assumption is that the narrator informs the reader there is an age difference between the two. When Laban later explains why he switches the daughters, he uses a different term to describe them, labeling Leah "firstborn," *bekorah* (29:26).[6] Legitimate translations include Leah is "great" or "big" and Rachel "little" or "insignificant." Here the narrator employs ambiguous terminology.

The reference to Laban's two daughters does not flow cleanly in the text (29:16). The text first recounts Jacob's meeting with Rachel at the well (29:4), his outburst at hearing who she is (29:11), and his reunion with Laban (29:13–14). The text then notes that Laban is concerned that Jacob, a member of his own family, is working for him for nothing and suggests that Jacob consider a wage (29:15). The reference to Laban having two daughters appears suddenly. The reader does not yet know what Rachel looks like, and Jacob is only about to announce his love for her (29:18). The references to Rachel are inserted to advise the reader about why Jacob wants to work for her, and the reference to Leah is awkward.

This description of Leah identifies her too as a child of Laban and part of the line that has been legitimated by the Deity as a good source of wives through Jacob's mother, Rebekah (Gen. 24). Thus far Laban is a positive character (28:46); Isaac and Rebekah send Jacob to Paddan-aram specifically to take a wife from among the daughters of Laban.

In Leah's introduction she is identified as a legitimate potential wife. Even here Leah is overshadowed by her sister since the reader and Jacob have already met Rachel (29:6–11). This verse raises the problem that her existence creates. The problem in this generation in Paddan-aram is similar to Rebekah and Isaac's situation—there are too many potential candidates for securing the Deity's promise (here mothers of heirs of the promise), thereby foreshadowing a problem for the generation of Jacob's children.

Leah's next description has troubled scholars because of the difficulty understanding what "soft (*rakkot*) eyes" means (29:17). The difficulty is magnified by the comparative description of Rachel that highlights her beauty. The

---

4. Frymer-Kensky is one of the lone scholars who does not focus on Rachel's beauty. Tikva Frymer-Kensky, "Rachel," in Meyers, *Women in Scripture*, 138–40.

5. Brown, Driver, and Briggs, *Lexicon*, 152–53.

6. Ibid., 114.

dictionary definition of the adjective for Leah includes "tender, delicate, soft,"[7] in a positive sense, such as words that are soft and gentle (Job 40:27), or in a more problematic sense, implying weakness (2 Sam. 3:39).

The NJPS translation is "weak," meaning tender, in the sense of dainty or delicate,[8] indicating refinement and delicacy of breeding.[9] Others consider the translation of her name as "cow," though still maintaining the translation of her eyes as "weak."[10] Some see her eyes as the one nice thing said about her, hence "lovely," but in contrast with Rachel's overall beauty.[11] Cotter's summary is useful: "However the word, so crucial and yet so difficult to understand, is translated, we still know that Leah suffers by comparison with her sister."[12]

Leah's next description is that she is "there" (Gen. 29:25). The text notes that Jacob works seven years for Rachel (29:20) and finally goes to Laban and says, "Give [me] my woman/wife" (29:21). Jacob does not explicitly ask for Rachel. Laban makes a feast (29:22), and when evening comes he takes Leah, brings her to Jacob (29:23), and Jacob sleeps with her (29:23). In the morning he realizes, "She is Leah."

Leah is the subject of this verbless clause, in which "there is no verbal marker of predication."[13] The word order marks this clause as one of identification, and its role is to identify a subject, in this case, "she is Leah."[14] Since it identifies Leah and she takes no action, here the clause is a description rather than an action.

The term identifies to the reader that the wife Jacob has been led to believe is Rachel is actually Leah (29:24), though the reader knows what is happening (29:23). Thus Leah is described as simply being there, and the ramifications are significant. It makes Leah the first and primary wife. It means, according to the Levitical laws adjudicating later Israelite marriages, that Leah is a legitimate wife, and Rachel will not be.[15] Despite all the evidence that Leah is the primary wife, she is never so labeled. On the evening in question, when she is brought to Jacob, the narrator states that he (Laban) takes his daughter Leah and brings her to him (Jacob) and he (Jacob) sleeps with her (29:23). Even Zilpah (30:9) and Bilhah (30:4) are given as wives, but Leah is not. Leah and

---

7. Ibid., 940.

8. Speiser, *Genesis*, 225; Lisa W. Davison, "Leah," in Freedman, *Eerdman's Dictionary of the Bible*, 797.

9. Gale A. Yee, "Leah," in Freedman, *Anchor Bible Dictionary*, 4:268.

10. Davison, "Leah," 797.

11. Cotter, *Genesis*, 222.

12. Ibid.

13. Bruce K. Waltke and M. O'Connor, *An Introduction to Biblical Hebrew Syntax* (Winona Lake, IN: Eisenbrauns, 1990), 72.

14. Ibid., 130.

15. Lev. 18:18, "Do not marry a woman as a rival to her sister and uncover her nakedness in the other's lifetime."

Rachel are referred to obliquely as wives (30:26), and Leah refers to Jacob as her husband, but Leah is never identified specifically as the wife of Jacob.

Though not named, Leah is described by her father as "firstborn" only after she is married to Jacob. Only when Jacob realizes it is Leah he marries does he remind Laban that he was in service for Rachel and feels that he has been deceived (29:25). Laban claims that in this place it is not done to marry the younger daughter before the firstborn (29:26).

Leah is Jacob's first and primary wife. Later she indicates this is how she understands her status (30:15). Laban, while deceiving Jacob, claims he is following custom (29:26). Genesis thus far understands the younger son's position as different from the older son's status, which is why the Deity speaks to Rebekah when she is still pregnant (25:23) and why Esau has a birthright to sell (25:31). Isaac is either playing favorites with Esau by giving him a special blessing or also understands the role of Esau as the oldest as one that signifies he should receive a special blessing (27:32). The Israelite Deity cares for Leah when no one else does, possibly indicating that she is blameless and the marriages are not organized incorrectly.

Leah, and possibly Laban, do nothing wrong in the eyes of their culture, the context of the Hebrew Bible, or the eyes of the Israelite Deity. Without Leah's marriage to Jacob, key tribes, Levi and Judah, would not exist, nor would Moses and David. The role of Leah's children is a recurring beat indicating that Leah is at least as important as Rachel.

Leah's final description, "unloved," is the painful reality of her marriage to Jacob (29:31). This description appears after Jacob marries Rachel (29:28), after the narrator notes that Jacob loves Rachel more than Leah (29:30), and immediately following the statement that Jacob serves Laban another seven years. Some argue that the text means not that she is "hated" but that she is "unloved," using Akkadian counterparts to make the case.[16] While carrying a gentler nuance and following the narrator's statement that Jacob loves Rachel more, the narrator employs *sane'*, a Hebrew term whose essence is stronger than loving someone less: it means "hate."[17] Others note that this verse employs legal terminology from Deuteronomy 21:15–17.[18] The Deuteronomy passage legislates how to treat the sons of a loved wife versus those of a hated wife and adjudicates that a firstborn son, even of a hated wife, still deserves the treatment of a firstborn son. The text never identifies who hates Leah, but the result leads the Israelite Deity to take actions on her behalf. Like Sarah and Rebekah, the Israelite Deity protects Leah and ensures her role in Israel's future.

Leah's descriptions are limited and the force of their meaning is unclear. When compared to Rachel, the force of Leah's birth order and the fact that

16. Speiser, *Genesis,* 230.
17. Brown, Driver, and Briggs, *Lexicon,* 971.
18. Von Rad, *Genesis,* 294.

she is not clearly identified as pretty are striking. Alone, Leah descends from the correct lineage, carries the power or authority of a firstborn, is a first and primary wife, and is, at best, not appreciated.

Leah as a Subject

Most of Leah's actions concern bearing children, naming children, or giving someone to Jacob to have more children on her behalf. While her actions are limited, the fact that she bears so often, the names she chooses for her children, and the roles her children play in the history of Israel are significant for how the Israelite Deity treats her and her role in the history of Israel.

Leah's first action is to conceive, followed quickly by bearing a son (29:32). This combination is repeated for the births of Simeon (29:33), Levi (29:34), Judah (29:35), Issachar (30:18), and Zebulun (30:20). The birth of her last son is the only case where the text explicitly states that the child belongs to Jacob.

In Leah's final birth sequence she bears Jacob a daughter. There is no reference to her conceiving nor is there an explanation for her daughter's name. This reference clarifies who Dinah is so that when she appears later in the narrative, who she is and how she is related to everyone need no explanation, though she is identified in the beginning of her own story as the daughter Leah bears to Jacob (34:1). In the Hebrew Bible and especially in Genesis, it is unusual to announce the birth of a girl. Thus far only Rebekah's birth has been announced (22:23).

Leah's final reference is a summary of her life's work and is connected to her primary actions. Genesis 46 contains the list of Israelites who go down to Egypt with Jacob (46:8), including the sons of Leah and their children (46:8–14), and Dinah (46:15). The text summarizes that they are the sons who Leah bears to Jacob in Paddan-aram (46:15). The text does not refer to Leah's death, and according to the numbers provided in the text, Leah cannot be included in the list of those who go to Egypt, and thus she must have died prior to the descent. This is confirmed when Jacob refers to her burial in the cave of Machpelah (49:31).

Leah's other significant action is speech. She understands the Deity as the source of her fertility, revealed by her first speech act: she names or "calls" her son Reuben because, as she says, "It means: The Deity has seen my affliction," adding that it also means, "Now my husband will love me" (29:32). Leah names her son and Jacob has little to do with it. The text does not even note that Leah bears a son to Jacob, as is the case with Sarah (21:2) and Hagar (16:15). As with many name explanations in the Hebrew Bible, the explanations are not always grammatically correct but more often are a play on words with the name and some action. Here there is a good explanation for the name, since it means "See, a son," playing on the verb *ra'ah*, meaning "to see,"[19] the first two letters of which are included in Reuben's name. The text is explicit that the Deity has "seen" that Leah is hated, thereby picking up on her state. Again, a matriarch recognizes the Israelite Deity and the role the Deity plays in her fertility without any sign of direct contact between the two.

Leah provides a meaning different from the actual name to bring in her own personal situation.[20] The noun Leah uses for "affliction," *'ani*, is from the same root used to describe Sarah's actions toward Hagar after Sarah is lowered in her esteem (16:6). She explains her son's name by describing her personal state.[21] These words are Leah's and reveal how she situates herself in the family.

For her second son, she says, "This is because the Deity heard I was unloved and has given me this one also," naming him Simeon (29:33). This son's name relates to "hearing," *shama'*.[22] Leah identifies the Deity as the source of her fertility and names the child after her personal life. Her situation has not changed, since she still feels hated, but the Deity listens to her.

For Leah's third son she says this time her husband will become attached to her since she has borne him three sons, explaining the name Levi (29:34). The root of the name is connected to the verb "be joined" and concerns her desire for her relationship with her husband,[23] revealing her continued focus on gaining Jacob's love.

For Leah's fourth son she says, "This time I will praise the Deity," explaining Judah's name (29:35). She connects the name with the verb *yadah*, meaning "throw, cast," but in the Hiphil it carries the sense, "give thanks, laud, praise."[24] This differs from the naming of her earlier sons. When naming Reuben and Levi, Leah does not focus on the child as much as on what the child will do for her relationship with her husband. Reuben and Simeon's names include recognition of the Israelite Deity in the process, though the focus is on her unhappy state.

The reason for Judah's name focuses solely on the Israelite Deity, not what the Deity can do, will do, or will change in her situation but simply praises, separating him somewhat from the others, whose names are a plea for change.[25] In Genesis all of Jacob's children presumably inherit the promise, but the reality is that Judah is the tribe that ultimately succeeds: Judah is the tribe of David, the tribe that continues past the Assyrian exile, and the tribe that returns following the Babylonian exile. The primary target audience of the

19. Brown, Driver, and Briggs, *Lexicon*, 906–10.
20. Von Rad, *Genesis*, 294.
21. Brown, Driver, and Briggs, *Lexicon*, 777.
22. Ibid., 1033–35.
23. Ibid., 530.
24. Ibid., 392–93.
25. Jeansonne, *Women of Genesis*, 75.

biblical text is the descendants of Judah. Thus from the beginning Judah's role is highlighted in a way the others are not.

Leah is involved in naming her maid's children. For the first Leah says, "What good fortune," and so she names him Gad (30:11). The explanation is straightforward since *gad* means "good fortune."[26] Leah declares, "What blessedness" (30:13), interpreting that women will deem her fortunate, so the second son her maid bears to Jacob she names Asher (30:12–13). The connection here too is simple, since the name Asher means "happiness" or "blessedness."[27] The implication is that Leah has given her maid as part of the contest Rachel claims to be in with her, though neither the narrator nor Leah claims she is procreating as part of a contest. Leah gives both children names that reflect positive things, though the name of the second reveals that she wants women to deem her fortunate.

Leah again speaks following the births of Zilpah's sons. The text shifts to the time of the wheat harvest when Reuben finds mandrakes in the field and brings them to his mother (30:14).[28] Rachel asks Leah to please give her some (30:14). Leah's response seems excessive for the simple question but it is a breaking point for her. She says, though one can imagine her yelling, "Was it not enough for you to take away my husband, that you also will take my son's mandrakes?" (30:15). The implication is clear: Leah considers Rachel the one who steals her husband. Rachel's response is not to deny the charges but to exchange a night in bed with Jacob for Leah's son's mandrakes (30:15).

Leah says, this time to Jacob, "To me you will come tonight, for I have surely hired you with my son's mandrakes" (30:16). There is no subtlety to her words. Her speech inverts the word order, stressing that "to her" he will go that night. She uses the term *sakar*, which means "to hire," to describe how she procures his services for that evening.[29] This is the root that Leah's father, Laban, uses when asking Jacob what his "wages" would be to work for him (29:15), which leads to Jacob's marriage to Laban's daughters. The verse uses grammar to stress its meaning by employing the infinitive absolute, which is a construction that often intensifies a verb. Thus Leah does not merely hire Jacob, but she does so surely, readily, and certainly: "will surely hire."[30] The narrator uses both terminology and grammar to emphasize Leah's bold words.

Her response hints that she and Jacob may no longer be having sexual relations. If Leah can hire Jacob's services for a few mandrakes, and Rachel

26. Brown, Driver, and Briggs, *Lexicon*, 151.

27. Ibid., 80–81.

28. Mandrakes (*Mandragora officinarum*) are a root, related to the potato, found in stony places. The root resembles a human figure, which probably led to its association with fertility rites, and was further wanted because it possesses narcotic properties for which it was esteemed. See Irene Jacob and Walter Jacob, "Flora," in Freedman, *Anchor Bible Dictionary*, 2:812.

29. Brown, Driver, and Briggs, *Lexicon*, 968–69.

30. Waltke and O'Connor, *Biblical Hebrew Syntax*, 580–97.

controls his sleeping pattern, then this verse reveals much about the household arrangement.

Leah acknowledges Elohim through her speech when naming her fifth son, the result of the evening with Jacob. She says, "Elohim has given me my wages for having given my maid to my husband," so she names him Issachar (30:17). The name Issachar includes the reference to *sakar* (or *sachar*), "hiring," Jacob for the evening. The text connects the name of the child with the means of procuring the child, and Leah associates the child as a wage for giving Zilpah to Jacob. Leah views her role as providing children for Jacob. She expresses her attitude toward her sister in the mandrake negotiations (30:15), but she does not bring it into the naming of her children.

Leah's reaction to her sixth son (30:19) is to say that Elohim has endowed her with a choice gift and this time her husband will exalt her, for she has borne him six sons, and she names him Zebulun (30:20). This wordplay connects Hebrew *zabad*, meaning "bestow upon" or "endow with," with *zabal*, meaning "exalt" or "honor."[31] This name reflects her joy in her sons mixed with her continuing hope that her husband will appreciate her. Leah names Dinah with no explanation (30:21).

The last time Leah speaks is with her sister. After working for Laban to marry his daughters, Jacob decides it is time to leave with his wives and children (30:26). Laban argues that he is blessed by the Deity because of Jacob and to name the wages due him (30:28). Jacob devises a complicated system so the animals promised him do well (30:31–43) and he becomes wealthy (30:43). This does not sit well with Laban's sons. Jacob notices a change in the way Laban relates to him (31:2) and is visited in a dream by the Deity telling him to go home (31:3). Jacob has both Rachel and Leah called to the field where his flock is, apparently to speak with them together, away from the rest of their family (31:4). Jacob tells them a story similar to but not identical with that recounted by the narrator, ending with Elohim of Bethel telling him to get up and return to his native land (31:13).

Rachel and Leah speak together. The sisters ask if they have a share in the inheritance of their father's house (31:14). They claim that Laban regards them as outsiders: he sold them and used their purchase price (31:15). They contend that all the wealth Elohim took from their father belongs to them and their children, and Jacob should do as Elohim says (31:16).

Their unified speech contains a fair amount of animosity, which they seem to share. First, they claim that their father sold them, though the text notes that Jacob worked seven years for each of them. Second, they claim Laban has used up their purchase price. Since the price, as recounted at the time of their marriages, is Jacob's labor, the only way for this to reflect that situation is if the new scenario, where Jacob's flocks are doing so much better than

31. Brown, Driver, and Briggs, *Lexicon*, 256, 259.

Laban's and his sons, refers to using up Jacob's time. Finally, they imply that what belongs to Jacob is theirs.

One problem with understanding all of the references in the daughters' speech is that, though the text provides many details, not all of them make sense. Possibly more precise is that the daughters are not happy with their father, feel they have not been treated well by him, and would rather go with their husband, who is now rich, than stay where they are. Rachel too has a son (30:23), and it is possible the sisters' relationship with each other has healed and they would rather be with each other than with their father. Whatever the true reasons and whether it is rooted in legitimate claims or not, the bottom line is that Jacob needs their approval to leave, and he receives it.

Following Judah's birth, Leah ceases to bear, temporarily (29:35). She first "sees" that she has stopped bearing (30:9). Even though Jacob loves Rachel more than Leah (29:30), he still had sex with Leah—she became pregnant four times (29:31–35). Though he also sleeps with Bilhah, he must have been maintaining sexual relations with Leah, for otherwise she would not realize that she is no longer bearing.

Leah's reaction is similar to her sister's and Sarah's, and she too gives her maid Zilpah to Jacob. The move is successful and Leah's maid bears Jacob two sons (30:10, 12).

The crude bartering for Jacob's sexual services in the mandrake episode contains another bold action of Leah: she "goes out" to meet Jacob (30:16). Her words and action are unusual for Leah. The action is important later for Dinah, who also meets a man when she "goes out," also leading to copulation (see chapter 10 on Dinah below).

When Jacob finally meets his brother Esau (33:1), Jacob arranges his children, in order of importance to him, with the children of the maids first, followed by Leah and her children, keeping Rachel and Joseph last (33:2). After Esau runs to greet him and embraces him, he asks who all the women and children are and each group comes forward. Leah comes forward and bows low before Esau with her children (33:7). Leah acts as do all Jacob's other wives, though in her presentation to Esau she appears as the second most important wife.

The bulk of Leah's actions concern bearing children, naming children, speaking, and giving others to Jacob so they bear him children. Her other action surrounds the mandrake situation, but even that is related to childbearing since she gains access to Jacob sexually so she can bear more children. In her last speaking role, Leah and Rachel speak with one voice in their assessment of how their father treats them, and they both are prepared to leave Paddan-aram (31:14). Leah's final action, bowing (before Esau), is also carried out by Rachel and the other mothers of Jacob's children. All of Leah's actions depict her as a dutiful, fertile wife. The naming of her children shows a movement from despair and desire for her husband's love to satisfaction and joy in her ability to bear children and the status it brings. Her children are the remnant who survive as a group with a cohesive identity through the tribes of Judah and Levi.

Leah as an Object

The references to Leah as an object do not alter her role in the text since most of the citations concern her being taken, her connection to her maid, or other characters' attitudes toward her. These references reinforce the concept of her as dutiful with a focus on bearing children.

The first reference to her as an object is when Laban, her father, takes her and brings her to Jacob (29:23). This case is different from other marriage situations in that the woman Jacob marries is not the one he thinks he is marrying, and the text never employs wife terminology. The narrator provides the reader with information before Jacob receives it. Thus the appearance of Leah is a surprise to Jacob (29:25). Later, when Leah answers her sister about the mandrakes, she accuses Rachel of stealing her husband (30:15). Rachel's response to Leah in the mandrake situation could be interpreted as her tacit agreement to Leah's accusation (30:15), meaning that Rachel too may have known that Jacob would first marry Leah.

The next case follows the first: Laban gives Zilpah to Leah (29:24). The gift seems superfluous but it lays the groundwork for Leah to give Zilpah to Jacob later (30:9).

After a week of marriage to Leah, Jacob marries Rachel, and the narrator notes that he loves Rachel more than Leah (29:30). The verse is usually translated, "indeed, he loved Rachel more than Leah" (e.g., NJPS); a more literal translation would be, "he also loved Rachel from Leah." The difference would be that he loved Rachel differently from Leah. The standard translation implies that Jacob loves Leah, just not as much as he loves Rachel. The later citations where Leah names her sons clarifies that she does not feel her husband loves her and she wants his love. Regardless of how little Jacob loves Leah, especially compared to his love for Rachel, it does not keep him from having sexual relations with her.

The Deity opens Leah's womb when the Deity sees she is hated (29:31), though she is never described as barren. The Deity's help appears in the verse stating that Rachel is barren, raising a contrast between the two and showing the Deity acting for Leah. Fertility, at least for the matriarchs, comes from the Deity.

The narrator notes that Leah is hated but not by whom. Only after that reference does the Deity open her womb (29:31). The same verse refers to Rachel's barren state. At issue is whether Leah is originally barren, as are the other matriarchs (11:20; 25:21). For the previous matriarchs the Deity takes some action allowing them to bear (21:1; 25:21). Both matriarchs believe that the Deity controls fertility (16:2; 25:22). In both cases the matriarch's spouse prays for fertility, in Abraham's case for Abimelech's house (21:17–18), and Isaac directly for Rebekah (25:21). If the Deity carries out actions to keep her from being barren, this would be the first case where the Deity acts to ease the matriarch's pain.

The Deity acts because Leah is hated, leading to her fertility and children, which causes her sister, Rachel, to become envious (30:1). The narrator relates that Rachel names the children of Bilhah after a contest she is waging with her sister, but Leah never addresses the baby contest. Leah responds by giving her maid to Jacob, but the narrator says that she does this because she sees she has stopped bearing (30:9), not because her sister's maid is producing. When Leah herself bears more children, she names them with the explanation that they are her reward for having given her maid to Jacob. The only time Leah raises the issue of Jacob's status as a dispute between the two is in the mandrake situation when Rachel wants, in Leah's eyes, even more than just her husband.

The next few actions where Leah is an object concern her maid, Zilpah. Leah does not appear as an object in the English translation, but in the Hebrew construction she is the object of a preposition. In 30:10 Leah's maid bears a son to Jacob, and in 30:12 Leah's maid bears Jacob a second son. Both concern providing children for Jacob.

Leah is an object when her son brings mandrakes to her. The text is explicit that the mandrakes belong not to Leah but to her son (30:14–15). Both Rachel and Leah refer to them as such. Leah's role in her children's lives is seldom conveyed in the text, other than it placing them lower in their father's esteem because they are not the sons of his more loved wife. This is the rare case of seeing Leah with one of her children. If everyone considers the mandrakes as playing a role in fertility, then Reuben's bringing them to his mother may indicate that he understands his mother's situation in the family, especially in relation to Rachel, and he is trying to help. This reveals a positive relationship that he would bring a prized object immediately to his mother, especially knowing his aunt's fertility problems.

Leah herself does not partake of the mandrakes, but their impact benefits her since it allows her to sleep with Jacob, or in the wording of the text, for him to "lay with her that night" (30:16). This follows Leah's bold move of going to meet him and informing him where he will sleep that night, but the narrator notes that it comes true—he does lie with her. The next verse, where Leah appears as an object, indicates that Elohim is still looking out for her by noting that Elohim listens to Leah, leading to her conceiving and bearing another son (30:17). Leah says nothing to Elohim in the interim, only to Jacob. Whether Elohim hears her comments to Rachel, her commands to Jacob, or simply understands her general situation is not clear. Regardless of what Elohim hears, Elohim again does something to allow Leah to bear children.

Leah is also an object when her father searches through her tent to find the missing teraphim (31:33; see chapter 4 on Rachel). Leah is only a bystander in this situation, but the narrator notes that Laban went into Jacob's tent, and Leah's tent, and the tent of the maids (31:33). Here Leah's tent appears to be different from that of Jacob and that of the maids. The narrator then notes that Jacob leaves Leah's tent and enters Rachel's tent (31:33). No order is expressed, but the implication is that Leah's tent is between Jacob's and Rachel's. Leah's tent is mentioned twice, though Rachel is the one who has the teraphim and toys with her father while he hunts for them.

Leah appears as an object when she is grouped with the other wives. To have a private conversation with Rachel and Leah, Jacob has them called to the field (31:4). When Jacob is about to meet Esau, he divides the children among Leah, Rachel, and the two maids (33:1). Here her position as second to Rachel is highlighted since he places the maids and their children first, Leah and her children next, and finishes with Rachel and Joseph (33:2).

Following Jacob's journey to Bethel (35:1), where Elohim changes his name to Israel (35:9), is a list of Jacob's children. This notice follows almost immediately upon Rachel's death (35:18), when Reuben lays with Rachel's maid, Bilhah (35:22). Leah's sons are listed first, then Rachel's, then Bilhah's, and finally Zilpah's. The order is not chronological (Rachel's sons are born last) nor is it in order of preference (Leah's are named first). The list appears immediately before Isaac's death announcement and is a summary.

Leah and her children rise to the top of the list and remain there in genealogical lists. Some are born before the children of the maids, and none is favored by Jacob, but the text from this point on treats all of Leah's children before the other children (46:8–14; 49:2–14).

The sons of Leah's maid are treated somewhat differently in the rest of Genesis. Following Rachel's death and preceding Isaac's death, the sons of Leah's maid are treated last (35:26). In the list of those who go to Egypt the sons of Leah's maid appear second in the list, following Leah's sons (46:16–18). In Jacob's blessing, the children of Leah's maid and those of Rachel's maid are intertwined (Dan, Gad, Asher, and Naphtali; 49:16–21), with Rachel's children listed last. While each list is designed for its particular context, in all of them Leah's children appear first.[32]

Leah's final appearance involves her death. When Jacob instructs his sons to bury him in the field of Machpelah that Abraham bought from Ephron the Hittite for a burial site (49:29–30), he explains that there Abraham and his wife Sarah are buried, and there Isaac and his wife Rebekah are buried, and there he buried Leah (49:31). The readers are not notified when it happens, but they are informed that she is buried there. Such is not the case with

32. For how different genres are modified by larger text-types see Finlay, *Birth Report Genre,* 245–46.

Rachel, who dies in childbirth and is buried by the side of the road. Thus in death Leah is treated by Jacob as the primary wife worthy of burial with the other matriarchs.

The actions characters carry out toward Leah in the story are not significantly different than those carried out toward most other women in the Bible, and some might argue that she is treated better by the men than most other women. She is only "taken" once, and that is by her father to marry Jacob. The Deity cares for her like the other matriarchs, by making her fertile. Like Sarah, she gives her maid to her husband; but unlike the Hagar situation, either her maid acts differently, Leah acts differently, or they both do, so no difficulties arise. The children are treated both as hers and as belonging to their mother (see chapter 8 below on Zilpah). The narrator elevates Leah's children by beginning with them when relating the descent into Egypt.

Leah's Relationships

The data about Leah's relationships reflect a slightly different character than revealed by examining her actions or texts in which she is an object. Her relationships reveal someone who almost ignores the actions of those around her and instead focuses on having children and gaining the love of her husband.

Leah's first relationship depicted in the text is her relationship with her father. When she is first introduced it is in the context of setting Jacob's wages. Laban asks what Jacob's wages should be, and here the narrator inserts the note that Laban has two daughters (29:16). Most of Leah's life is defined by being the firstborn sister, which leads her to be married to Jacob first, and the rest of her story focuses on the problems that emerge from Laban's action.

In general, scholars evaluate Laban negatively, to a large extent because of the daughter switch. His actions in the Rebekah episode are considered examples of his greed and insincerity.[33] These scholars assume Laban is greedy even though Laban does not consent to Rebekah's marriage until after hearing Abraham's servant's conclusive evidence that the Deity is behind the match (24:50).[34] Laban claims that he is following local custom (29:26), something not disputed by the narrator, and raises an issue behind Jacob's visit to Paddan-aram in the first place, the conflict between the older and younger sons.

Laban is accused of negative actions regarding Jacob's compensation for working for him beyond the fourteen years to pay for his two wives. Scholars raise a number of issues, but most consider everything Laban says as reflecting insincerity,[35] even while Laban admits that he knows the Deity has blessed

33. Speiser, *Genesis,* 184.
34. Von Rad, *Genesis,* 258.
35. Ibid., 300–301.

him because of Jacob (30:27) and asks Jacob to name the wages. Laban sets a scenario whereby his sons will benefit, making it difficult for Jacob to prosper. But Jacob manipulates the flocks to produce results that benefit him (29:30–37). Jacob later tells his wives that Elohim told him to do so (31:10), though the text never recounts such a dream. Laban can be accused of cheating Jacob, but Jacob does the same to Laban.

Jacob leaves Laban's house with his family and all his goods (31:17–18) while Laban is away (31:19). Unbeknownst to Jacob, Rachel steals her father's teraphim (31:19). When Laban catches up with Jacob, he claims he would have sent him off with music (31:27), and he laments that he did not have a chance to kiss his family good-bye (31:28). Only after claiming it is a foolish thing to do does Laban raise the issue of the missing teraphim (31:30).

Von Rad admits that Laban can only appear as the one injured by Jacob in this scene,[36] and later notes that the recovery of the idols is more important to him than the legal protection of his daughters,[37] even though Laban adds it almost as an afterthought. Yet Laban raises concerns about sending his children off properly, something that is also an issue when his sister Rebekah leaves immediately with Abraham's servant to marry Isaac (24:55). The debate between Jacob and Laban concerns their working arrangement. Laban's concern is his daughters and their children. His request of Jacob is that the Deity will watch over their arrangement when they are out of sight of each other because Laban wants to ensure that Jacob will not ill-treat his daughters or take other wives besides them when no one is watching (31:49).

With this slightly different view of Laban, his relationship with Leah appears not so bad. He guards their tradition, and possibly her reputation, by finding her a husband. That Jacob wants Rachel and what Rachel may have wanted do not change the fact that Laban finds a husband for Leah, which makes her a primary wife. This may create more problems than it solves for the family, but Laban does his duty to Leah.

Leah mentions her father only after the children are born and they are ready to depart. It is not clear what their relationship has been over the years. Laban is troubled that he does not have a chance to say good-bye to her, but both Leah and Rachel appear more than happy to leave him (31:14), though many of their complaints are not borne out by the text.

The story highlights through the naming of many of Leah's children how important it is for her to gain her husband's love (30:20). Yet her need for this lessens as the story progresses. In the original naming sequence it is the only goal, and by the time of Judah's birth it is not even mentioned. When Leah gives Zilpah to Jacob it is because she has stopped bearing, and

36. Ibid., 309.
37. Ibid.

neither of the children's names is directly connected to Leah's relationship with Jacob (30:11, 13). In the episode where Leah sells her son's mandrakes for a night with Jacob, she does not appear to want to sleep with him for any romantic rendezvous but treats the arrangement as a business transaction: she wants more children. That is certainly the Deity's understanding since the Deity's response to "hearing Leah" is to allow her to conceive (30:17). Jacob repeatedly places Leah after Rachel and Rachel's children, yet following Rachel's death the place of Leah's children shifts, maybe not in Jacob's affection but in their placement on the key lists of who is Israel. Finally, Jacob buries Leah in the cave with the patriarchs and matriarchs (49:31).

Rachel should be Leah's biggest nemesis. Leah is hated by someone, and Rachel is a good candidate, more because of what she says than what Leah says (30:1). Leah has one outburst where she accuses Rachel of stealing her husband (30:15), but that incident is never connected to a name or the explanation of her children's names. When the issue is Jacob or Laban, Leah and Rachel answer with one voice. Rachel has more problems with Leah than Leah has with Rachel, or Leah does not let her feelings about Rachel enter into the naming of children.

Leah's maid is also not an issue in this story. Contrary to the Sarah and Hagar situation, we know precisely how Leah acquires Zilpah—she is a gift from Laban (29:23). She reappears only when Leah stops bearing (30:9). The narrator raises no questions as to the legitimacy of Leah giving Zilpah to Jacob. No change in the relationship between Zilpah and Leah appears, and the text does not mention Zilpah conceiving—only bearing (30:10, 12). Though the children are always treated as somehow related to Leah (35:26; 46:16–18), they also always belong to Zilpah (33:2; 35:26; 46:16–18). Leah uses Zilpah to procure more children for Jacob but never lays full claim to them. Their names reflect nothing negative. That Leah considers giving her maid to Jacob difficult in some way is reflected in her considering Issachar a reward for it.

Little can be said about Leah's relationship with her children. Reuben understands the role of mandrakes and brings them to his mother (30:14). Jacob treats his children differently based on their mothers. His love for Rachel's children is felt by the other sons (37:4) and influences their relationship with Joseph (37:19–20) but not with their mothers.

Leah's relationship with the Israelite Deity is good. The Deity listens to her when she is hated and provides her with fertility. Like Sarah and Rebekah before her, Leah assumes the hand of the Deity in the good things that come her way. Leah recognizes the Israelite Deity and Elohim, though neither entity ever contacts her directly. Leah, like Sarah and Rebekah, never says or does anything against the Deity and does what she thinks the Deity wants from her.

Conclusion

Examining Leah before Rachel reveals a consistent picture. Leah is a legal and, through no scheming of her own, primary wife. Despite this, she is never labeled "Jacob's wife." The Deity recognizes her pain and protects her by giving her children. Despite the lack of love in her life prior to children and the animosity against her by her sister because of her children, she does not resort to the same devices as Rachel. She uses her limited means to procure more children. Her husband's love is what she seeks, but her character evolves and that need lessens as the story progresses. She recognizes the role of the Deity in providing the good things in her life. She is buried with the other matriarchs. It is Leah's children, Judah and Levi, who are the progenitors of the tribes that survive exile and are most likely the original target audience of the narrative.

4

Rachel

Rachel is usually viewed as the pretty and loved wife of Jacob. Rachel's stealing the family idols is treated as a side story, and her death in childbirth and burial along the road are addressed insofar as Jeremiah later refers to her grief watching her children go off in exile (Jer. 31:15). The focus here is on the legitimacy of her marriage to Jacob, how loving Rachel and Jacob's relationship is following their marriage, Rachel and Jacob's prophetic statements about children and death, and why she is not buried in the cave with the other matriarchs and patriarchs. Rachel appears different when viewed after considering Leah.

Rachel's Description

Rachel is first described like Leah in her connection to Laban: she is his daughter (Gen. 29:6). In Rachel's case the description is related to her activity. Immediately upon Jacob's arrival in the land of the easterners (29:1) he sees a well and asks the people if they know Laban, the son of Nahor (29:4). This scene is reminiscent of the scene concerning Jacob's mother, Rebekah (Gen. 24): he is in the right town, they know him, and Rachel is approaching with the flock (29:6). Rachel seems similar to Rebekah in that she first appears at the well; Jacob, like Abraham's servant, seeks Nahor's family; both seek wives for a descendant of Abraham; and the Deity's hand appears to be behind the meeting. The text suggests that Rachel is what Jacob seeks.

Rachel is next described as a shepherdess (29:9). Shepherds in the Hebrew Bible are not uncommon, with the role extending metaphorically to rulers and the Israelite Deity, yet Rachel is the only female shepherd in the biblical text. The status of shepherds ranges from lowly herdsmen (Amos 7:14–15) to master breeders of sheep (2 Kings 3:4). They were responsible for locating food and water for their flocks, often ranging far from home (Gen. 31:40) and guarding them against thieves (31:39) and wild animals (1 Sam. 17:34–35; Amos 3:12). Despite Rachel's somewhat dangerous career, commentators do not mention it.

Rachel's career is one Jacob adopts in the next few chapters. She is a woman alone in a place populated by men. Why is she the shepherdess rather than her older sister Leah? Is Leah raised to marry while Rachel works for the family? Is Rachel more capable?

Rachel is next described as the "smaller" daughter of Laban. The text includes this information when Laban raises the issue of Jacob's wages. Laban is uncomfortable with Jacob, a family member, working for no wages and asks Jacob to name them (29:15). The narrator inserts what appears to be irrelevant information: Laban has two daughters. Leah is identified as the bigger sister, and Rachel the smaller. Later the issue will be their ages (29:26), but at this point the narrator uses the term *qatanah* to describe Rachel. This term can mean "small" or "young" but carries the connotation "insignificant."[1] When the narrator wants clarity, he uses terminology defining their age situation, yet he employs different terms here.

Only after Rachel is described as Laban's smaller shepherdess daughter are her looks introduced. When describing the daughters, Leah has "soft eyes," compared to Rachel, who is described as "beautiful of shape and beautiful of appearance" (29:17). The first part of her beauty is described as *to'ar*, which translates as "outline, form,"[2] the same term used to describe Abigail (1 Sam. 25:3) and Esther (Esther 2:7). Deuteronomy uses the same description to define how one treats a captive woman who one might want to marry and make a wife (Deut. 21:11). Common to all these women is that a man would desire them because of their shape. The same is later applied to Joseph in Egypt and leads to a woman sexually harassing him (Gen. 39:7–20).

The legitimacy of desiring a woman for such reasons is questionable based on biblical examples. David marries Abigail, who is described as intelligent (1 Sam. 25:3). While some argue that she may also be David's sister,[3] and the text clarifies that her husband dies of somewhat natural causes (1 Sam. 25:37), the way she becomes David's wife is complex (1 Sam. 25). Esther's beauty, either her face or shape, wins her a beauty contest to become the

1. Brown, Driver, and Briggs, *Lexicon*, 882.
2. Ibid., 1061.
3. Jon D. Levenson and Baruch Halpern, "The Political Import of David's Marriages," *Journal of Biblical Literature* 99 (1980): 507–18.

queen of Ahasuerus (Esther 2:17), and she saves her people through her role as queen of Persia, despite the dangers she faces in this relationship (Esther 4:11). The Deuteronomy passage lists what one must do to the captive woman before marrying her: trim her hair, pare her nails, discard her captive's garb, and make her spend a month lamenting her father and mother (Deut. 21:13). The following line notes that should one no longer want her, she cannot be sold or enslaved (Deut. 21:14). The implication is that if one is drawn to her form, one may quickly tire of her. It may be no accident that the following instruction in Deuteronomy concerns what happens if a man loves one wife more than another wife (Deut. 21:15), the situation faced later by Leah (Gen. 29:30).

The second part of the phrase concerns her appearance, which the narrator identifies as "beautiful." This is the same phrase Abraham uses to describe Sarah when he fears that her beauty will cause his death upon their entry into Egypt (12:11). Here too the issue is whether her beauty is a burden, leading to a difficult situation. Rachel's beauty is usually considered positive. The text never states this but since the next verse reveals Jacob's love for Rachel, Bar-Efrat is probably correct in arguing that Rachel's beauty explains why Jacob loves Rachel.[4] What is seldom questioned is whether this is a legitimate reason for a patriarch to marry.

When Rachel is given to Jacob, the text states that Laban gives him his daughter as a "wife" (29:28). When Leah, her sister, marries Jacob first, she is not so identified. Leah is referred to as a wife obliquely, and Leah refers to Jacob as her husband (30:18), but the narrator does not. Thus the reference to Laban giving Rachel to Jacob as a wife is significant.

One major factor behind Rachel's actions concerns her last description: barren (29:31). The reference in this story comes as no surprise since the two previous matriarchs were also barren. Yet the barren reference differs somewhat because it is in contrast to Leah. Leah is hated and as a result the Israelite Deity "opens her womb," implying that up to this point she too is barren. The contrast is that while Leah may have fertility problems and the Deity intervenes, the Deity does not intervene in Rachel's case. The narrator emphasizes the comparison not of their state of fertility but of who does what to change it. Rachel may have Jacob's love, but Leah will have children.

Rachel's descriptions reveal her to be similar to her sister in that her first and most important attribute is that she is Laban's daughter. Her place in the family influences many of her attributes and actions since she is smaller or younger. Her other attribute is that she is beautiful, of form and of face. It is unclear if any of these attributes influences her job as a shepherdess or affects the Deity's decision not to undo her barren state quickly as the Deity does for Leah.

4. Bar-Efrat, *Narrative Art*, 49.

Rachel as a Subject

Rachel's first action is to come with her father's flock. This appears in the verse following Jacob's discussion with the locals about Laban's welfare (29:4–8). The locals note that Laban is well and his daughter Rachel is coming with the flock (29:6). The impact of Jacob's conversation with the locals and Rachel's actions verifying their comments is reminiscent of Abraham's servant's meeting with Rebekah, indicating that she is chosen by the Israelite Deity (Gen. 24). The thrust of this verse hints that Jacob's job may be as easy as the servant's and places Jacob in the world of Laban and his sheep.[5]

After her arrival, Jacob sees her, rolls the stone off the mouth of the well, waters the flock of his uncle Laban (29:10), kisses Rachel, breaks into tears (29:11), and tells her he is related to her father since he is Rebekah's son (29:12). Rachel's reaction is to run and tell her father (29:12). Here too there are great similarities with the Rebekah story, as well as significant differences. Like the meeting at the well, watering flocks is an element of the story, as is the account of what the visitor is doing there. Like Rebekah, Rachel also runs and tells the story to Laban (24:28–29 and 29:11). Rachel is compared to Rebekah through her actions.

Yet in Rachel's situation, Jacob, who is not a servant, does the work, whereas earlier Rebekah does the work for Abraham's servant (24:19–20). While Abraham's servant seems excited about his story (24:33), it does not pack the emotional punch that Jacob's kisses and tears evoke (29:11). The narrator is silent as to the impact of Jacob's kisses and tears on Rachel. According to the text she runs to her father only after Jacob tells her they are related.

The impact of Jacob on Rachel is not clear since she does not carry out another action until after Leah has borne four sons, making her next actions reactions. The first thing she does is to see that she has borne Jacob no children (30:1). This reference follows Leah bearing him four sons (29:32–35) and the narrator's comment that Leah has stopped bearing (29:35). Rachel becomes envious of Leah only when Leah is no longer fertile.

Rachel is envious because Leah has what Rachel wants. Her situation does not differ considerably from Hannah's (1 Sam. 1:2) or Sarah's (Gen. 16). Yet the difference between Rachel's reaction and those of Hannah and Sarah may be another marker that Rachel is not the designated mother for this generation. Sarah gives Hagar to Abraham, admits that the Deity has kept her from bearing (16:2), and brings the Deity in to judge in her argument with Abraham over Hagar's behavior (16:5). In Hannah's case she prays to the Deity (1 Sam. 1:10) and dedicates her future child to the service of the Deity (1 Sam. 1:11). Both women turn to the Israelite Deity in their distress.

5. Cotter, *Genesis*, 220.

Rachel's reaction to her infertility and envy of her sister is to speak to her husband, saying, "Bring me sons, for if not, I die" (Gen. 30:1). This is the first of many prophetic comments by Rachel about children and death, and highlights one of Rachel's issues: she asks for too much. Her speech is directed to Jacob, not the Israelite Deity, who thus far in the narrative has been the source responsible for fertility among barren women. That her comments are misdirected is reinforced by the text since, in the following verse, Jacob asks if he can take the place of Elohim (30:2). Rachel asks not for a son but for sons, perhaps simply multiple children. The ironic and prophetic element is that it is in childbirth with her second son that she dies (35:18); thus having children (plural) is why she dies.

Rachel's next action is a response to Jacob's angry reaction concerning her infertility (30:2). She gives him her maid Bilhah and claims that she may bear on Rachel's knees so through her she may have children (30:3). Rachel gives her maid Bilhah to him as a wife, and he comes to her (30:4). This is similar to Sarah's offer of Hagar to Abraham: a woman gives her maid to the patriarch and the children of that maid are considered somehow to belong to the wife. In each case the maid's status is identified both as a *shiphchah* and *'amah*.

Contrary to Sarah's maid, the reader knows how Bilhah comes into Rachel's possession: Laban gives Bilhah to Rachel as a wedding present (29:29). Hagar's Egyptian background is repeatedly raised in the earlier story (16:1, 3; 21:9, 21), and Bilhah's background is never described. Hagar reacts, so Sarah never claims her son (16:4–6); Bilhah's children are identified with Rachel throughout the rest of Genesis (30:6, 8; 35:25; 37:2; 46:26).

More significantly, Sarah gives her maid to Abraham because he has no children and his Deity has repeatedly noted that most of their deal concerns Abraham's descendants (12:2, 7; 13:15–16; 15:4–5, 13–14). When Rachel gives her maid to Jacob, he has four sons provided by his first and primary wife (29:32–35). The names she gives the children reveal that she views them not as fulfilling any need of the Deity, or even of Jacob, but as fulfilling her own need to win the contest with her sister.

Rachel again speaks to name the child Bilhah bears. She claims that Elohim has judged her, heard her plea, and given her a son, explaining why she names him Dan (30:6). The play on words concerns the Hebrew verb *dan*, which means "to judge," but in this case it is interpreted as, "God has pled my cause."[6] This identifies Rachel's concern with the Deity and views the birth of the child in that vein. Though Rachel claims that Elohim has heard her voice and judged her, such is not the case. When Leah conceives, the narrator states categorically that it is because of an action of the Israelite Deity (29:31). When Leah names her first son Reuben because the Deity "sees," the

6. Brown, Driver, and Briggs, *Lexicon*, 192.

narrator has just noted that the Deity "sees" her (29:31). In contrast, Rachel's claims are not reinforced.

Rachel speaks again to name Bilhah's next child, Naphtali, based on a contest she envisions with her sister, one in which Rachel claims to prevail (30:8). The contest between Leah and Rachel concerns Jacob's love, which Rachel has.

Rachel's next speech directly involves a reaction to something in Leah's life. Reuben, Leah's oldest son, finds mandrakes and brings them home to his mother, prompting Rachel to ask for some of them (30:14). Rachel's words are careful; she says "please," recognizing that she is asking for something from Leah, yet at the same time she refers to them as her (Leah's) son's mandrakes, not Leah's (30:14). Rachel believes that the mandrakes will help her conceive. Rachel's request is followed by Leah's outburst revealing Leah's analysis of the marriage situation: Rachel is an interloper in Leah's marriage (30:15).

Rachel's reply, saying Jacob will lie with Leah that evening in return for the mandrakes, indicates that Rachel controls access to Jacob (30:15). She is so desperate to have children she will give up time with her husband for the help the mandrakes might provide. Ironically, the incident results in more children for Leah (30:17, 19, 21). The narrator may hint that Rachel does not understand that the Deity is the source of children by her remaining barren even with the mandrakes.

For reasons never stated in the text, Rachel finally conceives and bears a son (30:23). She claims that "Elohim has taken away my disgrace" (30:23) and names the son Joseph, interpreted as, "May the Deity add another son for me" (30:24). The text never states why Elohim suddenly remembers Rachel. Elohim hears Rachel immediately after Dinah's birth, but the text makes no connection between the two incidents. What is clear from Joseph's name is, again, that Rachel is not satisfied. Rather than be content that she has a child, her name for the child is a request for more. Rachel does not know that what she desires, more children, will kill her.

Rachel's next speeches are made with her sister. Following the sheep- and goat-raising episode, Jacob calls Rachel and Leah out to the field to have a private conversation with them (31:4). The two sisters answer in unison (31:14; see chapter 3 above on Leah). They insinuate that they no longer have a share in the inheritance of their father (31:14) and that he regards them as outsiders, noting that he sold them and used up their purchase price (31:15). They note that all the wealth Elohim has taken away from their father belongs to them and their children, and Jacob should do as Elohim told him (31:16).

Leah may have been as upset about their perceived insults from their father as Rachel, but Rachel does something about it. After she and Leah converse with Jacob, while Laban is away shearing sheep, Rachel steals her father's teraphim (31:19).

There has been much discussion about what the teraphim are, what Rachel thinks she will gain by stealing them, and why she takes them. The problem begins with how Rachel takes them. The narrator uses the term *ganab*, which means "to steal."[7] Speiser argues that "appropriate" is a better term because the issue is bound up with the purpose of Rachel's act. If Rachel meant to undo what she regarded as a wrong, and took the law into her own hands, then "stole" would be misleading. Speiser understands the term *teraphim* to refer to "household images" that were figurines in human shape (1 Sam. 19:13) and were in popular use for purposes of divination (Ezek. 21:21). He relates them to the practice at Nuzi, where possession of the household gods could signify legal title to a given estate, particularly in cases out of the ordinary involving daughters, sons-in-law, or adopted sons.[8] Thus he connects her actions directly with the sisters' statement that they feel they have been robbed by their father. The difference between the sisters is that Rachel takes action against their father, whether legal or not.

The problem with them only being "household images" is that the narrator always refers to them as "teraphim" but both Jacob and Laban refer to them as *'elohim*. It is not surprising that the narrator does not refer to them as *'elohim* since that term is used for Israel's Deity in this chapter. By referring to them with another term the narrator keeps a distance between Israel's Deity and other gods, especially those represented in an image that can be physically moved. Since Rachel primarily uses *'elohim* when referring to the Divine, it is not clear how she understands the teraphim, especially since she never speaks about them.

Laban goes after Jacob to say good-bye to his children (Gen. 31:22–29) and to retrieve his gods (31:29). Jacob states that anyone with whom he finds his gods shall not remain alive (31:32). The narrator recognizes the problem, noting that Jacob does not know that Rachel has stolen the idols (31:32). Rachel again acts in a way that the narrator treats as a prophecy of her early death.

Rachel next hides the teraphim from her father while he searches for them. Laban first goes to Jacob's tent, then Leah's, and then the maids' tents. After leaving Leah's tent he enters Rachel's tent (31:33).[9] The text notes that Rachel takes the teraphim and places them in the camel cushions and sits on them (31:34). Laban cannot find them, and Rachel says to her father not to be angry with her that she does not get up for him, but the way of women is upon her (31:35).[10]

---

7. Ibid., 170.

8. Speiser, *Genesis*, 245.

9. The apparent contradiction regarding the search order of the tents will be discussed later in this chapter under "Rachel as an Object."

10. The narrator does not provide enough information to confirm this. Rachel gives birth to Benjamin a few chapters later; thus it is possible there is even more irony in this story, since she claims to be in the way of women when she is pregnant.

Since most scholars consider Rachel a good and favored wife, her actions in this scenario receive a mixed reception, viewed as funny, a "literary gem," and ironic drama.[11]

All of this avoids addressing that she takes something that is not hers, endangers the entire family by having them, compounds the incident by lying about having them, and possibly lies about having her period. This is another example of the family of tricksters again tricking one another. Yet Rachel's motivations are not clear. Why trick Laban now? When she is in competition with her sister the reader understands that she wants children. In this case, even following the Nuzi connection, if she thinks there is legal meaning to the idols it is not clear how she thinks she can act on legal precedent, as she is leaving the land where they would be relevant.

Other reasons why she might take these idols do not burnish her image. She could have taken them simply out of anger at her father, and tricking him about why she is sitting is simply a last laugh on the father she resents (according to 31:14–16). Lapsley notes, "Whatever the precise significance of the teraphim, the connection between Rachel's anger toward Laban and the theft of the teraphim cannot be denied."[12] This is reinforced by her comments to him: when he is rummaging around in her tent, she calls him "my lord," 'adoni, pretending to treat him with respect while she intentionally sits on what he seeks (31:35).[13] Another option is that she believes in the power of local deities. Rachel invokes 'elohim, a generic reference to the Israelite Deity, rather than the Tetragrammaton. Her reference to 'elohim is not consistent with the Deity's actions, and when she should invoke the Deity or 'elohim, she does not (30:1). Is this another example of Rachel's misuse or misunderstanding of any and all deities?

Rachel acts like her sister and the rest of the family when meeting Esau. The text notes that she and Joseph, like the other wives and children before them, bow low before Esau (33:7).

Rachel's next action is her death (35:19). Rachel's death follows immediately upon Jacob's instructions to build an altar to Elohim at Bethel. The incident begins with Elohim telling Jacob to go to Bethel and remain there (35:1). Jacob prepares for the incident by telling all who are with him to rid themselves of the foreign gods in their midst, purify themselves, and change their clothes (35:2). The text confirms that the people do so (35:4). The only individual in Jacob's group who the reader knows has a foreign idol is Rachel (31:35). Thus, either the teraphim are not considered foreign gods, or Rachel rids herself of them without the text mentioning it, or she reveals that she has them at this

11. For the first see von Rad, *Genesis*, 309; for the last two see Speiser, *Genesis*, 250.

12. J. E. Lapsley, "The Voice of Rachel: Resistance and Polyphony in Genesis 31.14–35," in Brenner, *Genesis*, 237.

13. Sarah uses the term 'adoni to refer to Abraham at the moment when she wonders whether he can impregnate her.

time. The silence of the text does not bother most scholars; yet why refer to the alien gods at this point in the story, when Elohim does not demand it and Rachel is the only individual known to the reader to have such an item?

Elohim appears to Jacob, changes his name to Israel, notes that he should be fertile and increase, that kings shall issue from him, and that Elohim is assigning the land given to Abraham and Isaac to him (35:11–12). Elohim's command to be fruitful and multiply is odd since Jacob already has twelve children. The only child yet to arrive is the one whose birth will cause the death of his mother (35:18). If there is anything to the timing of the stories, it is likely that Rachel is already pregnant when the blessing is made.[14]

Following that scene they set off, but they do not say where they are going or why (35:16). The group is still some distance from Ephrath when Rachel dies, though Ephrath does not seem to be their destination. The text notes that as she breathes her last (literally "her soul goes out"), letting the reader know she is dying, she names the child Ben-oni, but his father calls him Benjamin; thus Rachel dies and is buried on the road to Ephrath (35:18–19).

Rachel's last breath and last speech are used to name the child, so she has no opportunity to explain his name (35:18). The meaning of the name is obscure.[15] *Ben* means "son," and the *'oni* element may signify "my vigor," though most treat it as some kind of misfortune or suffering (from a different root).[16] Most scholars assume that what Rachel names her son must be stating something bad about her death, explaining why Jacob changes it. The text provides no reason for Jacob's decision to change the name or evidence that it is a better name ("son of the right").

The death of women is rarely recounted in the Hebrew Bible, and this one is striking. The scene has Jacob traveling, for no apparent reason, when his wife, who has had trouble conceiving for years, is about to give birth. Rachel's last act is to name her son. Jacob, who has not named any of his children thus far, changes the child's name, reversing Rachel's last action. With these last actions, Rachel's utterance that without children she will die (30:1) and Jacob's claim that whoever has Laban's idols will die (31:32) come true.

Rachel's actions do not depict her as the model matriarch one expects. Her initial actions establish the means for the reader to expect her to be chosen by the Deity, showing her at the well and as one who moves quickly, like Rebekah. Rachel's actions may be similar to Rebekah's, but readers will learn that Rachel's *character* differs from Rebekah's. Rachel is envious of her sister, demands children, and uses her maid to engage in a battle with her sister. She assumes Elohim's role in places where the text does not confirm her words and never invokes the help of the Deity. Rachel steals her father's idols, incurring a

14. Von Rad, *Genesis*, 339.
15. Speiser, *Genesis*, 274.
16. Ibid.

death sentence from her husband, who knows nothing of her actions. Her final action, naming her son with her last breath, is not respected by her husband, who changes the child's name.

Rachel as an Object

The cases where Rachel appears as an object explain and highlight the apparent disconnect between Rachel's actions, which are not always in line with an ideal matriarch, and why she is so favored by Jacob and later scholars. Most of the sentences in which Rachel is an object have Jacob as the subject, and he is blinded by her looks or by his love for her.

The first place where Rachel is an object is at the well. Jacob has a conversation about Laban with the others at the well, who tell him that Laban's daughter Rachel is coming (29:6). The text then notes that Jacob sees Rachel, qualifying her as the daughter of Laban (29:10). The reader does not yet know that Rachel has a nice form and face. Because the text focuses on his relationship to her, Jacob appears to move the stone because she is his relation and he has arrived at his destination.

After moving the stone and watering the flock, Jacob kisses Rachel and lifts up his voice and cries (29:11). There is not much kissing in Genesis, and it is not clear how appropriate such an action would be. After his emotional and physical outburst Jacob tells Rachel that he is the brother of her father, the son of Rebekah (29:12). Her reaction is similar to Rebekah's: she runs home to tell Laban (29:12). There is no indication how Rachel feels about Jacob.

The narrator reveals that Jacob loves Rachel (29:18). This reference follows Laban's request of Jacob that he name his wages, and the information about Leah, Rachel, and Rachel's beauty. Since Jacob's love for Rachel is expressed immediately after referencing her beauty, the connection seems direct.[17] Jacob's love for Rachel is listed as part of the background information for Jacob's answer to Laban about his wages. Following Laban's initial request for Jacob to name wages, the narrator inserts a number of points. Laban has two daughters. One is "bigger" or "older" than the other. The narrator names them and lists attributes for each. Jacob's love for Rachel is identified (29:15–18). Only once the reader has all this background information does Jacob answer Laban's question about wages: Jacob will serve Laban seven years for his younger/smaller daughter Rachel (29:18). Jacob's reference to Rachel as Laban's younger/smaller daughter confirms that Jacob knows about Leah. The narrator confirms that Jacob serves seven years for Rachel but comments that they seemed but a few days because of his love for her (29:20). Rachel's attitude toward Jacob is never expressed.

17. Bar-Efrat, *Narrative Art*, 49.

Between the reference to Jacob's working for Rachel out of love for seven years and her next appearance as an object, Jacob marries Leah (29:23). In the morning he says to Laban, "What have you done to me?" protesting that he was in his service for Rachel (29:25). His choice of words has been heard before in Genesis: it is precisely what Pharaoh and Abimelech say to Abraham when learning that Sarah is his wife (12:18; 20:9). Here too a woman has been offered under false pretenses but, contrary to the previous cases, Jacob marries the wrong sister.

Laban is not bothered by Jacob's words and responds that it is not the practice of the place to marry off the younger before the older (29:26), something Jacob should know after living there for seven years. In his original negotiation with Laban (29:18), Jacob had specified that he was working for Rachel, the younger/smaller daughter, but when Jacob asks Laban for his wife after completing his years of service, he does not specify which woman he will marry (29:21). Jacob is fully aware of the role custom plays in his new temporary home from the moment of his initial arrival, since the chapter begins with a recitation of how the flocks are watered in the area (29:2). Everyone there knows everyone else, made apparent in Jacob's initial introduction to Rachel (29:5–6), as is the case with Rebekah and Abraham's servant as well (Gen. 24). The ways of the place and how Laban functions should come as no surprise to Jacob.

Laban counters with the offer that Jacob will receive Rachel at the end of the bridal week if he agrees to serve another seven years, to which Jacob agrees. Laban gives him his daughter Rachel as wife (29:28). As with Leah, Laban gives a maid, Bilhah, to Rachel (29:29). These arrangements work for Laban, and Jacob accepts the terms, though they are in violation of Leviticus 18:18 (NJPS), "Do not marry a woman as a rival to her sister and uncover her nakedness in the other's lifetime." Thus, in the eyes of the biblical text, the marriage is not legitimate.

It is not unlikely that the reason for the law in Leviticus is a result of the problems that stem from the situation in which Leah and Rachel now find themselves. The next verse emphasizes the problem, noting that Jacob comes to Rachel also and loves Rachel more than Leah (Gen. 29:30). Thus Jacob establishes a difference between the two sisters that becomes a major issue in Leah's life. The text never states Rachel's feelings toward Jacob, but her knowledge that she has power over him through his love for her appears in her speech to him (30:1) and in her control over his sleeping partners (30:15). Rachel is an object when her maid conceives and bears Jacob a second son (30:7) in what Rachel labels a fateful contest with her sister (30:8).

Rachel is next the object of actions by Elohim (30:22). Immediately following the birth of Dinah, Elohim remembers Rachel, listens to her words, and opens her womb. What words of Rachel Elohim hears and how are not clear. In this verse the narrator reiterates that fertility comes from the Deity or Elohim, not as a result of mandrakes.

Rachel is not an object again until Laban enters her tent in search of his gods (31:33). This sequence is one where the text offers more details than usual, and the details confuse the situation. Jacob tells Laban to point out what Jacob has that belongs to Laban and to take it, also reminding the reader that Rachel has stolen the gods (31:32). First Laban goes into Jacob's tent, then Leah's tent and the tents of the two maids, but does not find them (31:33). The text then notes that he leaves Leah's tent and enters Rachel's tent. Thus it is not clear if Laban goes to Jacob's tent, Leah's tent, the maids' tents, and returns to Leah's tent again before going to Rachel's tent, or if the narrator is summarizing that Laban went into everyone's tent before Rachel's. This minor detail may say something about either Rachel's status or Leah's. If the order listed refers to tent placement, then Leah's tent is next to Jacob's, possibly a place of honor and not what one would expect. If it is simply remarking on the order the tents are entered, then is Rachel's last because she is younger or does it build suspense and give Rachel time to hide the gods?

When preparing to meet Esau, Jacob divides the children among Leah, Rachel, and the two maids (33:1). The text emphasizes that Rachel and Joseph are last (33:2), probably because of their more beloved position in the family.

Rachel is an object in her death scene. When her labor is at its hardest, the midwife tells her not to fear, for it is another boy for her (35:17). The family knows that Rachel is pregnant and has a midwife with them. This woman is the only person who is with Rachel when she dies. She is the one to hear what Rachel wants to name her son. The woman's words are meant either to encourage her to hold on or to comfort her as she dies, knowing that she has what she wants—children. Rachel appears as the first matriarch to have a midwife and the first to die in childbirth.

Rachel's midwife appears only a few verses after Deborah, Rebekah's nurse, dies and is buried under an oak that is below Bethel and has a name, Allon-bacuth (35:8). The mention of Deborah's death and her burial site contrasts somewhat with Rachel's next appearance as an object: Jacob sets up a pillar over her grave, and it is the pillar at Rachel's grave "to this day" (35:20).

Rachel is not buried in Hebron, with the rest of the family, but is buried on the spot, on the road to Ephrath. Jacob does not even try to bury her in Hebron, in the burial plot purchased by Abraham. It is so important for Jacob to be buried there that he commands his sons to carry him up from Egypt to be buried there with his parents, grandparents, and Leah (47:30). Jacob later claims that Rachel dies "to his sorrow" (48:7), though here, as Cotter notes, "Without any notice that he mourns for the wife for whose sake he labored twenty years and who has borne him two sons, Jacob buries her at Ephrath/ Bethlehem, erects a pillar, and continues to travel on. This is surprising given the tenderness with which his earlier love for her was noted in the text."[18] In the

18. Cotter, *Genesis*, 260.

account of her actual burial, not only does Jacob not mourn but he journeys on and pitches his tent beyond Migdal-eder (35:20–21).[19]

Rachel's sons are referred to after her death (35:23–26). From this point on, Leah's children are always listed first. Immediately following her death, when Jacob's sons are listed, her sons appear right after Leah's (35:24) but before the maids' sons. In the list of those who go down to Egypt with Jacob, "the sons of Rachel, the wife of Jacob," are identified following the sons of Leah and the sons of her maid (46:19). In the final blessing of Jacob's children, Rachel's biological sons are last, following even her maid's children (49:2–27). Leah's children are always first, contrary to the place of Rachel's children, which is not fixed and is set by context, not by their mother.

The image of Rachel as an object is dominated by Jacob's love for her. It governs why she is married, when he takes her, and where she is placed by Jacob. In death her placement is somewhat lowered.

Rachel's Relationships

Rachel and Leah are sisters married to the same man, but their relationship with everyone in their shared life is different. Rachel has the attention on her, so she focuses on her sister and father. Because she dies at her second son's birth, her relationship with him is limited. Rachel and Leah's relationships appear to be ordered differently, and so I will treat them differently here.

Rachel is first introduced as the daughter of Laban, and the reader understands that as a primary description. The first character in the story with whom Rachel interacts is Jacob, who becomes her husband. When Jacob first sees her he knows who she is, though she does not know who he is. Thus, in her eyes, his first actions with her may appear strange (moving the rock, kissing her, and crying, 29:10–11). On some levels this becomes the paradigm of their relationship: Jacob loves her and carries out a series of actions throughout his lifetime based on that. Rachel's feelings toward Jacob are never expressed, and the knowledge that he will do anything for her could be seen as a guiding principle in her life.

When the text describes Rachel, it also introduces Leah (29:16–17). The reader already knows Rachel. The information about Rachel's beauty may explain why Jacob loves her, as the next verse mentions (29:18). That statement explains why he would be so distressed at marrying Leah instead (29:25), why he would work another seven years for Rachel (29:27), and why he would love Rachel more than Leah (29:29–30). It would also show Rachel that he would do anything for her.

19. Jacob's building a pillar could be considered a special gesture separating Rachel as unique, but the only other references to it are in Jeremiah as she mourns her descendants leaving the land in exile.

Thus it is no surprise that Rachel would be forceful in her relationship with Jacob and demand children of him (30:1). What is surprising is his response, that he would become angry with her. His response, asking if he can take the place of Elohim, reflects his idea that the Deity is responsible for fertility but may also express his frustration of not being able to provide her with all that she wants. There is no question that, whether he needs or wants more children, since he already has sons through Leah, he will impregnate Bilhah to follow Rachel's wishes (30:4, 7). He does not question either Leah or Rachel in the mandrake incident.

Despite references to Joseph and Benjamin as favored children, following Rachel and Jacob's argument, there is little evidence of any special relationship between Jacob and Rachel. Jacob follows Rachel's orders when told to have sexual relations with Bilhah and Leah. When he calls the sisters to discuss leaving, he speaks to them together (31:4–13) and thus they respond (31:14–16). Rachel endangers Jacob by stealing her father's gods (31:19). When Jacob meets Esau, Rachel and Joseph are kept closest to him, presumably because he loves them more and wants them to be most protected and closest to him (33:2), though the narrator never explains the arrangement. Rachel's next episode is her death scene. Her midwife is with her, but Jacob is not (35:17). Rachel's last action is to name her child, which name Jacob changes (35:18). Jacob does not mourn her and buries her by the side of the road, not in the family burial cave. Evidence of their love affair fizzles out completely.

Rachel's relationship with her father is not great, but she has better reasons than Leah for having problems with her father. Rachel is first identified as Laban's daughter, the sign she is a legitimate marriage partner for Jacob (29:6). In the description of her and the introduction of her sister, new elements appear that are clearly of prime importance to Laban: Rachel is the smaller/younger daughter. Since the text never reveals Rachel's feelings for Jacob, it is not clear whether she is bothered by Laban's switch of wives on the wedding evening or whether she is informed of it in advance. Laban's actions establish that he views his responsibility to Leah, as firstborn, as overriding his agreement with Jacob, something that Rachel could view negatively.

Both sisters reflect negative feelings toward their father when Jacob discusses his desire to depart and his fears about doing so (31:14). The sisters speak in unison to Jacob, but Rachel carries out an action against their father (31:19). It is a hostile act when she calls him "lord" and tells him she cannot rise because of her period, but she is hiding what he seeks (31:35). It is impossible to explain Rachel's feelings toward Laban as anything but negative, and there is little evidence of any strong feelings of Laban toward Rachel.

Rachel's negative feelings toward Leah are different since they stem from something concrete: Leah's fertility. When Leah is first introduced, her only importance appears to be as Rachel's sister, and her marriage is arranged for the same reason. This never appears to bother Rachel; her problem with

Leah concerns fertility. The narrator states categorically that Rachel becomes envious of her sister when she sees that she has borne no children to Jacob (30:1). When Rachel has a child, through Bilhah, immediately after (30:4), she names the second child based on a contest she envisions herself having with her sister, indicating that her two sons are not enough or that not having her own biological son is still a problem for Rachel.

The mandrake incident reveals continuing tension between the sisters. Rachel recognizes that Leah has something she wants and requests the mandrakes politely (30:14). Rachel's response to Leah's outburst is tacit agreement with her, and she controls Jacob's cohabitation schedule (30:15). Following this incident or because of Joseph's birth, their arguments seem to cease. After Rachel bears her own biological child, the only time the sisters are together they speak against their father and agree to leave together (31:14).

Rachel is more explicit about what she wants from her maid than Leah is, but that may be because Rachel's maid is used before Leah's and establishes the paradigm (30:3). Also, Rachel has not produced children for Jacob and is more in need of her maid than Leah is. She wants Jacob to sleep with her so "I will be built up from her" (30:3), using the same wordplay Sarah employs (16:3). For the significance of Reuben sleeping with Bilhah after Rachel's death (35:22), see chapter 9 on Bilhah.

It is difficult to discern Rachel's relationship with her children. She names her children based on issues in her life, primarily concerning her sister (30:8). When she has Joseph, her explanation for his name is that she wants more children (30:24). Her relationship with Benjamin is brief since she dies naming him. Though she names him, he is not allowed to retain that name (35:18), and it does not reveal any relationship she has with him or his brother.

Rachel's final relationship concerns the Deity, with whom she has little to no contact. In the Jacob stories, "Elohim" tends to be used more often than "the Deity," though not exclusively (see the chapter on Leah). Even where the narrator and characters refer to the Israelite Deity, Rachel does not. Rachel brings Elohim into the story when the narrator does not, and does not recognize Elohim's role when it is there.

The first case concerns the reference to Leah being hated. The Deity opens Leah's womb, not Rachel's (29:31). Leah names her sons in ways that recognize the Deity. Rachel turns to Jacob in anger asking for children (30:1). He suggests that it is not his fault, for Elohim is the source of children, and Rachel takes action (30:3).[20] She claims that Dan's birth is vindication from Elohim, something the narrator does not reinforce (30:6). She recognizes the Israelite Deity when naming Joseph but requests more (30:24). Elohim remembers, listens, and opens her womb (30:22), and Rachel notes that Elohim takes away her disgrace.

20. Sarah does also, but Abraham has been promised children, he has none, and she identifies the Deity's role first.

There is no contact between Rachel and the Deity after that, though there is between Rachel and her father's gods. Rachel takes her father's gods (*'elohim*), so named not by the narrator (who calls them "teraphim") but by her father (31:30) and husband (31:32). While she does not treat them with respect, she does handle foreign idols, which Jacob realizes should not be with anyone in his group, at least when they visit Bethel (35:2). Her possession of these idols, and Jacob not knowing it, may lie behind her early death (31:32). At best, Rachel's relationship with Elohim is slight and misguided. Her relationship with the Israelite Deity is one where she only asks things of the Deity. She does not respect other gods, yet she steals them.

Conclusion

Examining Rachel after Leah reveals a more complex character than a pretty girl whose husband loves her but who cannot have children. Her depiction in the text is the least favorable of the matriarchs, and in light of what happens to her descendants, the northern kingdom, it is not clear that any of her children inherit the full promise. She is not motivated by nor does she take actions on behalf of the Israelite Deity. She is not a primary wife, and her marriage, in the eyes of Leviticus, is prohibited. She does not honor her father and keeps foreign gods.

5

Review of Part 1

Matriarchs

In this chapter I review the matriarchs to determine if there are characteristics, actions, or relationships common to all of them. Commonalities or
repeated themes will determine if these individuals function collectively
as "matriarchs" or if it is a name scholars should avoid.

Matriarchs' Descriptions

The one characteristic applied to all four matriarchs concerns their looks.
Three of the four, Sarah, Rebekah, and Rachel, are labeled as attractive:
Sarah, "beautiful of appearance" (12:11); Rebekah, "very good of appearance" (24:16); and Rachel, "beautiful of form and beautiful of appearance"
(29:17). Leah's eyes are "soft" (29:17), and it is difficult to determine what
is meant by the term. Since it focuses on her eyes and is used in comparison
with Rachel's appearance, it likely refers to her looks, though because the
term "soft" is not usually an adjective referencing looks, the term may carry
a different connotation. Thus the text describes some physical attribute of
each of the matriarchs.

One might argue that the text identifies at least one parent for all of the
matriarchs, if one accepts Abraham's comment that Sarah is his biological

sister through their father (20:12). There are reasons to doubt this comment, however. Sarah's parentage is less significant since she and Abraham are the first matriarch and patriarch. The text hints that Terah's line is the important one, since he has a genealogy (11:27), and all the other mothers of the patriarchs descend from his line.[1] Terah's role is difficult to determine since the Deity never speaks with Terah and never makes promises to him.

For the later matriarchs, their parentage is an important element of the story, marking them as the right women. In Rebekah's case Abraham's servant is sent to find a wife from the land of Abraham's birth (24:4), not from the specific family line of Terah or Nahor. That she is Milcah's daughter is one of the many signs the servant notices identifying Rebekah as the chosen one. Jacob is specifically instructed to find a wife from the daughters of Laban (28:2). In Leah and Rachel's case, Laban has too many daughters that fit the bill, and the question is, which one (or both) is correct?

Three of the matriarchs are identified as barren (Sarah, 11:20; Rebekah, 25:21; Rachel, 29:31). Leah might also fit this category, because the Deity opens her womb, allowing her to conceive, taking action to make her fertile. The implication is either that she too is barren, or that everyone is barren until the Deity takes actions to reverse that state. Sarah's barren state begins as the major story line, and the last generation of patriarchs has too much fertility, or too many heirs. The essential element of the fertility description is that it helps define the women's relationship with the Israelite Deity, a key factor in understanding the women married to the patriarchs.[2]

Only three matriarchs are labeled as wives. The text states that Laban takes Leah and brings her to Jacob, and he sleeps with her (29:23), but the text never says that Jacob takes her as wife. Despite this, the text hints that she is more legitimate than Rachel, for she is the one who is buried in the family burial cave, and her children ultimately inherit.

Aside from those few characteristics, there is no other descriptor that applies to all four matriarchs, or even a majority of them, that separates them from other women in the text. Both Rachel and Rebekah are identified as moving quickly, but that cannot be applied to Sarah or Leah.

Matriarchs as Subjects

The most obvious action all the matriarchs carry out is childbearing. All of them conceive and bear sons, although there is considerable difference within each of their stories as to when they bear. Most of Sarah's story is over

---

1. He has a *toledot* that begins with a *waw* consecutive, meaning it is one of the coordinating *toledot* that serve to link them into the larger textual blocks to which the independent forms are the major headings. See Thomas, *These Are the Generations*.

2. Finlay, *Birth Report Genre*, 37.

before she bears Isaac (21:2), and after bearing him and securing his place in the inheritance structure of the Deity's promise (21:9–10), she dies (23:2). In Rebekah's case the children happen early in the story and the reference to her barren state is quickly reversed (25:21), since the issue in her generation concerns which son will inherit the promise. With the sisters, Leah's children arrive almost immediately in her story (29:32–35), while Rachel must wait (30:22). When and how many they bear are parts of their individual stories, highlighting different legal and emotional issues involved in childbearing.

The other key element in the matriarchs' ability to bear children is that they all do it with help from the Deity. The Israelite Deity tells Abraham directly that Sarah will be the mother of the relevant heir (17:19). Rebekah conceives only after her husband prays on her behalf (25:21). The text states that the Deity sees that Leah is hated and therefore opens her womb (29:31). While Rachel must wait longer, Elohim too remembers Rachel, listens to her, and opens her womb (30:22). The text hints that each of these women is the correct wife to marry a patriarch, but the narrator is explicit that the Israelite Deity is personally responsible for each of these women conceiving. The Israelite Deity carries out specific actions to make each woman a mother. The importance of the mother in the Hebrew Bible contrasts with the relative absence of the mother in the birth reports from the literature of the ancient Near East.[3]

The other actions of the women cover a range of issues, from helping the Deity's promise come true to taking foreign idols. Three of the four suggest that their husbands sleep with their maids (Sarah, Rachel, and Leah). All of the other actions taken by the matriarchs concern details of their story rather than a defining action for the group. A defining characteristic of childbearing is not shocking; what this method of assessing these women clarifies is not just that they all bear but that they bear with the explicit help of the Israelite Deity. This is the only action all the matriarchs share.

Matriarchs as Objects

This category holds some commonalities and some aspects that are shocking because they do not carry throughout all the women in the book. All of the matriarchs are taken from somewhere outside Canaan and brought to Canaan. Both Sarah and Abraham are newcomers. Isaac is not even allowed to leave the land, and his bride must be brought to him, whereas Jacob must leave the land, and luckily finds his wives and can still return home. This geographical point relates to their parentage. Neither Abraham (24:3) nor Rebekah (27:46) wants their child to marry a local woman. This means the women must be brought from elsewhere. The way the women are brought to

3. Ibid., 41–42.

the land differs, but they are all from outside the land, even when the men are born in the land.

With the exception of Rebekah, the Deity either tells someone else to "listen," or the Deity "listens" to Sarah, Leah, and Rachel. In Sarah's case the Deity tells Abraham to listen to Sarah's voice (21:12) to protect Isaac's inheritance. Elohim hears Leah when she hires Jacob with her son's mandrakes and she conceives (30:17). Elohim also hears Rachel when remembering her and opens her womb, and she too conceives (30:22). Rebekah is the only one who Elohim does not hear, as well as the only one to inquire of the Deity and to whom the Deity responds directly (25:23). In each case the result of hearing leads to different actions on the Deity's part. All the women request something related to having children or protecting them.

No reference to a specific sexual encounter is named prior to conception for any matriarch.[4] Such is not the case with Sarah's and Rachel's maids. The text states explicitly that Abraham "came to" Hagar, leading to her conception (16:4), and Jacob "came to" Bilhah (30:4). Such is not the case with any of the matriarchs.

In some situations it appears as though the Deity directly makes the woman pregnant with little participation by the spouse. The text is explicit that Abimelech does not touch Sarah (20:4), because immediately after leaving Gerar the Deity takes note of Sarah and does for her as the Deity has said (21:1). She conceives and bears (21:2) with no reference to Abraham until the narrator mentions that he is the father, after the fact (21:3). In Rebekah's case Isaac pleads on her behalf and the Deity responds to his plea; but again, Rebekah conceives as the Deity's response to Isaac's plea, not as the direct result of any specifically mentioned sexual encounter (25:21).

With Leah's first four sons, the text never mentions any interlude between Leah and Jacob, and the text never names to whom Leah bears (29:32–35). Instead, Leah is hated, the Deity opens her womb (29:31), Leah conceives, and she names the children (29:32–35). So too is Rachel's case. The Deity remembers Rachel, listens to her, opens her womb (30:22), she conceives and bears a son, and nowhere is Jacob's name mentioned in the process. The text highlights that most of the children of the matriarchs are conceived in the same way: the Deity decides that after they have been barren they are ready to be mothers of the heirs of the Deity's promise. The Deity, not the patriarchs, causes women to conceive.

The matriarchs' burials are not consistent. Three of the four are buried in the cave of Machpelah: Sarah, Rebekah, and Leah. Rachel is buried on the side of the road. Her last act, naming her son, is changed immediately (35:18). No mourning is carried out for her, though a pillar is erected. This separates Rachel in a physical way from the rest of the matriarchs and the clan.

4. Ibid., 37–38.

Matriarchs' Relationships

This category is complex since each matriarch has a different set of characters with whom she interacts. There are few commonalities, making those that exist striking.

There is no consistency in the relationships of the women to their families. We know nothing about Sarah's family. The most central figure of Rebekah's family that the reader meets is the same as that of Rachel and Leah: Laban. Because his relationship with them is so different, it is difficult to draw any conclusions.

The relationship of the women to their husbands is also difficult to assess. Sarah and Abraham have few discussions, and the actions that Abraham takes concerning his wife do not reflect much kindness toward her. Isaac loves Rebekah from the beginning of their relationship and does not appear to change throughout the story. Jacob loves Rachel before they are married and loves her children more than his other children, though the text says little about how loving their relationship is after Leah bears children. Leah wants Jacob's love but never gains it.

The relationships of each woman with her children are also not consistent. Sarah, who has only one child, is protective of his position concerning his older half brother (21:9–10). The narrator notes that Rebekah loves Jacob but does not state her feelings toward Esau (25:28). Leah has an interaction with one of her children (30:14) following the births of her first four sons (29:32–35) and it provides little insight. Rachel dies giving birth to her last son (35:18).

The one consistent factor in the relationships of the women is with the Israelite Deity. The Deity has chosen all of them because the Deity is the one directly responsible for the birth of all of the children, in some cases even to the exclusion of mentioning the father. Three of the four are actively connected with the Israelite Deity (Sarah, Rebekah, and Leah), and even Rachel refers to Elohim, though never in a context where the narrator agrees with the association. Both Sarah and Rebekah ensure that the Deity's promise to the correct son is carried out, even when their fathers may not help. Leah recognizes the role of the Deity in her ability to conceive and praises the Deity through the names of her children.

Conclusion

This review indicates that the defining characteristic of the matriarchs is that they are picked by the Deity to bear children who inherit the Deity's promise to the men. The men have a limited role in choosing their wives. Only Rachel is picked by her future husband, and that does not go smoothly. With the exception of Sarah, the other women are picked as wives through signs.

The Israelite Deity decides when the women will conceive and does so in a way that highlights the Deity's role, almost to the exclusion of the patriarchs.

One of the first things the reader learns about two of the mothers concerns their physical appearance. Despite claims that reference to their looks is included only as it helps explain the story, in all of the cases it explains only a minor part of the story. Sarah's beauty causes trouble for her in Egypt, landing her in Pharaoh's house, but that turns out to be a small, almost insignificant element of the story. So too, Rebekah has all the right characteristics for Abraham's servant, but the reference to her looks serves only as a reason why Isaac lies about his relationship with her, a minor story line. Jacob may initially love Rachel for her looks. On some levels the reference to their beauty is almost a red herring. It does not seem to benefit the women, leads their husbands to put them in harm's way to protect themselves, and contributes little to nothing to the story line.

PART 2

Mothers of Potential Heirs
(or Slaves, Concubines, Daughters, and Daughters-in-Law)

This section investigates the women of potential heirs whose descendants do not inherit: Hagar, Esau's wives, Zilpah, Bilhah, Dinah, Mrs. Judah, Tamar, and Asenath. All of these women are in a relationship with a man that could lead to the inclusion of their child in the inheritance of the promise. Hagar, Zilpah, and Bilhah have sexual relations with a patriarch resulting in offspring. Esau is the descendant of a patriarch and a matriarch and has children. Dinah is the offspring of a patriarch and a matriarch and has sexual relations. Mrs. Judah, Tamar, and Asenath have children with a son of a patriarch and a matriarch.

One issue with this group is who inherits, especially difficult in light of the questions raised in the previous section. If Rachel is not a legitimate wife, do her children inherit the promise? If Rachel's children inherit the promise, do Zilpah and Bilhah's children? If their sons inherit, what differentiates them from the matriarchs? What of the next generation? If all of Jacob's children inherit, then the roles of Bilhah, Dinah, Tamar, and Asenath lay the foundation for who are legitimate mates for their generation, who cannot return to Paddan-aram and must find partners in Canaan and/or Egypt.

Zilpah and Bilhah's status shows how women in this category fall into a wider range of situations than the matriarchs. This group includes women who are legitimate wives, slaves, a daughter of a matriarch and a patriarch, the daughter-in-law of the next generation, and a wife from Egypt. What unites these women is the threat their children pose to those who inherit.

Matriarchs are compared less with their contemporaries and more with other women of their status, and that type of comparison will continue here. Our attention will focus on how Hagar compares to Zilpah and Bilhah, how the wives of Esau compare with Zilpah and Bilhah and with Hagar, and on their children.

6

Hagar

Hagar has a unique position in the Hebrew Bible. She is treated with special honors because the Deity speaks with her directly, part of her story is conveyed sympathetically by the narrator, and she does things for her child few other women in the text are able to do. Yet she is treated harshly by Sarah, Abraham, and even the Israelite Deity. One important question in examining Hagar is, do her actions precipitate how she is treated?

Other issues complicate understanding the already complex character of Hagar. She appears in the New Testament, where, again, she is not treated well (Gal. 4:22–27). Here we will consider Hagar's character as it appears in the Hebrew Bible. Additional elements from the New Testament that may affect her character will be considered only as an element of the history of scholarship rather than as part of her character in the Hebrew Bible.

Hagar's Description

Hagar's first description is as a *shiphchah* (Gen. 16:1), translated numerous ways: "maidservant," "slave-girl," or "handmaid."[1] Trible translates the term as "maid" but in a footnote comments that the term refers to a "virgin, dependent

---

1. For the first see Brown, Driver, and Briggs, *Lexicon*, 1046; NJPS; for the second see NRSV; and for the third see KJV.

maid who serves the mistress of the house."[2] The heart of the problem is the number of different terms for slaves, and female slaves in particular. Female slaves differ from male slaves in that they also serve sexual and procreative functions, raising the issue here as to whether these functions are inherent in the type of slavery conveyed by this term. The sexuality of women so designated is legislated in Leviticus 19:20, especially concerning their freedom and sexual activity with them. Often the individual who bears this designation belongs to a female.

What is clear from Genesis 16:2 is that Hagar belongs to Sarah and is subservient to her. This point is emphasized by the repetition of *shiphchah* to describe Hagar six different times in chapter 16 and only once after this chapter. The reader never learns how Hagar comes into Sarah's possession. Such is not the case later with Zilpah (29:24) and Bilhah (29:29), both of whom are wedding presents from Laban, described as gifts on the daughters' wedding nights. It is thus not unusual for matriarchs to have a *shiphchah*, and the other matriarchs use their women for the same procreative functions as Hagar was used.

Hagar is labeled a *shiphchah* when Sarah suggests to Abraham that he go in to her (16:2) for procreative purposes. Sarah hopes she may be "built up"[3] through a *shiphchah*, someone subservient to her. Sarah's plan for Hagar, that she bear a child who will somehow belong to Sarah, reinforces the idea that the term *shiphchah* includes the possibility of a procreative role for that woman, since Sarah uses that term, as opposed to other terms for slaves, in 16:1.

Verse 3 is more emphatic about Sarah and Hagar's relationship: Hagar is labeled "her *shiphchah*." So too Hagar belongs to Sarah in verse 5 when Sarah complains that she gave Hagar to Abraham's bosom and now Sarah is "lowered" in Hagar's eyes.

Sarah is not the only one who recognizes and labels Hagar a *shiphchah*. Abraham's response to Sarah's request that the Deity judge between the two of them is to tell Sarah, "your *shiphchah* is in your hands," recognizing Hagar as belonging to Sarah (16:6). When Hagar is given to Abraham she may receive a change in status,[4] and so in this verse, according to von Rad, Abraham uses legal terminology and "severs his relationship with Hagar and thereby restores the old legal relationship."[5] So Abraham's words do not simply recognize Hagar as belonging to Sarah but are the means by which she reverts to that status.

The messenger of the Deity also designates Hagar a *shiphchah*. Hagar's reaction to Sarah's oppression is to run away (16:7). When the Deity's messenger finds her at a spring of water in the wilderness, he asks her a question by addressing her as "*shiphchah* of Sarah" (16:8).

2. Trible, *Texts of Terror*, 30n9.

3. For more on what Sarah thinks will happen as a result of this situation see above, chapter 1 on Sarah.

4. See below in the discussion of other descriptions of Hagar.

5. Von Rad, *Genesis*, 192.

The next and final reference to Hagar as a *shiphchah* is in the summary of the line of Ishmael (25:12–18). Ishmael is described as the son of Abraham whom Hagar the Egyptian, Sarah's *shiphchah*, bears (25:12). The reference to her as such here is odd since between 16:8 and this verse she appears with a different slave term and, as will be argued below, following Frymer-Kensky, she is freed. This reference summarizes Ishmael's line, confirming that the Deity does as promised and makes him a nation. It may include reference to the relationship of Hagar to Sarah to remind the reader how and why Abraham fathers Ishmael in the first place.

Many treat the reference to Hagar as a *shiphchah* as evidence that the narrator is trying to demean her, but its use by the narrator, Sarah, and Abraham functions to explain her status and relationship to the other figures in the text. Later Sarah will refer to Hagar with a term that may be more demeaning, but in the beginning of Hagar's story the narrator uses *shiphchah* to describe what the situation is. Sarah uses it to identify who she means to give to Abraham. The messenger of the Deity uses the term so Hagar knows who is being addressed. The final reference identifies the relationships of all the parties, explaining why and how those relationships exist.

It is also important to remember that slavery is acceptable in the Hebrew Bible. The children of Israel being slaves in Egypt has negative connotations and is a situation they strive to and eventually do leave behind, but the idea that all slavery would be abolished does not appear in the Hebrew Bible. There are a number of terms for slaves and slavery, and many are used in the biblical text to reveal piety and submission to the Israelite Deity. Furthermore, slavery in the ancient world was not the same as that conducted in the United States.[6]

Hagar is defined as a *shiphchah* because it shows her status in the context in which she is living, highlights some of the functions she is intended to perform, and establishes the legitimacy of those around her to use her in that way. It does not mean that it is nice, nor does it mean that Hagar is in a good situation, but the references are to situate her rather than to demean her.

When Hagar is first introduced as a *shiphchah* she is also identified as Egyptian, another description frequently applied to her (16:1). This reference labels her not just as foreign. When Sarah and Abraham visit Egypt (12:10), he claims he will be killed because of Sarah's beauty. The implication is that non-Egyptians are not safe in Egypt, and Abraham fears the Egyptians (12:13). For his words to be convincing, Sarah has to fear foreigners in general or Egyptians in particular. Thus from the beginning of the patriarchal story there is a negative association with the Egyptians in the text.

6. For slavery in the ancient Near East see I. M. Diakonoff, "Slave Labour vs. Non-Slave Labour: The Problem of Definition," in *Labor in the Ancient Near East*, ed. Marvin A. Powell, American Oriental Series 68 (New Haven: American Oriental Society, 1987), 1–3.

The negative identification of Egypt for Sarah can only have been enlarged when she was taken to Pharaoh's house (12:15), where she was given to Pharaoh, a situation not far off from how Hagar will later be used. Sarah has a person in her possession functioning in a way similar to how Sarah functions in Egypt.[7] The later associations with Egypt, where Israel will be enslaved, must be considered background music for all references to Hagar. The term implies she is foreign, from a place that already enslaved Sarah and will later enslave the Israelites.

Hagar is referred to as Egyptian in 16:3, where the narrator recounts that Sarah gives her to Abraham. This verse is explicit in determining who is related to whom and how. Sarah is Abraham's wife, and Hagar is Sarah's Egyptian maid.

Hagar is not described as Egyptian again until 21:9, when Sarah sees Hagar's son "playing" with Isaac, Sarah's recently weaned son. The narrator notes that Sarah sees the son of Hagar the Egyptian. Again, the term highlights that Hagar is foreign and from Egypt in particular, and this Egyptian connection ties into the end of the episode: after the Deity shows Hagar the water in the desert, she finds her son a wife from Egypt (21:21). Trible notes that this action ensures that Ishmael's descendants will be Egyptian.[8] Ishmael's descendants are identified in a number of different contexts. Esau, when he realizes that Isaac has blessed Jacob and sent him off to Paddan-aram to find a wife, goes to Ishmael and takes one of his daughters for a wife, in an effort to marry an insider (28:9). Three times in the Joseph story the Ishmaelites are named as the ones to whom Joseph's brothers sell him, making the Ishmaelites one of the ways the Israelites land in Egypt (37:25, 26, 28).[9]

The final reference to Hagar as Egyptian is in the summary of Ishmael's line (25:12). The reference to her as a *shiphchah* here is odd, but the reference to her as Egyptian is not. Hagar, from the beginning to the end, is Egyptian—foreign—and that affects her relations with those around her and her future descendants.

Hagar's next description, as an *'ishah*, is controversial because scholars cannot agree whether, when Sarah gives Hagar to Abraham, she gives her to him as a "concubine" or "wife" (16:3).[10] The translation "concubine" stems from Speiser's treatment of the phrase connecting it to the Akkadian cognate *ashshatum*. Speiser agrees that *'ishah* may signify either "wife" or "concubine" but opts for "concubine" here because Akkadian uses the term *hirtum* for

---

7. The similarity is not exact. In Gen. 16 Hagar is given to Abraham for procreative purposes. Sarah is taken by Pharaoh's courtiers because of her looks, indicating that his intentions are not procreative but sexual.

8. Trible, *Texts of Terror,* 27.

9. The complication in the Joseph story is that three times the text identifies the Ishmaelites as the ones to whom they sell Joseph, but two times the Midianites are implicated (37:28, 36).

10. NJPS and Speiser (*Genesis,* 116, 117) translate it as "concubine," whereas KJV and NRSV translate "wife."

"the principal wife" in nonlegal contexts, meaning "chosen woman."[11] He is influenced by Nuzi texts in which a childless wife is required to provide a concubine to her husband to procure children.[12] In his translation Sarah gives Hagar to Abraham without including marriage rights.

Von Rad argues in the opposite direction. He claims that in order to understand the conflict "one must refer to legal customs that were apparently widespread at that time."[13] Contrary to Speiser, this is a legal context and 'ishah must be understood as "wife." At issue is whether Hagar is promoted to wife. The problem is exacerbated by the Hebrew Bible's silence on legislation for different types of wives.

The text has used a similar construction and will again. When Pharaoh refers to what happens to Sarah in Egypt, he claims, "Why did you say 'she is my sister' so that I took her to me for a wife?" (12:19). Thus the status Hagar receives is identical to that given to Sarah when Abraham gives Sarah to Pharaoh.

Both Zilpah and Bilhah are given to Jacob by their female owners using the same terminology as is used for Hagar when she is given to Abraham. Von Rad says it is the same situation, yet he does not address why the inheritance system of their children is different.

In light of the terminology, the legal qualifications, and the need for Abraham to later refer to Hagar again as a *shiphchah*, it seems likely that some status change is implied in this verse. What is unclear is whether she is a "second" wife, or a "co-wife," or some other status not adjudicated by the biblical text. Trible points out that, though Sarah takes this action to build herself up (16:2), she in fact diminishes her status and Hagar receives a promotion.[14]

Hagar is next described as an *'amah*, another term for a female slave. The term appears two times in 21:10. Sarah has just seen that "the son whom Hagar the Egyptian had borne to Abraham was playing" with her own recently weaned son (21:9). Sarah's response is to tell Abraham to banish "that slave" and her son because the son of "that slave" will not inherit with her own child (21:10). In the context of the verse the term carries negative connotations. Hagar's name is not used, and the use of "that" when referring to a person can be an effort to objectify them. Furthermore, Hagar's son is also a son of Abraham, and Sarah refers to Hagar as a slave to highlight why Ishmael must be banished.

Trible identifies *'amah* as a more oppressive term than her previous identification as a *shiphchah*.[15] Meyers claims that a *shiphchah* is more servile than an *'amah*.[16] The lexicon of Brown, Driver, and Briggs states that *'amah* can be

11. Speiser, *Genesis,* 117.
12. Ibid., 121.
13. Von Rad, *Genesis,* 191.
14. Trible, *Texts of Terror,* 11.
15. Ibid., 30n9.
16. Carol Meyers, "Gen 12:16; 20:14; 24:35; 30:43; 32:5; Exod 11:5; 1 Sam 25:41; 2 Kgs 5:26; Esth 7:4: Female (and Male) Slaves," in Meyers, *Women in Scripture,* 178–79.

translated "maid, handmaid," as is her earlier description, but sometimes the term is more servile.[17] If so, this reinforces Frymer-Kensky's suggestion that in chapter 16 Hagar is "promoted," but Hagar's reaction to her pregnancy (see below) leads Sarah to act in accord with paragraph 147 from the Code of Hammurabi, which stipulates that if the slave wife has borne a child, her mistress can demote her to an ordinary slave.[18]

The problem understanding the implications of 'amah is exacerbated by its use in association with the women belonging to Leah and Rachel. In 30:1 Rachel refers to Bilhah as her 'amah when she suggests that Jacob lay with her so she may bear children through her (30:3), though when Bilhah is originally given to Rachel she is a shiphchah (29:29), and when she carries out the plan she reverts to a shiphchah (30:4). When Laban searches for his teraphim he goes to the tents of the 'amahot (plural of 'amah), referring to Bilhah and Zilpah. Do they receive a change of status too, even though there is no precipitating incident? It is hard to imagine that Rachel would refer to Bilhah with a more demeaning and oppressive term precisely when she is trying to have children through her. It is difficult to discern whether there is something innate in the term that is offensive or if it is the way Sarah uses the description that conveys something negative.

The same term, 'amah, is used in 21:12–13 but this time in the mouth of the Israelite Deity. The Deity tells Abraham not to be distressed over the boy or his slave, for the Deity will make a nation out of the son of the 'amah. In both verses the Deity says nothing negative about Hagar or Ishmael but uses consistent terminology.

Hagar's final description is as "mother" (21:21). This verse concludes the episode in the desert where the Deity reveals the well to Hagar, saving her and her son. The text focuses on Ishmael, noting that the Deity is with him, that he dwells in the wilderness and becomes a bowman (21:20), and ends with "his mother took a wife for him from Egypt" (21:21). In her final act she is not a slave—she is a mother of a nation and is the one who finds the wife who will bear that nation. Hagar returns to Egypt. Her experience is the opposite of the Israelites: she leaves Egypt a slave and returns free.

Hagar's description is not consistent. She is a shiphchah, she is a wife, she is an 'amah, she is a mother, and she is free. The one consistent description of her is that she is Egyptian.

Hagar as a Subject

Most of Hagar's actions are similar to those of the matriarchs and concern procreation. Those that differ are open to a range of interpretations concerning their legitimacy.

---

17. Brown, Driver, and Briggs, Lexicon, 51.
18. Frymer-Kensky, Reading the Women, 228.

Hagar's first action is that she conceives (16:4). She does nothing prior to this; in the earlier verses where she appears she is an object. Conception is the first verb for which she is the subject, and it defines her role in the story: she is fertile compared to her barren owner.

The same verse recounts that she "sees" that she has conceived. It is her reaction to that sight, or insight, that leads to conflict. Her reaction to "seeing" she is pregnant is that her mistress is "lowered in her esteem." As Trible points out, many scholars try to make Hagar the subject of the following verb (*qalal*), though she is not (thus I will address the verb itself later in this chapter).[19] In 16:5 Sarah says to Abraham almost the same thing, "now that she sees that she is pregnant I am lowered in her esteem." The new information in this verse is that Sarah knows what Hagar sees. The text does not clarify whether Sarah realizes this through unspoken code or through overt actions by Hagar. Sarah is upset about it and blames Abraham.

The next time Hagar "sees" is different. After she has been in the desert, Elohim calls to her, tells her to lift the boy and hold him by the hand because the Deity will make him a great nation (21:18). The Deity opens her eyes and she "sees" a well of water (21:19). The Deity causes her to see, leading her to save both herself and her son.

Hagar "flees" (16:6). Her action is not out of context, since Sarah's oppression of her in the previous verse is the impetus. Her action is bold: she is a slave running away from her master.

In the modern world many respect the bravery of a slave running away from sexual and physical abuse, but runaway slaves were not universally viewed as brave in antiquity. There are a number of responses to runaway slaves throughout the ancient Near East in different times and periods. According to paragraphs 49–50 in the Laws of Eshnunna and paragraphs 12–13 in the Code of Lipit-Ishtar there is a fine for not returning a fugitive slave.[20] Paragraphs 15 and 16 in the Code of Hammurabi recommend death for stealing or harboring a runaway slave.[21] The book of Deuteronomy takes the opposite tack, instructing that one not turn over to his master a slave who seeks refuge, and recommends that a slave can choose to live among them and that he not be mistreated (Deut. 23:16). There is no evidence in Genesis that the laws of Deuteronomy are recognized, and Hagar is not going toward a place where Deuteronomy may function but is leaving such a place.

Hagar's next action is a response to the Deity's messenger. The question is, "Where have you come from and where are you going?" She answers, "From before my mistress Sarah I am fleeing" (Gen. 16:8). This is not a bad answer to the first part of the question and confirms why she flees in the first place.

19. Trible, *Texts of Terror*, 12.
20. Roth, *Law Collections*, 66–67 and 28, respectively.
21. Ibid., 84.

It does not answer the second part of the messenger's question, where is she going, unless she has no obvious goal in mind, in which case fleeing is not only the action that occupies her but the location: away from there. The previous verse notes that the messenger finds her on the road to Shur, generally understood as on the way to Egypt.[22]

Despite all that has happened to Hagar, this is the first time she speaks, and it is not with another human but with a messenger of the Deity. No person ever speaks directly to Hagar, only the Deity or the Deity's messenger.

Hagar's relationship with the Deity continues in her next action when she "calls the name of the Deity, the one who speaks to her, 'you are *'el-ro'i*,' because she says, '[something] after seeing me'" (16:13).[23] The Hebrew of this verse is complicated, and much of it is related to explaining what Hagar means by her name for the Deity. Speiser explains the problem by noting, "MT is pointed defectively (*'El-r°'ī*), perhaps on purpose, to leave the reader a choice between this, i.e., 'God of seeing,' one whom it is permitted to see, and the *rō'ī* of the last clause, 'one who sees me.'"[24] Speiser here provides an explanation of the root of the problem, and his conclusion is more to the point, "The explanatory gloss that follows is hopeless as it now stands."[25]

Hagar "calls." The Hebrew verb is *qara'*, with a base meaning of "to call, proclaim, read."[26] Hagar is either proclaiming a name for the Deity or calling the Deity by it, something other women in Genesis do not do. Hagar comes up with a name for the Israelite Deity that is rooted in her personal experience. She does this because she is pleased with what the Deity or the Deity's messenger just conveyed to her: the Deity will increase her offspring (16:10); she is pregnant with a son, whom she will name Ishmael; and the reason for this is that the Deity has paid attention to her suffering (16:11). Hagar is happy with the Deity's words, though the messenger of the Deity notes that Hagar must go back to her mistress and allow herself to be oppressed. Hagar is allowed to name the Israelite Deity, receives no reprimand, is granted offspring, and is still forced back into slavery by the same Deity.

Hagar's next actions stem directly from this episode: she bears a son. In 16:15 Hagar is referred to twice as bearing a son to Abraham. In both cases her name is used, and she is characterized neither as a slave nor an Egyptian. In the next verse Hagar, again with no negative qualifications, is identified as bearing a son to Abraham, this time highlighting Abraham's advanced age of eighty-six when this happens (16:16).

The next time Hagar is referred to as bearing a son to Abraham the phrase is not as positive and raises other issues. In 21:9 Sarah sees Hagar's son "playing,"

22. Speiser, *Genesis*, 118; Trible, *Texts of Terror*, 16.
23. My translations are aimed to reflect the Hebrew, especially when it is complicated.
24. Speiser, *Genesis*, 118.
25. Ibid.
26. Brown, Driver, and Briggs, *Lexicon*, 894.

either at or slightly after Isaac's weaning event. The difference between this reference to Hagar's childbearing and that in Genesis 16 is extreme. Contrary to the references in Genesis 16, here Hagar is identified as Egyptian, and the emphasis on her bearing a son to Abraham is not highlighted as something positive but functions to identify her child too closely with Sarah's son. Though the verb for which she is a subject is the same as in Genesis 16, the surrounding elements, her Egyptian identification, and Sarah now having her own son change the impact of the statement.

Sarah's seeing Hagar's son and her suggestions to Abraham result in Hagar and her son being banished. Despite this situation, Hagar is the subject of only a few verbs even in this episode. The first verb is the simple *halak*, meaning "to go, come, walk" (21:14).[27] Hagar is the female singular subject of the verbs, even though she is with her son Ishmael. This verb is followed by another (discussed below), and it is not clear why two verbs are needed. One reason may be that it shows she does not fight Abraham's previous action of sending her. Trible notes that the verb "go" or "depart" describes what the Hebrews want to do in the exodus traditions but in Hagar's story defines what the slave woman must do.[28] This point will become important later because another way of reading this verb is to tie it to the exodus traditions but emphasize not what Hagar must do but that she too is now free.

Hagar again "goes" or "departs" after leaving the child (21:16). The narrator even tells the reader how far she goes, a bowshot away from the child. This occurrence of the verb differs considerably from the earlier instance because in the previous case her action is a response to Abraham's action; here she chooses to do so. The narrator explains why (to be discussed below), but the point here is that Hagar intentionally goes. Hagar's explanation, not wanting to see the child die, and the fact that the Deity, not Hagar, later hears the lad (21:17), indicates that she goes far enough away to neither hear nor see the child.

The final time Hagar "goes" saves her son. After Elohim opens her eyes and she sees the well of water, she goes to it. The first time she carries out this verb it is the reaction to something Abraham, with the help of Sarah, imposes upon her; the second time she takes the initiative; and the third time it is in response to the actions of the Deity, which save both Hagar and her child.

After noting that Hagar "goes" the first time, the text states that she wanders in the wilderness of Beer-sheba (21:14). The next verb, *ta'ah*, is usually translated as "wander" and has a base meaning of "err"; even in the contexts where "wandering" is clear, it may carry the sense of going astray, especially in the sense of not knowing where to go.[29] The question is, does

27. Ibid., 229–37.

28. Trible, *Texts of Terror*, 23.

29. Brown, Driver, and Briggs, *Lexicon*, 1073. In Genesis this verb is used to refer to Joseph when he is found "wandering" in a field in search of his brothers. He is "going astray," in that he does not know where to find them (37:16).

Hagar have an intended path and plan for where to go and how to get there before the water runs out, or does she lose her way, go astray, thereby creating her predicament?

The intentionality of her course is at the heart of the difference between this flight of Hagar and the previous one. Earlier Hagar initiates the action (16:6). Hagar's location when the messenger of the Deity finds her, on the road to Shur, indicates that she is on her way back to Egypt and that her flight is not completely haphazard.[30] Trible notes that the territory of Beer-sheba, unlike that of Shur, provides no water at all.[31] Yet such is not the case. Immediately following this episode is an incident between Abraham and Abimelech concerning wells in Beer-sheba (21:22–33). The incident is instigated by servants of Abimelech seizing a well that Abraham argues is his (21:25). The two sign a pact concerning the well, which ultimately belongs to Abraham, but the incident is narrated in the text immediately following Hagar and Ishmael's wandering in this region. At the very least, it proves there is water in the territory of Beer-sheba. And nothing in the text says that the well Abraham claims to be his is not the same well that is revealed to Hagar by Elohim.

The verb "wander" does not imply that Hagar wants to leave. It reveals, whether she originally has a plan or a destination, that in the process of leaving she becomes lost and is wandering. The emphasis on Hagar alone as the subject places the blame on her for the predicament and isolates her. She is responsible for herself and her child and has no one to whom she can turn.

Hagar's next action occurs after their water is gone, and while it is painful to translate "cast," that is what she does: she casts the boy under a tree (21:15). Hagar is the subject of the verb *shalak*, with a base meaning of "throw, fling, cast," and it usually has a human subject.[32] Again, the closest use of the verb is in the Joseph story, where Reuben recommends that his brothers not kill Joseph but cast him into the pit (37:22), which they do (37:24).

The verb Abraham uses to "send" Hagar away and that places her in this circumstance is *shalach*, a homonym of the verb used with Ishmael (21:14). The verb Sarah uses when she tells Abraham how to deal with Hagar is *garash*, meaning "drive out, cast out."[33] Sarah demands that Hagar and Ishmael be "cast out," Abraham "sends them," and Hagar does "cast out" Ishmael. Trible translates Hagar's action as "left" in order to distinguish Sarah's action from Hagar's.[34] The meaning of the verbs used by Sarah and Hagar varies considerably in the ways and places they are used, but both carry the similar connotation of casting out. This is in contrast to the verb describing what Abraham does to Hagar (*shalach*), which sounds like the verb describing what

---

30. Speiser, *Genesis*, 118; Trible, *Texts of Terror*, 16.
31. Trible, *Texts of Terror*, 24.
32. Brown, Driver, and Briggs, *Lexicon*, 1020–21.
33. Ibid., 176. This verb will be discussed in more detail below.
34. Trible, *Texts of Terror*, 34n62.

Hagar does to Ishmael (*shalak*), and is less harsh than what Sarah suggests and Hagar does.

Hagar's next actions are all in one verse. After she casts the child and goes some number of bowshots away, she "sits" and "says" (21:16). Her words are chilling and include her next verb, "I will not look at the death of the child" (21:16). Her motivation is clear: she leaves the child because she is convinced he will die and she does not want to see it. Trible notes how Hagar distances herself from the child by referring to him not as "her" child but as "the" child.[35] Thus Hagar's actions and words distance her from the child mentally as well as physically. Painful as this scene is, it is beautifully depicted by the narrator: Hagar abandons her child when she thinks he is dying. The problem is, one might argue, the only thing worse than watching one's child die is abandoning the child so the child dies alone.[36]

Hagar's next actions continue to emphasize the beauty of the scene and reinforce her distress: Hagar sits and lifts up her voice and cries (21:16). Her pain and distress are clear; what is not clear is whether they concern her own personal situation or the child's. This may seem a harsh question to ask of a woman in a horrible situation, but it is one the narrator may use to evaluate her. If the primary role of women in Genesis is mother and being proper mothers is more important than their roles as wives, this may be important in how the narrator evaluates her.

The last verbs with Hagar as subject focus on things she does for her child. In 21:19 she fills the skin with water and "waters the lad," thereby saving him. Hagar's final action is to "take" an Egyptian wife for Ishmael. This action is unusual for a woman. Speiser notes that it is usually the job of the father, who must assume the costs involved, and here Hagar must take over the responsibility, in which case one could view this action negatively.[37] Another way to view the act is positive: she is allowed to do something other women are not permitted to do.

Finding a wife for her son and choosing an Egyptian woman highlight the unique status of Hagar and how foreign she is. She is allowed to find a wife for her son, implying that she is free to make this choice, so it is likely that she is free at this point in the narrative. This final action brings Hagar's story full circle because just as she is foreign, causing her son to be not of the right line to inherit the promise, so too will her descendants be foreign.

Hagar's actions cover a wide range from standard verbs of going and bearing to unique actions for a woman like fleeing and taking a wife for her son. Her actions show her taking such brave steps as running away from oppression to naming the Deity. Her role as a mother is emphasized by the numerous times

35. Ibid., 24.
36. I would like to thank D'ror Chankin-Gould for pointing this out.
37. Speiser, *Genesis*, 156.

she is the subject of the verb "to bear." Most of her actions are in response to actions carried out on her, yet other characters are the objects of similar verbs and do not act the same. Hagar's actions and descriptions reveal a complex character.

Hagar as an Object

Hagar appears as an object of Sarah when she is first introduced as her Egyptian maid (16:1). Where Hagar appears as an object emphasizes a fundamental element at the beginning of her story: she belongs to someone else. This element of her character is reinforced by the next few references to her as an object, such as 16:2, where Sarah suggests that Abraham consort with "her maid," and 16:3, where Sarah "takes" Hagar and "gives" her. In all these cases Hagar is a physical object that can belong to someone and be given away.

The next reference to her as an object may change this designation. In 16:3 Sarah takes Hagar and gives her to her husband, but when she gives her to him, is she simultaneously promoting her to a different status with the usage of *'ishah*? Proof she is given a promotion is in the following verse when Abraham sleeps with her: he sleeps not with "a maid" or "an Egyptian" but with Hagar (16:4).

After conceiving and seeing that she has conceived, Hagar's esteem is the object of the verb *qalal* (16:4). Hagar does something to convey this action, though she is not the subject of the verb. The phrase is translated in NJPS, "was lowered in her esteem." The base meaning is "be slight," and here as a stative verb it means "to be trifling, of little account."[38] The first appearance of the term is in the narrator's voice, though later Sarah claims she feels the same from Hagar (16:5). The verb in the Piel can mean "curse"; according to 12:3, those who "curse" (Piel of *qalal*) Abraham will be subjected to the more severe curse (*'arar*) by the Israelite Deity. Hagar's reaction to her pregnancy provokes a strong response from Sarah, who prior to this speaks only with entreaty.

Abraham's response reinforces the idea that Hagar previously receives a promotion because he says to Sarah that her maid is in her hands and Sarah should do to her what is right in her eyes (12:6). Hagar may have previously had a promotion from one form of slavery to some category of wife, but this is now rescinded. She is again a servant and is returned to Sarah. The language of the encounter reinforces the idea that Hagar is an object to be handed back and forth.

Abraham also tells Sarah, "Do to her what is good in your eyes" (16:6). This phrase appears in a number of places in the Hebrew Bible, and seldom

38. Brown, Driver, and Briggs, *Lexicon*, 886.

is the result positive. One of the most famous appearances of this phrase is at the end of Judges: "and every man did what was right in his own eyes" (Judg. 21:25).[39]

Sarah reinforces the negative results in her response: she "oppresses" Hagar (Gen. 16:6). The verb is a harsh one; it carries with it connotations of slavery. Frymer-Kensky asks what precisely Sarah does; since Hagar has previously been a slave, what more could she do?

After fleeing from Sarah, Hagar is an object for the messenger of the Deity, who "finds" her by a spring of water (16:7). The messenger speaks to her, and asks her where she comes from and where she goes (16:8). Though the messenger speaks to her directly and calls her by her name, even the messenger adds that she is the *shiphchah* of Sarah. The messenger, knowing she is fleeing from her mistress, tells her to go back (16:9). When the messenger tells her to return, the messenger acknowledges she should allow herself to be oppressed by her (Sarah's) hand.

What the messenger offers Hagar is the opportunity to greatly increase her offspring, so many they will be too many to count (16:10). This promise "makes Hagar the only woman to receive a divine promise of seed, not through a man but as her own destiny."[40] The promise to Hagar is the same promise made to all the patriarchs.[41] Hagar is sent back to what will knowingly be more oppression and is granted something other women are not.

Hagar is again an object when the messenger explains the reason for Hagar's destiny: she shall have the child because the Deity has listened to her suffering (16:11). Later, when the Deity saves Hagar and Ishmael in the desert, it is because the Deity hears the cry of the child (21:17). Here the Deity recognizes Hagar's suffering and offers her something other women do not receive. Is her suffering worse than other women's or is she more special? The text indicates, as with the matriarchs, that something about the mother establishes the child's destiny. Ishmael will not ultimately inherit the promise in the same way the progeny of the matriarchs do; however, he still inherits, according to this verse, because of his mother, not his father.

Hagar is not the object of any other verses in this chapter because she becomes active, bearing the child the Deity promises. Only at Isaac's weaning feast does Hagar again appear, and she is an object before she is a subject there too. In 21:10 Sarah tells Abraham, after seeing Ishmael "playing" with Isaac, to "cast out that slave, for the son of that slave shall not inherit with Isaac." Sarah does not use Hagar's name, though she is clearly intended. She also uses a different term for Hagar, *'amah* rather than *shiphchah*.

39. For more about how this phrase and variations of it are used in the book of Judges, see Schneider, *Judges,* 31, 125, 203–6, 273, and especially 284.

40. Frymer-Kensky, *Reading the Women,* 230.

41. Trible, *Texts of Terror,* 16; in 32n27 she lists the references of 15:5; 22:15; 26:4; and 28:3.

Most discussions of this scene highlight the brutality of Sarah and question her motivation. Trible entitles the heading for this section, "A Line to Exile," referring to Sarah "debasing Hagar" and calling the scene "Sarah's triumph."[42] Abraham's role in the scenario is also suspect, though he seems to agree only when the Deity assures him it is the right thing to do (21:12). The assumption is that the Deity is not watching out for Hagar, just as she is earlier sent back to oppression when she is pregnant. Frymer-Kensky emphasizes what results from Hagar being sent away: she is emancipated.[43] Ishmael and Hagar leave Abraham's protection but they leave free. Again, an episode with Hagar is fraught with complexity.

That few have noticed Sarah's emancipation of Hagar may concern Hagar's last reference, where she is a *shiphchah*, and how she appears in the New Testament. The last reference to Hagar is in the summary of Ishmael's line (25:12), which follows the summary of Abraham's life (25:1–11). Referring to Hagar as a *shiphchah* reminds the reader how and why discussing Ishmael in Abraham's context is relevant and different than Isaac and children from his later wife and concubines (25:1). The reference defines not Hagar's final status but her introduction (16:1).

Such is not the case in the New Testament. Romans 9:6–9 evaluates the role of Abraham's two sons by noting, "not all of Abraham's children are his true descendants, but it is through Isaac that descendants shall be named for you," not identifying either Ishmael or Hagar. According to Briggs, "Paul's description of Hagar and her fate is significantly more negative than the original Genesis account."[44] Reference to the expulsion of Hagar and Ishmael is explicit in Galatians 4:21–31, where Hagar appears in an allegory.[45] This text notes that Abraham has two sons, but one is singled out as a slave and the other is free. Hagar becomes the present Jerusalem because she is a slave, as the Jews are slaves to the law, while Sarah, not named, becomes the Jerusalem above because she is free. The chapter ends by referencing the banishment of Hagar: "But what does scripture say? 'Drive out the slave and her child: for the child of the slave will not share the inheritance with the child of the free woman.'" Such a portrayal contains no room for Hagar, representing the Jews, to be freed, other than by faith in Jesus.[46]

Hagar and Ishmael's freedom is not easy, and she is faced with many difficulties, just as will be the case when the Israelites leave Egypt. Genesis 21:14 reveals this by noting that Abraham takes bread and a skin of water and gives them to Hagar. He places them on her shoulder together with the child and

---

42. Ibid., 22–23.
43. Frymer-Kensky, *Reading the Women*, 235.
44. Sheila Briggs, "Hagar in the New Testament," in Meyers, *Women in Scripture*, 88.
45. Ibid.
46. For a more in-depth discussion on the ironic representation of Sarah and Hagar see Schneider, *Sarah*, 131–33.

sends her away. The narrator draws the image of the woman sent away with little to sustain them in the desert. The picture is two-sided. In the original promise to her by the Deity's messenger, she is promised a child and *she* has the child—Abraham does not. This contrasts with Sarah, because in the following chapter Abraham will take Sarah's only child and would have sacrificed him if not for the messenger of the Deity (22:12). This parallel is warranted not only because of the proximity of the incidents to each other and the focus on sons of Abraham but also because both the expulsion of Hagar and Ishmael and the sacrifice of Isaac begin with the same verb for Abraham: he "rises early."[47]

The last two instances where Hagar appears as an object highlight the deep connection between Hagar and the Israelite Deity. In 21:18 Elohim calls to Hagar from heaven, asking what troubles her and telling her not to fear. In contrast to the situation in Genesis 16, the Deity here refers to her only as Hagar. She is no longer anyone's slave, confirmation that with her banishment from Abraham she is freed.

To prove she should not fear, Elohim opens her eyes (21:19). She sees the well of water and saves herself and her son. Hagar earlier names the Deity based on "sight" words, and this theme is picked up here in that Elohim opens her eyes so she can see. Elohim speaks directly with Hagar and saves her. The Deity recognizes her freedom and refers to her by name.

The occurrences of Hagar as an object reinforce her character's complexity. She is a slave treated poorly by her owner, her owner's husband, the Deity, and the narrator. The Deity hears, speaks to her, and is concerned about her suffering. She is promised a child. She is freed.

Hagar's Relationships

Hagar's complexity is revealed in her relationships, which follow a pattern similar to her description. She is a slave and even then does not follow the normal script of a slave. Humans treat her only as an object, never addressing her by name, yet the Deity addresses her by name.

Hagar's primary relationship is with Sarah, and it is a bad one. There is no data about their relationship prior to when Sarah gives her to Abraham. The reader does not learn how she came to be in Sarah's possession.

Using Hagar to provide children who would count as Sarah's and Abraham's is not out of line with ancient Near Eastern or biblical custom. There are numerous laws and contracts from Mesopotamia legislating this. Genesis has two more cases where women with the same title as Hagar are given to other women to bear children (see below, chapters 8 and 9 on Zilpah and

47. See Schneider, *Sarah*, 103–4.

Bilhah). The difference is Hagar's reaction. Her reaction causes Sarah to feel debased, and the relationship sours. Sarah abuses Hagar. Hagar runs away. These women who thus far have not carried out many actions use all the tools available to them to hurt one another. The issue between them is not Abraham but concerns children.

It is unclear whether the relationship between Hagar and Sarah improves between the birth of Ishmael and Isaac since Hagar disappears from the story after Ishmael's birth.[48] Not even Isaac's birth is noted as affecting their relationship, but only at or after the weaning ceremony is their relationship again the focus. Sarah does not respond to the presence of Hagar but focuses solely on her son and his actions, his "playing." This demeans Hagar even more since she is objectified, and yet it suggests that the issue is not Hagar the person, or even the slave, but the mother. She refers to Ishmael as "the son of that slave," focusing on Hagar's status as it impacts her son (21:10).

Sarah's last act regarding Hagar, where Hagar is simultaneously banished and freed, highlights Sarah's complexity. Sarah has the most to gain from Hagar but also has the most to lose from her; Sarah is the one who promotes, enslaves, oppresses, and frees Hagar.

The only insight the reader has into how Hagar feels about Sarah is through her actions. When Sarah oppresses her she flees, and tells the Deity's messenger the same (16:8). In the second situation she never addresses any element of her situation other than grief at not wanting to see the child die, and she sobs about her predicament.

Less is revealed about Hagar's feelings toward Abraham than her feelings toward Sarah. Abraham is concerned about his son Ishmael but that never engulfs Hagar. Abraham does not quarrel with Sarah about going to Hagar to impregnate her (16:2). When Sarah quarrels with him about feeling demeaned by Hagar's pregnancy, Abraham puts up no fight and says immediately that Hagar is in Sarah's hands to do with her what she thinks is good (16:6). There is no reference to contact between Hagar and Abraham upon her return, only the statement that she bears a son to him (16:15, 16).

Between the births of Ishmael and Isaac, Abraham pleads on behalf of Ishmael before the Deity (17:18) and circumcises him (17:25), but Hagar is not mentioned. Presumably, Hagar is with the family since she is with Ishmael in the text following Isaac's weaning.

After Abraham's conversation with Sarah, the narrator specifies that Abraham is upset because Ishmael's banishment concerns a son of his (21:11). There is no concern for Hagar. The departure scene can be interpreted as a sad good-bye, with Abraham placing food, water, and the child on Hagar's shoulder as he sends them off. Yet in the next chapter, when Abraham takes

---

48. Note that this is not the case with Ishmael, who is referred to as a significant player in Gen. 17.

Isaac to Moriah, the text lists two servants, an ass, wood, and a knife they take with them (22:3). Despite Abraham's concern, he sent Hagar and Ishmael off ill-prepared.

Following Genesis 21, Hagar has no contact with Abraham's family. The text never notes if Abraham learns that they survive their desert ordeal. The one time Ishmael has contact with Abraham is at Abraham's funeral, when he and Isaac bury him together (25:9).

Hagar's relationship with Ishmael is not described in the text. She returns to what she knows will be oppression in order to bear him (16:9). She does not want to watch him die and so abandons him (21:16). The Deity hears the boy's cries and opens her eyes, allowing her to save her child (21:19). Hagar finds him a wife, one of her own, an Egyptian (21:21).

Hagar's relationship with the Deity is complex. Elohim and the Deity's messenger speak to her, though to people she is an object. The Deity promises her a future through her son (16:10) and sends her back to be oppressed (16:9). She names the Deity (16:13–14) and accepts the future that the Deity declares for her. The Deity hears her son's cry in the desert and opens her eyes to save her and her child. There is no indication that the Deity hears Hagar's voice, though the text states explicitly that she lifts up her voice and cries. When the Deity opens her eyes, Hagar's thoughts are not expressed by the narrator or through conversation, but her actions reveal that she listens to the Deity since she follows the Deity's instructions (21:19). The next verse notes that Elohim is with the boy but does not mention Hagar (21:20). The Deity's focus on Ishmael suggests that, like the matriarchs, Hagar's role as mother is the important one.

Conclusion

Hagar is a complex figure. She is a mixture of opposites: slave and free, subservient and arrogant, favored by the Deity and oppressed, foreign to and part of Israel. Her role as a mother is her most important one, since that is her primary role from her introduction to her last reference. Her background stands in stark contrast to the matriarchs. The Deity views her with sympathy and gives her help, but only a limited measure. This mix of characteristics is what makes it difficult to determine precisely who Hagar is, and highlights with her actions and those of the people around her how difficult the human situation can be.

7

Esau's Wives

Esau, Jacob's brother and son of Isaac and Rebekah, has a number of wives, though the text is not consistent with their names. The text provides little about Esau's wives other than their patronyms. Since the background of the matriarchs is a major element in their characters' approval by the Deity, the background of Esau's wives may serve to discount them.

In this chapter I will treat these women as one group. Methodologically each should be treated as an individual, but all of these women are the subject of only one verb, are objects of the same verb, and are described similarly.

Description of Esau's Wives

Esau's first wife is Judith, daughter of Beeri the Hittite (26:34). She is introduced with Basemath, the daughter of Elon the Hittite. This verse follows Isaac's trip to Gerar (26:1–33), during which the Deity tells Isaac for the first time that the Deity is the Deity of his father Abraham, and that the Deity will bless Isaac and increase his offspring for the sake of Abraham (26:24). Isaac responds by building an altar and invoking the Deity by name (26:25). Immediately after, Abimelech comes to Isaac and now recognizes that the Deity is with Isaac, so he makes a pact with him (26:28). The agreement is sealed with a feast (26:30).

The text has already indicated that Esau is Isaac's favorite (25:28), and Esau first marries women immediately following Isaac receiving the recognition of the Deity and of the inhabitants of the region that he is the next patriarch. The connection between Esau marrying and Isaac being recognized as patriarch may not only be a referent so Rebekah can later be upset by it, but is timed because only now is there something tangible for Esau to inherit.

Esau later marries another woman, Mahalath, the daughter of Ishmael and sister of Nebaioth (28:9). The timing of this marriage is relevant. This reference appears after Jacob impersonates Esau and receives his father's blessing (Gen. 27). It follows the second incidence of Rebekah expressing distress over Esau's choice of wives, noting their Hittite and native background as the problem (27:46). Isaac's response is to bless Jacob and send him to his mother's brother to find a wife in Paddan-aram (28:2), instructing him, as his father's servant is instructed (24:3), not to take a wife from the Canaanites (28:1).

After Jacob leaves to find a wife that would please his parents from the daughters of his maternal uncle, the narrator states explicitly that Esau realizes his wives are not pleasing to his father (28:6–8).[1] His response is to marry Ishmael's daughter. This appears to be a good choice, since Ishmael is his paternal uncle. Yet clearly this wife is not the right one. Mahalath is not really a Canaanite since Ishmael is a descendant of Abraham and Hagar, who is Egyptian (16:1), and Hagar takes an Egyptian wife for Ishmael (21:21).[2] Both the timing and the woman directly relate to Esau's attempts to marry a woman who will please his father. What neither the narrator nor Esau ever states is whether he is trying to inherit the promise from the Deity, which is not identical with either his birthright that he sells (25:32) or the blessing his brother receives by impersonating him (27:27–29).

Two other women are identified as Esau's wives in the list of his generations (36:1). Esau takes wives from the "daughters of Canaan" (36:2),[3] a definition of Canaanites that incorporates other designations since none of their parents are named as Canaanites.

Reference to these women as "daughters of Canaanites" carries more weight than just using the plural of "daughter" rather than the singular.[4] Thus far the phrase "daughters of Canaanites" appears only in contexts where patriarchs state that their children should not marry them. In 24:3 Abraham makes his

---

1. Rebekah and Isaac are bothered by the first set of wives (26:35). When Rebekah complains to Isaac about Esau's wives, Isaac is the one who sends Jacob to Paddan-aram (28:5). Jacob obeys his mother and father when he goes to find a wife in 28:7. In 28:8 Esau is only concerned that the Canaanite women displease Isaac.

2. Nebaioth is listed as Ishmael's firstborn son in 25:13.

3. This author understands the reference here to the daughters of Canaan, and later the daughters of Heth, not to refer to individuals called Canaan and Heth but to the place and people since their father's names are identified.

4. I would like to thank Leah Rediger Schulte, who researched the occurrences of that phrase and its implications.

servant swear not to marry Isaac to one. The servant repeats the same (24:37). In 27:46, when Rebekah complains about Esau's wives, she refers to them as the "daughters of Heth." When Isaac instructs Jacob not to marry, he states that he should not take a wife from the daughters of Canaan (28:1).[5] The same is repeated in 28:6 when Esau realizes the impact of his other wives on his father (28:8). The only time the phrase "daughters of" appears in reference to someone other than a personal name, it highlights how these women are not legitimate marriage partners for patriarchs or the one to receive the Deity's promise. The text plays with the meanings because when Isaac instructs Jacob to go to Rebekah's brother to find a wife, the text identifies these women as the "daughters of Laban," showing how Leah and Rachel are acceptable by contrasting them with the daughters of Heth.

The first in this list of Esau's wives is Adah, daughter of Elon the Hittite (36:2). Earlier, Adah is identified as the daughter of Beeri the Hittite (26:34). In this same list Oholibamah, daughter of Anah, daughter of Zibeon the Hivite, is identified (36:2), whereas in the previous introduction (26:34) the second wife was Basemath, and she is the daughter of Elon the Hittite, while the first wife is Judith, the daughter of Beeri the Hittite. Ishmael's daughter, previously named Mahalath, here appears as Basemath.

Scholars offer little discussion about these women, and those who refer to them attempt to solve the conundrum, situating them with what is known about Edomite tribes.[6] Steinberg changes this trend by noting that the list represents "the women who, from the Israelite perspective, prevented Esau from continuing Isaac's line."[7] She also notes that more "study is needed in order to understand better the social function of the placement" of their names. For her, "The appearance of these names suggests the importance of women and marriage for analyzing the formation of kinship groupings."[8] Steinberg begins such a study by examining each of the named wives of Esau, and she focuses on what their background suggests about marriage and kin relations in ancient Israel.

Esau's wives indicate that, compared to the matriarchs and in light of Hagar, the background of the wife and future mother is a key factor in the promise. Esau has the correct parentage; his wives do not. That the names of the wives and their patronyms are not consistent does not matter since the point about them is that they are not descendants of the line of Terah. The difference is not in the actions the two brothers carry out toward each other or which parent favors them but in the women they marry. This is not an issue when the woman belongs to a woman with a legitimate background, such as Zilpah and Bilhah—or is it?

---

5. There are only two references to "daughters of Israel" in the Hebrew Bible, Judg. 11:40 and 2 Sam. 1:20.

6. Speiser, *Genesis*, 279.

7. Steinberg, *Kinship and Marriage*, 118.

8. Ibid., 118n5.

The previous descriptions appear in places where Esau is positioning himself in the family either immediately after his father receives the promise from the Deity (26:34) or upon learning that his wives are a significant factor in how his father evaluates him (28:6). The last list (Gen. 36) appears immediately after the death of his father (35:27–29). Esau's brother Jacob does precisely what his father suggests (28:2): he marries daughters of their mother's brother Laban (29:23, 28). As Thomas has shown, in Genesis the "generation" lists tend to appear for lines that do not continue to inherit the promise, such as Ishmael and here Esau.[9] The purpose of the list of the descendants of these women is to preserve their line since they will no longer be the focus of the text.[10]

Esau's wives have only one description, the name of their father. The women's names and patronyms are not consistent. What is consistent is that they are not from the right line and their children are not eligible to inherit. Again, the mother and her background are a defining characteristic of who is legitimate to inherit the Deity's promise.

Esau's Wives as Subjects

The first action of Esau's wives appears to refer to Esau's first two wives when the narrator notes that "they" were a source of a "bitter spirit" to Isaac and Rebekah (26:35). The narrator does not elaborate on any actions they take to become a "bitter spirit," and because all we know about them is that they are "Hittite," the reader must assume that their background is the problem. Esau does not realize that these women are a problem until 28:6. This indicates either that his parents did nothing to reveal this to Esau or that he did not pick up the signals. The reference means that even without Jacob impersonating Esau there is reason to send Jacob to Paddan-aram.

The next action appears in Esau's *toledot*, meaning "generation list," and is carried out by all the wives listed there. Adah bears to Esau Eliphaz (36:4), Basemath bears Reuel (36:4), and Oholibamah bears Jeush, Jalam, and Korah (36:5). Later, where the other wives are identified only as the source of their children, Oholibamah "bears to Esau" Jeush, Jalam, and Korah (36:14). In this reference she is identified by her matronym, daughter of Anah, daughter of Zibeon.

Following reference to these wives bearing children, the text notes that these were the "sons of Esau born to him in the land of Canaan" (36:5). Jacob's children, with the exception of Benjamin, are not born in the land of Canaan (29:31–30:22; 35:16–19). The emphasis on being born in the land is interesting since presumably Isaac, Jacob, and Esau are all born in the land and it does not make them Canaanite. The reference contrasts all

---

9. Thomas, *These Are the Generations*, 142–44.
10. Ibid., 145–46, 158.

of Jacob's children, except Benjamin, with those of Esau because Jacob's children are not born in the land. The reference to their birthplace highlights that even being born in the land does not change the impact of having the wrong mother.

The wives of Esau are responsible for only two actions, disappointing his parents and childbearing. Only the first two wives are identified as causing a bitter spirit for his parents, while his marrying the daughter of Ishmael is a reaction to their disappointment. The other action they all share is that they bear children. Again the role of the women as sources for future children is more important than any other.

Esau's Wives as Objects

Esau's wives appear as objects, as the wife of Esau or as the daughter of someone else. When Esau is forty years old he "takes" both Judith, daughter of Beeri the Hittite, and Basemath, daughter of Elon (26:34). Rebekah complains that she is disgusted with her life because of those daughters of Heth (27:46), resulting in Esau "taking" Mahalath, the daughter of Ishmael and sister of Nebaioth (28:9).

The line of Esau also refers to Esau's sons as the sons of his various wives. Eliphaz is the son of Esau's wife Adah, and Reuel is the son of Esau's wife Basemath (36:10). There are also summary statements: "those were the descendants of Adah, the wife of Esau" (36:12); "those were the sons of Basemath, the wife of Esau" (36:13); "these were the sons of Oholibamah, daughter of Anah, daughter of Zibeon, the wife of Esau" (36:14); "these are the descendants of Basemath, wife of Esau" (36:17); and "these are the descendants of Esau's wife Oholibamah" (36:18). A list claiming "those were the descendants of Adah" (36:16) does not name Esau as Adah's spouse, though he is elsewhere.

Every time the wives of Esau appear as objects they are both mothers who have borne children and the wives of Esau. These contexts do not add any new information.

Relationships of Esau's Wives

The text provides little to no evidence of the relationship between Esau's wives and anyone else, because the wives are flat characters. Nothing is known about Esau's relationship with them or of them to one another. The only information regards Rebekah and Isaac with Esau's first two wives, and that is negative. They are upset about the women, though the text does not state why. The use of "daughters of Hittites" combined with the following instruction to Jacob to take a wife from Rebekah's brother's daughters implies that the Canaanite/Hittite element is the problem. Despite Esau's marrying another woman later, there is no indication that he rids himself of the earlier women.

Conclusion

Esau's wives highlight one element that separates the matriarchs from other women: their background. Esau's wives are labeled as Canaanite, Hittite, and Ishmaelite. They are referred to as "daughters" of those labels, emphasizing them as inappropriate. They bear children, seemingly without trouble. They do not have the right lineage and thus cannot mother the future heir to the Deity's promise.

8

Zilpah

Zilpah and Bilhah are not treated thoroughly in most studies of Genesis. When they are discussed they are grouped together, as though they are identical except that they belong to different sisters.[1] The reasons for this are that they carry similar descriptions, belong to sisters who are wives of Jacob, provide children for the sisters to Jacob, and have primarily a procreative function. When and how the sisters give them to Jacob differs, as does the treatment of Bilhah after Rachel's death; hence they are different enough to need separate chapters.

How they compare and contrast with Hagar is rarely considered. Both Zilpah and Bilhah are in the same relationship to a matriarch, yet the status of their children differs. In this chapter I examine Zilpah alone first and then where Zilpah and Bilhah function as a pair. Zilpah is not a fascinating character since she does very little. She will be treated before Bilhah because, as the "maid" of Leah, she is introduced first.

Zilpah's Description

Zilpah, like Hagar, is described using terms whose precise meaning is difficult to ascertain. One descriptor never assigned to Zilpah is an ethnic iden-

---

1. Jeansonne, *Women of Genesis*, 135n22; Steinberg, *Kinship and Marriage*, 122–34.

tification. This contrasts to Hagar, whose Egyptian background is a defining characteristic.

Zilpah is first introduced as a *shiphchah* belonging to Laban, who gives her to Leah, his daughter, as a wedding present (29:24). The text identifies all the individuals' relationships to one another. When Abraham's servant is charged with finding a wife for Isaac, Abraham states that the woman is to be from the land of Abraham's birth; he does not say the woman must be a descendant of Terah (24:4). According to Abraham's charge, nothing in Zilpah's description would make her an unacceptable wife for Isaac. In Isaac's charge to Jacob, he states that Jacob should take a daughter from among the daughters of Laban, his mother's brother. In Abraham's understanding of a legitimate wife for Isaac, Zilpah counts, though not in Isaac's estimation.

After Leah sees that she has stopped bearing and gives Zilpah to Jacob, Zilpah is still a *shiphchah* (30:9). Does the reference to a *shiphchah* alert the reader that this woman may have the responsibility for procreation?

Zilpah, like Hagar, may receive a status change since she is given to Jacob as a wife (30:9). But, unlike Hagar, whose status appears to revert back to a *shiphchah* when Sarah is angered by Hagar's reaction to her pregnancy and Abraham gives Hagar back to her (16:6), with Zilpah there is no interceding incident other than conception. Yet when the text notes this it again labels Zilpah Leah's *shiphchah* (30:10). Zilpah is identified as Leah's *shiphchah* in 30:12 when she bears a second son to Jacob. What is different in Zilpah's case is that her children are counted as hers and as Leah's, something that never happens with Hagar. The last reference to Zilpah as Leah's *shiphchah* appears in 35:26 in the summary of Jacob's twelve children following Rachel's death.

Zilpah is a *shiphchah* without being named in 30:18. Leah has just borne a son, and in the process of naming Issachar she reveals that the son is her reward for having given her *shiphchah* to her husband. Leah hints that giving her *shiphchah* to her husband is not easy, hence the reward.

The plural of *shiphchah*, *shephachot*, occurs four times, and presumably both Zilpah and Bilhah are intended, though neither one is named. Before Jacob meets his brother, Jacob takes his wives, his "maids" (*shephachot*), and his eleven children across the river (32:23). Jacob divides the children and separates the children of Leah and Rachel from those of the maids (33:1). He places the maids and their children first, followed by Leah's children and Rachel's children (33:2). When Jacob meets his brother Esau, he lines up his family in this same order. The maids (*shephachot*) with their children come forward. These references treat the women and their children as a unit.

A similar reference treats Zilpah and Bilhah together without naming them, but designates them *'amah*. This appears when Laban seeks his teraphim (31:33). He goes into the tent of Jacob, Leah, and the two *'amahot*.

They do nothing and are not named, and he does not find anything in their tent.

Both Zilpah and Bilhah are identified as *nashim* (plural of *'ishah*, "wife/ woman") in the beginning of the Joseph story (37:2). Here Joseph is an attendant to the sons of Bilhah and Zilpah, the *nashim* of Jacob. This is the only time they are so identified. Most scholars assume that Bilhah and Zilpah are referred to as "wives" here, though this is the first time the text has done so. This contrasts with Hagar, who is never identified as a "wife" other than when she is given to Abraham for procreative purposes (16:3), as are Zilpah and Bilhah. Steinberg claims, "through the initiative of Leah, Zilpah became a secondary wife," and refers to both Bilhah and Zilpah as secondary wives.[2] Speiser, who when a *shiphchah* is given to a man "as a wife" argues that they are concubines, translates here "wives" without comment.[3]

Earlier, when both of Jacob's wives are alive and they are about to meet Esau, the narrator distinguishes between the two sets of women, using the term *nashim* to refer to Leah and Rachel, and reserving *shephachot* for Zilpah and Bilhah (32:22). It is not clear what happens in the interim, other than Rachel's death (35:18) and Reuben's encounter with Bilhah (35:22). This is the last description of Zilpah, and it appears after Rachel's death. If the women are wives at this point, when and how does this happen?

Unlike Hagar's case, when Zilpah is identified as an *'ishah*, equal to Bilhah, there appears to be a definite meaning to the term. When the term is applied to Hagar, there is confusion, and her precise status remains unclear.

Zilpah as a Subject

Zilpah is limited in the actions she performs, with the focus on childbearing. Genesis 30:10 notes that Zilpah bears Jacob a son, and shortly thereafter Zilpah bears Jacob a second son (30:12). In the list of those who go down to Egypt, Zilpah's descendants are identified as those she bore to Jacob (46:18). Like Esau's wives, Zilpah never "conceives," she only "bears."

Zilpah's only other action reinforces her role as a mother of Jacob's children, though she is not named. The text notes that the maids, here *shephachot*, approach with their children and bow low before Esau (33:6). While they are not named here and are grouped with Bilhah, this text reinforces the importance of Zilpah and her children because they are introduced as Jacob's children with his other children. When the text omits the names of the "maids," it highlights their importance in bearing children to Jacob while at the same time it shows their lower status by not needing to name them but only grouping them as a category.

2. Naomi Steinberg, "Zilpah," in Meyers, *Women in Scripture*, 122, quotation on p. 170.
3. Speiser, *Genesis*, 287; cf. 117 and 230 for "concubine."

Zilpah as an Object

The places where Zilpah appears as an object coincide with her descriptions. When she first appears, Laban gives her to Leah (29:24), reinforcing that a *shiphchah* can be treated like an object and handed over to others. So too Leah gives Zilpah to Jacob (30:9). Genesis 30:18 points out the difficulty Leah has giving her *shiphchah* to her husband while still treating her *shiphchah* as an object to be transferred.

While not named, Zilpah is "taken" one time, but it is not sexual: she is grouped with Bilhah, Leah, and Rachel when Jacob takes them across the ford of the Jabbok (32:23).

Zilpah is likely one of the women identified as an *'amah* in 31:33 when Laban looks for his teraphim. The text notes that he goes into "the tent of the two maids." Their shared tent is another example of Zilpah and Bilhah having lower status than Leah and Rachel. The two are treated as a category, emphasizing the difference in their status compared to their mistresses.

Zilpah is grouped with Bilhah prior to Jacob meeting Esau (32:23). Jacob rises in the night and takes his wives and maids. Rachel and Leah are juxtaposed with Zilpah and Bilhah: the narrator reserves the terminology *nashim* for Rachel and Leah and *shephachot* for Zilpah and Bilhah. They are not named and are grouped together, just as Leah and Rachel are. In the same episode, Zilpah and Bilhah remain unnamed when they are divided (33:1) and placed in order (33:2) and brought before Esau (33:6), whereas Leah and Rachel are named (33:1, 2, 7).

In 35:26 Zilpah is an object in two ways: she is the *shiphchah* of Leah but is also identified as the mother of her sons. While she functions primarily to provide children for Jacob, who are treated as Leah's, the text is clear that they belong to Zilpah. Zilpah is identified with her sons again when she and Bilhah are called Jacob's "wives" (37:2). Joseph works with the sons of his father's wives and so Zilpah is associated with her sons and Jacob. Zilpah is again labeled the mother of her children in 46:18, where the text lists her descendants. Here the narrator notes that it is Zilpah whom Laban gives to his daughter Leah, and her status is not qualified.

Zilpah's Relationships

There is little information about any relationships Zilpah has. She belongs first to Laban, who gives her to Leah (29:24). Leah gives her to Jacob (30:9). When Leah gives her to Jacob (30:9) Leah already has children (29:32–35) and is trying to get more for her spouse, especially since Bilhah has recently borne children to Jacob (30:5), though she never claims that as the reason for giving Zilpah to Jacob. Leah's names for Zilpah's children are positive, explaining them as "luck" (30:11) and "good fortune" (30:13). Leah hints that giving Zilpah was difficult for her in the explanation for her fifth son's name: she claims that the Deity has given her a reward for giving her maid to her husband (30:18). There is no sign of anything negative in Zilpah's relationship with her children, Leah, or Jacob, though Zilpah's feelings are nowhere mentioned.

Zilpah is grouped with Bilhah, sometimes not even named, yet they are not identical since Bilhah bears children before her owner, Rachel; and immediately after Rachel's death Reuben lays with her (35:22). Zilpah's children, like those of Bilhah, do not receive the pride of place when meeting Esau, and it may be because of her status. The text notes that the differing treatment of Jacob's sons affects their feelings toward Joseph (37:4), but nothing indicates how that affects their relationship with their mother. This lack of information on Zilpah's relationship with anyone reinforces the notion that her importance is in her ability to bear children.

Conclusion

Zilpah, like Esau's wives, is a flat character. Esau's wives have backgrounds that keep them, or their husband, from inheriting the Deity's promise. Such information is not provided about Zilpah, leaving open the possibility that she is an acceptable mother to an heir to the promise. It is difficult to identify her status since she is labeled a *shiphchah*, *'amah*, and *'ishah*. Still at issue is whether her children inherit the promise. If the end of Genesis indicates that all Jacob's children inherit, then the later reference to her as a wife and the final one with no title indicate that she is an acceptable mother.

9

Bilhah

Bilhah and Zilpah carry out similar functions in the story because they receive similar titles and are grouped together in the text. Despite this, Bilhah's "owner" has a different relationship with Bilhah because of her barren state. Bilhah receives a different designation than Zilpah: *pilegesh*. This designation is used when Reuben, Leah's son, lies with Bilhah immediately after Rachel's death. Thus not all of Bilhah and Zilpah's situations are identical.

Bilhah's Description

Bilhah, like Hagar and Zilpah, is described using a range of terms whose precise meaning is difficult to ascertain. Like Zilpah, Bilhah's ethnic identity is never mentioned.

Bilhah is first introduced when Rachel marries Jacob. After waiting out the bridal week, Laban gives Jacob his daughter Rachel as wife (29:28). The narrator turns to Bilhah, telling the reader that Laban gives his *shiphchah* to his daughter Rachel (29:29). Only after the reader knows that Rachel too has a *shiphchah* does the text note that Jacob "came" to Rachel. Jacob sleeps with Rachel only after Bilhah is mentioned, whereas in Leah's case Jacob comes to Leah (29:23) before the reader learns of Zilpah (29:24). This parallels the order in which children are born to Jacob in each set: Leah, then Zilpah; Bilhah, then Rachel.

Bilhah is a *shiphchah* when Rachel gives her to Jacob for procreative purposes because Rachel has no children and her sister Leah has already borne four sons (30:4). Bilhah is labeled a *shiphchah* not when Rachel first proposes the plan (30:3) but when they enact it. Bilhah again becomes pregnant by Jacob and there too she is identified as Rachel's *shiphchah* (30:7).

The next time Bilhah alone is identified as a *shiphchah* is in the summary of Jacob's children in 35:25, where she is named the *shiphchah* of Rachel. This contrasts with a mere three verses earlier where she is labeled Reuben's father's *pilegesh*, Rachel is dead, and Reuben is laying with her (35:22), a scene that will be discussed below.

As noted in the discussion of Zilpah above, the plural of *shiphchah*, *shephachot*, occurs four times, and Zilpah and Bilhah are the unnamed referents. These happen when Jacob meets Esau: they cross the river (32:23), Jacob divides the children and distinguishes the children of Leah and Rachel from those of the maids (33:1), Jacob puts the maids and their children first (33:2), he meets his brother Esau and "orders" or arranges his family. The maids and their children function as one unit.

Bilhah receives the designation *'amah* in the singular, whereas Zilpah only receives it when grouped with her. Following the birth of Leah's first four sons, Rachel pleads with Jacob for children (30:1). Jacob becomes angry for her insinuating that he can take the place of the Deity, who Jacob claims has denied her fruit of the womb (30:2). Rachel suggests he take her *'amah* Bilhah, adding that she (Bilhah) will bear on her (Rachel's) knees (30:3). When Jacob follows Rachel's suggestion, Bilhah is again identified as a *shiphchah*. Many scholars claim that when Sarah labels Hagar an *'amah* prior to banishing/freeing her, the term is more oppressive than *shiphchah*.[1]

It is possible the reference to Bilhah as an *'amah* here is meant to be insulting since when Sarah makes the request of Abraham, she repeatedly employs the particle *na'*, making her request an entreaty (16:2), and *na'* is not found in Rachel's speech. Rachel's suggestion appears in the midst of an argument with her husband, who the narrator claims is already angry (30:2). The problem is that Rachel also adds that Jacob should sleep with Bilhah so Rachel too will be built up through her (30:4). It is unclear why, when Rachel clearly intends to use this woman to do things she cannot and to be bettered by the process, she would insult the person who will achieve this status for her. The previous reference to Bilhah as a *shiphchah* (29:29) is an aside by the narrator, and so is the following reference to Bilhah as a *shiphchah* (30:4). The only time Rachel refers to Bilhah's status is here, and she uses the term considered more demeaning unless, as Meyers suggests, *shiphchah* is more servile than *'amah*.[2]

1. Trible, *Texts of Terror*, 30n9; Brown, Driver, and Briggs, *Lexicon*, 51.
2. Meyers, "Gen 12:16 . . . : Female (and Male) Slaves," 178–79.

When Leah refers to her reward for giving Zilpah to Jacob, she refers to her maid as *shiphchah*, not *'amah*.

Bilhah and Zilpah are both identified as *'amahot* when Laban searches for his teraphim in 31:33. Laban goes into the tent of Jacob, that of Leah, and that of the two *'amahot*. The description is in the voice of the narrator and does not carry negative connotations.

Bilhah, as is the case with Hagar and Zilpah, is given "as a wife" (*le'ishah*) to Jacob before he comes to her (30:4). As in the case of the previously discussed *shephachot*, scholars are not in agreement whether this terminology reveals a change in status.

Bilhah and Zilpah are defined as *nashim* (plural of *'ishah*, "wife/woman") in the beginning of the Joseph story (37:2). The assumption is that Bilhah and Zilpah are "wives," though this is the first time they are so named.

There is little in Zilpah's background that could be responsible for this change in status, but such is not the case with Bilhah. Bilhah is named a *pilegesh* in 35:22, something never ascribed to Zilpah. This appears immediately following Rachel's death. The text states that Laban gives Bilhah to Rachel (29:29), and she "belongs" to Rachel two other times (30:4, 7). To whom does Bilhah belong following Rachel's death (35:18)? The scene describes Reuben "laying" with her, using the term *shakab* and labeling her the *pilegesh* of Reuben's father, implying that with Rachel dead she belongs to Jacob (35:22). This is reinforced when the narrator claims that Israel (i.e., Jacob) hears of it. Jacob does nothing about the situation but refers to it much later, in Reuben's "blessing," where he states that he (Reuben) mounted his father's bed, thereby bringing disgrace (49:4). The implication is that Jacob considers Bilhah as belonging to him, at least after Rachel's death.

Bilhah is considered a minor figure and commentators have little to say about this scene. Most scholars view the situation through Jacob's later reaction to it, ignoring the new term referring to Bilhah. The assumption is that Bilhah belongs to Jacob and Reuben commits a crime.

According to the rules of Leviticus 18:8, if Bilhah were a proper wife, Reuben would violate Israelite law. It is also true that Jacob violates Israelite law, as expressed in Leviticus 18:18, by marrying a wife as a rival to her sister. Frymer-Kensky focuses on the specific use of the word *pilegesh* in this instance, stating that the text refers to Bilhah as a *pilegesh* to diminish the gravity of the act.[3] If Bilhah is a "concubine," something not regulated by Levitical laws, there is less of a problem with Reuben's actions. In the discussion about the legitimacy of Jacob marrying Rachel, most assume that the laws of Leviticus are not functioning in Genesis.

Trying to understand Bilhah's role based on the term *pilegesh* is a complex endeavor. Two issues are highlighted in biblical stories about a *pilegesh*: what

---

3. Tikva Frymer-Kensky, "Bilhah," in Meyers, *Women in Scripture*, 62.

the status of their children is compared to the children of wives, and what a *pilegesh* of a ruler means politically.[4] Most scholars focus on the political aspect of Reuben's action. The problem is that Reuben's move has no political significance at that point in the story; all the political ramifications pertain to the status of future descendants of the tribe of Reuben, expressed in Jacob's "blessing" (Gen. 49:3).

At this point Rachel, Bilhah's former owner, is dead (35:22). To whom Bilhah now belongs is unclear. The next time Bilhah is mentioned, both she and Zilpah are identified as "wives" of Jacob (37:2). Whether Leah is alive is unclear. Perhaps, because of the Reuben incident, Jacob clarifies the women's relationship to him to protect his reputation, the lives of the women, or the status of his other children.

Bilhah's status is more complex than Zilpah's because she is named an *'amah* by Rachel and a *shiphchah, pilegesh,* and *'ishah* by the narrator. We no longer know whether these terms are used interchangeably as a stylistic concern or whether each term carries a different connotation.

Bilhah as a Subject

Bilhah's actions vary from those of Zilpah slightly. In 30:6 Bilhah conceives and bears Jacob a son. In the next verse she carries out a similar action, conceiving and bearing Jacob a second son (30:7). Zilpah does not "conceive"; she only "bears." The addition of Bilhah conceiving may relate to the difference in the status of the mothers. When Zilpah bears, Leah already has children of her own and Zilpah's are extras. In Rachel's case, and therefore in Bilhah's, the children are the first Rachel provides for Jacob, and from the names she gives them one sees that she views them as part of a contest she wages with her sister (30:7–8).

Bilhah and Zilpah are treated together in a way that reinforces their role as mothers of Jacob's children, though they are not named. Both maids (*shephachot*) approach with their children and bow low before Esau (33:6).

Bilhah, like Zilpah, provides children to Jacob. This is summarized using the term "bear" in 46:23 with a list of Bilhah's descendants and the note that she bears them to Jacob. The children belong to Bilhah, Jacob, and Rachel. Bilhah's feelings are never expressed.

Bilhah as an Object

Bilhah is treated primarily as an object. Laban gives her to Rachel (29:29), Rachel gives her to Jacob (30:3–4), and Jacob takes them all with him (32:23).

4. Schneider, *Judges,* 248.

Bilhah and Zilpah are identified as *'amahot* in 31:33 when Laban searches for his teraphim. The two are treated as a category, emphasizing that their status differs from that of Rachel and Leah. The two are grouped in contrast to Rachel and Leah in the preparations for meeting Esau (32:23). The maids are juxtaposed with the wives as the narrator reserves the terminology *nashim* for Rachel and Leah and *shephachot* for Zilpah and Bilhah. The two maids remain unnamed when they are divided (33:1), placed in their order (33:2), and brought before Esau (33:6), in contrast to Leah and Rachel, who are named (33:1, 2, 7).

In 35:25 Bilhah is an object, the *shiphchah* of Rachel, but also identified are her sons. Bilhah functions to provide children for Jacob, who are treated as Rachel's, though the text is clear that they belong to Bilhah. In contrast with Zilpah, Bilhah's children are part of a contest Rachel wages with her sister Leah, though the children are the first Rachel can claim.

Bilhah is the object of a verb never associated with Zilpah. Following Rachel's death, Reuben "lays" with her (35:22). The verb is *shakab*, meaning "to lie down," but it carries the connotation of lying down for copulation.[5] Two different prepositions meaning "with" may accompany the verb, and often when the preposition associated with the verb is *'et*, as it is here, the verb refers to a sexual encounter against the wishes of the person identified as the object of the verb, such as the case of Dinah (34:2) and Tamar (2 Sam. 13:14). The Dinah case occurs in the previous chapter and, as here, though Jacob "hears" (same verb, *shama'*) of the incident, he does nothing at the time (Gen. 34:5). Later, when Jacob provides a less than glowing "blessing" for Reuben and references this encounter as the reason, Bilhah is not named, but the text refers to Reuben "mounting his couch" (49:4). In Jacob's understanding this incident is not about Bilhah and her status but is an attack on him.

The timing of this episode may be relevant to its meaning. In this chapter the Deity instructs Jacob to go to Bethel and build an altar to the Deity (35:1), which Jacob does. The text notes that Deborah, Rebekah's nurse, dies and is buried under the oak below Bethel (35:8). The Deity again appears to Jacob, blesses him, changes his name to Israel (35:10),[6] and, for the first time, assigns the land to Jacob/Israel (35:12). Jacob sets up a pillar at the site and names it Bethel (35:13). Immediately thereafter Rachel dies, and Jacob sets up another pillar, this time over her grave (35:20). It is after this event that Reuben lays with Bilhah.

Reference to Deborah, Rebekah's nurse, is considered odd and "displaced."[7] Despite von Rad's claim, "One may not ask what Rebekah's old nurse, who

5. Brown, Driver, and Briggs, *Lexicon*, 1011–12.
6. The Deity changes Jacob's name to Israel after he wrestles the Deity's angel (32:29), but no land is given.
7. Speiser, *Genesis*, 270.

belonged in Isaac's house, was doing on Jacob's wandering,"[8] it is important to ask that question. The text does not state what she is doing with Jacob, or how or when she joins up with him. Deborah, Rebekah's nurse, is the only link to which son should receive the promise. Presumably she is there when they are born and is the witness to which son should receive the blessing (25:23–26). Rebekah puts forward Jacob as the son to receive the Deity's promise because he is born second (25:23). Her death notice appears immediately before the Deity bestows the blessing upon Jacob. With the death of the only person who could know the reality of which son fulfills the Deity's announcement to Rebekah (25:23), the Deity carries out the blessing. This is reinforced a few lines later when Rachel dies. From the brief account of Benjamin's birth, which is also Rachel's death, the only person with her is Rachel's midwife. A different noun is used than that referring to Deborah, but the passage highlights that it is a woman, not Rachel's husband, who witnesses the birth and, in this case, death.

Jacob's name is changed and he is given the land. The text moves from there to Benjamin's birth and Rachel's death. Without this intervening scene, the cycle of events would play identically to that between Isaac and Esau. After Isaac receives the Deity's promise (26:23) there is a scene between him and Abimelech of Gerar where they settle on wells, make peace (26:26–33), and Esau takes two wives (26:34). Esau is the oldest, and the assumption in most biblical texts is that the oldest inherits. With one intervening scene, after Jacob receives the Deity's promise, his oldest son "takes a wife/woman."

The intervening scene is not a casual one. Bilhah belongs to Rachel, who has just died. The narrator hints that she now belongs to Jacob by referring to her as "his father's [Reuben's] *pilegesh*." While not questioning Jacob as Reuben's father, the narrator does not mention Jacob's name in describing the relationship between Bilhah and Jacob; and when Leah conceives Reuben, nowhere in the process of conception, bearing, or naming is he called Jacob's son (29:32). In the pattern set by Isaac and Esau, the immediate action after inheriting the father's promise is for the oldest son to marry to create a new line of people who will inherit. Various parents denounce marrying Canaanites. The family is now in Canaan. The family sneaks out of Paddan-aram, the primary source for wives for the last two generations of patriarchs. They leave on bad terms (31:17). Their parting words imply that neither Jacob nor Laban is allowed to go where the other resides (31:52). With the bridges to Paddan-aram and the house of Laban burned, where are the sons of Jacob going to find legitimate wives? Bilhah is from the area where Rebekah, Leah, and Rachel originate. Both she and Zilpah would be legitimate wives for Isaac. Does Reuben consider Bilhah a legitimate wife?

8. Von Rad, *Genesis,* 338.

Bilhah and Zilpah are identified with their sons when they are described as Jacob's "wives" (37:2). This scene follows Reuben's actions toward Bilhah, and reference to her as a wife may be an attempt to clarify the women's status. Is some action taken to change their status, either the death of both of their owners or Jacob's concern about how his sons treat mothers of his other sons? Since it is unclear whether Leah is alive, and the text provides no information about Jacob carrying out an action to change their status, any conclusion is conjecture.

In the summary list of those who go down to Egypt, seven individuals are named as Bilhah's descendants. It continues by noting that Laban gives her to Rachel and does not include a title or a description of her. Like Zilpah, in her final reference she is simply Bilhah.

Bilhah is more of an object than Zilpah since Bilhah is passed among Laban, Leah, and Jacob, and Reuben feels that he has the right to take her sexually.

Bilhah's Relationships

There is little information on Bilhah's relationships. In contrast to Leah's excitement and pleasure toward Zilpah's children, expressed in the naming process (30:11, 13), Rachel names Bilhah's children in relationship to the contest she is waging with her sister (30:6, 8). If the term *'amah* is more oppressive than *shiphchah*, then Rachel has little respect for Bilhah, even at the moment when she needs her most (30:3).

Regardless of how well Bilhah and Rachel do or do not get along, it is clear that with Rachel's death Bilhah loses protection. It is unclear to whom she belongs, though the narrator hints that she belongs to Jacob by referring to her as his (Reuben's) father's *pilegesh* (35:22). What Reuben thinks will result from this action, which Jacob considers is against him, is never stated.

It is not clear what Bilhah's relationship with Jacob is. The title "wife" reveals that she gains status after the Reuben episode. It is unclear if this results from Rachel's death, the Reuben episode, or an effort to legitimate her sons. She is not buried in the cave of Machpelah.

Conclusion

Bilhah is not interchangeable with Zilpah. Bilhah is given to Rachel in a different sequence than Zilpah is given to Leah. Rachel and the narrator label Bilhah differently. Bilhah's children serve a different function for Rachel than Zilpah's children serve for Leah. Rachel and Leah view the children of their "maids" differently. The biggest difference is that Bilhah's "owner" dies, making her a sexual object to be taken by Reuben. Jacob objectifies her in a battle with Reuben when he likens her to a couch. Bilhah achieves the status of wife, and her children are treated like those belonging to Zilpah, Leah, and Rachel.

10

Dinah

Dinah is the daughter of a patriarch and matriarch who has a sexual encounter and a marriage arranged. With the family in Canaan it is unclear how to find an acceptable spouse following the conditions established by the previous patriarchs. Dinah is the only possible legitimate mother, and the question becomes, what is more important, the father or the mother? She is also the first female child of a patriarch or matriarch. The focus has been how to find the right wife for a male heir of the promise. This is the first instance where the reverse is at issue: How does one find an appropriate spouse for a possible female heir to the promise? The common denominator necessitating her treatment here is the potential of her heirs to inherit.

Dinah's Description

Dinah's first description is as the daughter who Leah bears to Jacob in the first line of the story where she is a focus (34:1). In this case the reference is almost a parenthetical note.[1] She is the first and only daughter born to a matriarch and is important enough for a birth notice (30:21). This reference places her as more than simply Leah's daughter since her brothers, full brothers who Leah also bears, take the lead to protect their sister's honor. Her first

---

1. Finlay, *Birth Report Genre*, 124.

and only description as the daughter of Leah appears before she is raped; afterward her mother disappears.[2]

Her next description is still as a daughter but this time she belongs to Jacob (34:3). She is identified as his daughter a number of times, all occurring after her rape. She is so labeled immediately after she is raped when Shechem is strongly drawn to her. She is identified as Jacob's daughter when he hears she has been defiled (34:5). When the "men" (her brothers) are distressed and angry about what has happened to her, they note that an outrage was committed in Israel by lying with Jacob's daughter; they label her a daughter but do not name her (34:7).

The references to Dinah as Jacob's daughter after the rape highlight a difference between Dinah and other clear rape victims in the Hebrew Bible: the *pilegesh* in Judges 19 and Tamar in 2 Samuel 13. In neither story is the woman labeled a daughter. In Judges 19 the woman goes to her "father's house" (19:2), she admits him (the Levite) to her father's house (19:3), and the text refers to the "girl's father" five times (19:3, 4, 5, 6, 8) but never is she named the man's daughter. All texts refer to her as *na'arah*. For Leeb, "Close reading of the Hebrew texts in which this term occurs, however, suggest that the word connotes a girl or young woman who is away from home, perhaps in danger or at risk in some way."[3] So too is the case with Tamar. Absalom is the son of David (2 Sam. 13:1), but Tamar is described only in relation to her brothers (13:2, 4, 5, 6, 7, 8, 10, 11, 12, 20, 22), never as David's daughter, and she never gains his protection. References to Dinah as Jacob's daughter place her in a unique category.

In marriage negotiations Dinah frequently appears as a daughter. Dinah's name is absent when Hamor asks Jacob if his son can marry her, referring to her as "your [Jacob's] daughter" (Gen. 34:8). Negotiations with the brothers are complex, and they, without naming her, tell Hamor and Shechem that if they do not listen to them and become circumcised they will take their "daughter" (though she is their sister) and go (34:17).

Dinah next appears as a daughter when "the youth" wants Jacob's daughter (34:19). This is the only time Shechem is labeled a *na'ar*.[4] Leeb's investigation of the terms *na'ar* and *na'arah* indicates that the terms usually apply to an individual when they are outside the protective sphere of the father's house, including facing mortal danger or illness.[5] She notes that this is another example where the father appears to be present, but the narrator knows that the individual in question will not survive to the end of the story.[6] In this verse

2. Some question whether she is raped; see Lyn M. Bechtel, "Dinah," in Meyers, *Women in Scripture*, 69–70.

3. Leeb, *Away from the Father's House*, 125.

4. Ibid., 100.

5. Ibid.

6. Ibid.

she is protected by her father's house when the male, the son of a ruler and rapist, is not so protected.

Dinah, as a daughter, appears in the list of those who go down to Egypt. The text lists the sons of Leah and their offspring who come to Egypt and ends by stating that they are the sons who Leah bears to Jacob in Paddan-aram in addition to his daughter Dinah (46:15). Following Genesis 34, Dinah disappears from the narrative. Her appearance in Genesis 46 indicates that she is alive when the family goes to Egypt, and the lack of descendants indicates that either she is never again married, since no spouse is named for her, or she never bears children. It is critical for the narrator that she is listed as going to Egypt. If she were to stay in the land, a descendant of a matriarch and a patriarch, what would her offspring in the land mean regarding the Deity's promise?

Dinah's next description is as a *na'arah* (34:12). Leeb notes that this term is applied to her first when she goes outside her protected environment, immediately after Shechem rapes her and falls in love with her (34:3).[7] His emotions shift precisely when she is most vulnerable, reinforcing that the use of the term *na'arah* applies to women when they are unprotected. The multiple terms used for Dinah by the various speakers in the narrative emphasize the different points the parties try to make. Leeb suggests that when Shechem addresses her father he attempts to excuse his behavior by naming her a *na'arah*, calling attention to Jacob's failure to keep his daughter confined to "women's spaces."[8]

Dinah is labeled once a *yeldah*, usually translated as "girl."[9] After Shechem rapes Dinah he tells his father, "Get me this girl as a wife" (34:4). He is referring to her not as unprotected but possibly as young.

Dinah's final description is as a sister. The term's first appearance is when Jacob's sons answer Shechem with guile because he defiles their "sister" Dinah (34:13). The text does not identify which brothers are involved. The reader knows that Dinah will have twelve brothers from the same father, including six full brothers. Later the narrator will elaborate on how particular brothers respond, but here the narrator treats the brothers as one group. This is the first time Jacob's sons act as a unit.

The brothers state that they cannot give their sister to those who are "uncircumcised" (34:14). Most translations refer to the situation of the Shechemites as uncircumcised, though the brothers literally say that they cannot give their sister to "a man who to him is a foreskin." The issue is not that the Shechemites are missing some procedure but that they possess something Dinah's brothers do not. When the phrase is used regarding the Philistines, it is intended to depict the Philistines as barbaric (e.g., Judg. 14:3).[10] Here

7. Ibid., 136.
8. Ibid., 138.
9. Brown, Driver, and Briggs, *Lexicon*, 409.
10. Schneider, *Judges*, 204.

they make a big deal of the issue so they can keep their sister from marrying him or, if Shechem agrees to do it (which he does), attack them when they are vulnerable. Another option is that they originally, or at least all but Levi and Simeon, are interested in creating a way to make Canaanites acceptable marriage partners by making them follow the rules of their ancestors (Gen. 17:12–13).[11] This is relevant for the other brothers since future marriage partners in Canaan are an issue.

Shechem's circumcision does him no good. Dinah is referred to as a sister when, after her brothers Levi and Simeon slay all the males and her other brothers take part in the plunder, the reason the narrator provides is that their "sister" has been defiled (34:27)—their actions are on behalf of their sister.

Dinah's last appearance as a sister appears in the brothers' rhetorical question (34:31). Answering Jacob's response to Simeon and Levi that they have brought trouble on him, making him odious to the inhabitants of the land, the brothers ask whether their sister should be treated like a whore.

Some scholars have used 34:31 to show that it is not rape but consensual sex, and the only issue is whether to have sex is Dinah's decision to make. That reasoning does not flow from the brothers' rhetorical question. If she is raped there should be some punishment of Shechem, and that does not happen. Instead, Jacob is prepared to marry her to her rapist. The implication of the brothers' comment is that Jacob is treating her like a whore by selling her to Shechem. Shechem says to Jacob and her brothers that he will pay whatever they tell him (34:13). The issue here is not whether she is raped (she is definitely raped) but whether marrying her off, with a monetary transaction, is treating her like a whore.[12] The brothers are not revealing anger toward Shechem; they have already dealt with him. They are reacting to the reprimand of their father, who does nothing when their sister is initially raped.

Dinah's description differs from those of the other women in this section because the reader knows her background. She is Leah's daughter, meaning she has full brothers. She is Jacob's daughter, meaning someone should protect her. She is a *na'arah*, hinting that she is unprotected. She is a sister, meaning someone will act in her defense, regardless of the legitimacy of the action.

Dinah as a Subject

Dinah carries out one action, yet for many scholars it marks her as at fault. According to 34:1, Dinah "goes out to visit the daughters of the land." The

11. Compare the terminology here to that used by the Deity when commanding Abraham to practice circumcision (Gen. 17:10–14). There foreskin terminology is only used in terms of explaining the process of circumcision.

12. Suzanne Scholtz, *Rape Plots: A Feminist Cultural Study of Genesis 34*, Studies in Biblical Literature 13 (New York: P. Lang, 2001).

verb used is *yatsa'* and has the sense "to go or come out."[13] It is a common verb with specialized meanings. Leeb surmises, as with Rebekah and others, that "this was a trip to the local water source or well, since we do not know of other gathering places for women in ancient times."[14] There is nothing outrageous in her actions, yet, Leeb continues, "her ability to initiate action is ended after the first verse in which she took the fateful step of 'going out.'"[15]

Other scholars see more in Dinah's simple action. Von Rad explains: "The story describes very realistically how Dinah once stepped outside the small circle allotted to the life of the ancient Israelite woman, how she looked around rather curiously at the 'women of the land,' that is, at the settled Canaanite women, and how she thus loosened the stone which became a landslide."[16] Von Rad is prepared to consider what happens to Dinah as rape, but he hints that she begins the process through her "curiosity." Those who do not consider this a rape also claim they know what is behind Dinah's actions. Fewell and Gunn note, "Dinah seeks company elsewhere, among the women of the land, literally, among the 'daughters' of the land. Her search for connection, and perhaps for worth, however, meets a tragic end."[17] Bellis suggests, "Dinah's story is a sad tale of a woman who dares to leave the safe confines of her tent."[18] She does not blame Dinah but "dares" to hint that Dinah is not blameless.

Thus far Dinah is the only daughter of a patriarch and matriarch and is one of the few unmarried nonslaves depicted. Her actions are not out of line with how other matriarchs act. Both Rebekah and Rachel are first presented alone at the well (24:15; 29:9). There may be some hint that Rebekah is not well protected because she is labeled a *na'arah*, but her action does not lead to rape. There is no negative connotation to Rachel's going out by herself. Leah goes out (same verb) to meet Jacob and tell him he is sleeping with her that night, leading to Dinah's birth (30:16). If Dinah's one action is problematic, then all of the matriarchs, with the exception of Sarah (18:6, 9), are daring and unsafe.

The text notes that she goes out "to see" the daughters of the land. The verb may include a wider range of meanings such as perceive, but nothing innate in the verb demands significant contact. The text refers to the people she sees as the "daughters of the land." The question is, why does Dinah want to see them and are they a threat to her or to her brothers? The threat from the "daughters of [something other than a personal name]" has been for men

13. Brown, Driver, and Briggs, *Lexicon*, 422.
14. Leeb, *Away from the Father's House*, 136.
15. Ibid.
16. Von Rad, *Genesis*, 331.
17. Fewell and Gunn, *Gender, Power, and Promise*, 81.
18. Alice Ogden Bellis, *Helpmates, Harlots, and Heroes: Women's Stories in the Hebrew Bible* (Louisville: Westminster John Knox, 1994), 87.

marrying them; with the first daughter of a matriarch/patriarch, however, the threat is not from the "daughters" but from the sons of the land.

Dinah never marries, never conceives, and never bears a child. The only thing she does is "go out to see." All the matriarchs, except Sarah, "go out," and going out gets them their husbands or sexual access to their husband for procreation. The same is done here, yet the consequences are not positive. This raises the question as to what is different about Dinah. Is Dinah's problem the same raised earlier for Reuben: how can this generation find legitimate marriage partners?

Dinah as an Object

Dinah is an object numerous times. This is a case where the character is acted upon more than she acts, and one can show that Dinah appears in Genesis as an object.

Dinah's first appearance as an object is not negative but unusual since it records her birth. Leah last bears Jacob a daughter and names her Dinah (30:21). There are two unusual elements here. The first is that she is mentioned. She is the only identified daughter of a matriarch and patriarch. The other element is that Leah provides names for her biological sons and those borne by Zilpah, who belong to her, with an explanation. Dinah's name has no story.[19]

Dinah is identified as the daughter who Leah bears to Jacob in the beginning of the chapter when she goes out (34:1). This is the last time that she belongs to Leah and is safe.

In the next verse Dinah is the object of a number of violent verbs that occur in quick succession (34:2). She is seen, taken, laid with, and abused. Dinah goes out to see the daughters of the land; what leads to her rape is that she is seen.

The next verb of which she is the object is *laqach*, which has a base meaning of "to take."[20] The term is the standard one for "to take a wife" but also to take a thing. Standing alone the word does not mean rape, but when used with a woman as the object the connotation is that a sexual encounter of some sort is involved, even marriage.

Dinah is the object of this verb later when Shechem says to his father, "Take for me this girl as a wife" (34:4).[21] Shechem is depicted as crass in using the imperative with his father, "Take for me." The verb he uses for what he wants his father to do is what Shechem has already done, "taken" Dinah.

---

19. Finlay uses this to explain how the naming is a parenthetical note (*Birth Report Genre,* 124).

20. Brown, Driver, and Briggs, *Lexicon,* 542.

21. I do not include the phrase describing Dinah as a wife as a description because "wife" does not describe how she appears in the text but how someone wants her to be.

Dinah is the object of this verb again but her brothers are the subject (34:17). The brothers tell Shechem that if he does not circumcise himself and his whole town they will "take" their "daughter" and go. Here is an example where *laqach* simply means "to take." After Dinah's brothers kill all the males and plunder the city of Shechem, they take Dinah out of Shechem's house and go out (34:26). In this context Dinah is not the object of the verb "went out," the same verb Dinah is the subject of in the beginning of her story (34:1).

Shechem's next action against Dinah is that he "lays with" her (34:2). As in Bilhah's incident with Reuben, the verb used is *shakab*, meaning "to lie down," with the preposition *'et* connoting a sexual encounter against the wishes of the person identified as the object of the verb, such as Tamar (2 Sam. 13:14).[22]

Dinah is again the object of this verb but is labeled "the daughter of Jacob" when her brothers find out about the incident (Gen. 34:7). The narrator notes that the outrage is that Shechem has lain with the daughter of Jacob. The implication is not that she is unclean, or that she has been raped, but that he has "laid with" a daughter of Israel. Here too the narrator depicts Shechem laying "with" her by using the preposition *'et*. The implication is that sleeping with a daughter is the thing not to be done, raising the problem of who is a legitimate marriage partner for a daughter of a matriarch and patriarch.

The Dinah reference was used earlier to support the implication that force may be implied with the use of *'et* in Bilhah's case because in Dinah's context (34:2) the next verb is *'anah*, meaning "to be bowed down, afflicted."[23] The same verb is used when Sarah afflicts Hagar (16:6). Those who do not want to consider this scene a rape translate this verb "shame her," with "shame" or "intense humility" relating to failure to live up to societal goals and ideals.[24] If the word carries the connotation of slavery and physical abuse, as some argue for Hagar, why here does it refer to disappointing one's parents? The reason, for those who do not consider this rape, has to do with the following verses, not because of what the words of the verse actually mean.

The next places where Dinah is an object follow immediately upon her rape and mitigate, for some, the previous words. Shechem is "strongly drawn to Dinah" (here defined as Jacob's daughter), he "is in love with the *na'arah*, and he speaks to the heart of the *na'arah*" (34:3). Fewell and Gunn, two scholars who exonerate Shechem's actions, note, "The verbs of violation merge with terms of affection, commitment, courtship, and marriage."[25] Bechtel argues, "From this description Shechem appears to be a man in love, not a man committing an exploitative act of rape."[26] Fewell and Gunn go on to suggest, "Moreover, the last expression—'to speak to the heart of'—may move us beyond the account

22. Ibid., 1011–12.
23. Ibid., 776.
24. Bechtel, "Dinah," 70.
25. Fewell and Gunn, *Gender, Power, and Promise*, 81.
26. Bechtel, "Dinah," 70.

of Shechem's affections to those of Dinah."[27] Despite Shechem's love, the reader is not moved to the affections of Dinah because they are never described.

None of these discussions flesh out the meanings and connotations of the verbs used for which Dinah is an object. The first, "was drawn to," concerns Shechem's bonding with Dinah. This verb is what the Deity intends men to do to women, as in the explanation why a man leaves his father and mother to cling to his wife, according to 2:24. It may not follow in modern cases of rape, but it is what the Deity intends, according to the book where the case appears.[28]

The second verb is "loves." She is identified as a *na'arah*, an unprotected girl. There are few cases in the Hebrew Bible where one individual loves another and the love is reciprocated. Samson loves Delilah and it does not bode well for him (Judg. 16:4). The one example of a woman loving a man is Michal, who loves David, and the results are not beneficial for Michal (1 Sam. 18:20). Jacob loves Rachel, but as I argued above the results are problematic for Rachel, Jacob, and the whole family. Shechem's love for Dinah cannot be assumed to be good.

The text notes that Shechem "speaks to her heart," that of a *na'arah*, an unprotected female. The phrase, while it sounds romantic, does not bode well for characters. The raped *pilegesh* in Judges is telling. There too the Levite goes "to speak to her heart" (Judg. 19:3). The debate is whether he is making an appeal to her mind or to her heart.[29] If the mind is intended, there is nothing romantic in his words. Trible studied the use of the term in other biblical contexts centering on the actions of a man toward a woman and found that it is used either by the offended or by the guilty party, and thus does not exonerate Shechem.[30] I have noted that Samson tells Delilah "all of his heart" (Judg. 16:18), the secret to his strength, leading to his capture and death.[31] The term is one that leads not to romantic unions but to betrayal and death. Thus none of Shechem's actions in Genesis 34:3 change what he does to her in the previous verse.

The next verse recounts how Jacob hears that Shechem has "defiled" Dinah (34:5). The verb *tame'* means "to be or become unclean"; it has purity connotations. The verse is in the voice of the narrator, but it is difficult to discern whether Jacob hears that she has been made unclean, if that is his interpretation of her rape, or if it is the narrator who defines the rape as making her unclean. The verb "make unclean" with Dinah as the object appears again prior to her brothers' answer to Shechem over the marriage price. The text notes that the

27. Fewell and Gunn, *Gender, Power, and Promise*, 81.

28. Bechtel notes that rapists feel hostility and hatred toward their victims, not unlike the Tamar and Amnon case ("Dinah," 70). This is the case in the modern world and likely was the case in the ancient, as evidenced by Tamar and Amnon. The verb here employed, according to the book of Genesis, carries different connotations.

29. Robert G. Boling, *Judges: Introduction, Translation, and Commentary*, Anchor Bible (Garden City, NY: Doubleday, 1975), 110.

30. Trible, *Texts of Terror*, 67.

31. Schneider, *Judges*, 253.

brothers speak with guile because Shechem has made their sister unclean. This aspect of Shechem's action, making her impure, is a factor in the minds of the brothers, and the narrator's point is straightforward: this action is the motivation for their reaction. When the brothers plunder the town they do it because their sister has been made impure (34:27).

Hamor, Shechem's father, suddenly appears and speaks with the brothers to say that his son longs for their "daughter" and to please give her to him in marriage (34:8). The tone here is very different from Shechem's demand that Hamor get her for him. Dinah is described as a daughter, and he uses the particle *na'*, making his statement an entreaty. She is not a little girl but a daughter, someone who should have people watching out for her welfare.

The text shifts abruptly, and Shechem is speaking with the brothers. He drops the polite talk and moves to the economics of the situation, claiming he will pay whatever they say as long as they give him the *na'arah* for a wife. Again, Shechem is depicted as crass and desperate. He refers to Dinah as a *na'arah*, implying she is not protected.

Dinah is the object of the verb "to give" when her brothers respond that they cannot give their sister to a man "who to him is a foreskin" (i.e., an uncircumcised man; 34:14). The brothers presume that they are able to make marriage arrangements, outside the authority of their father Jacob. This would not be the first time this appears in Genesis, as Laban, the brothers' grandfather, is the one who negotiates their grandmother Rebekah's marriage (24:50), though Bethuel appears to agree with Laban there.

Shechem expresses his desire for Dinah by quickly doing what the brothers say because he delights in Jacob's daughter (34:19). Here she is "Jacob's daughter," not "Dinah," or "the girl." The implication is that her connection to Jacob is desirous rather than just Dinah herself.

Dinah's role as Simeon and Levi's sister is emphasized in 34:25 when they kill the men of Shechem, who are still in pain from their circumcisions. Their relationship as full brothers of Dinah is highlighted, explaining why they are more bothered than the others. Dinah's final appearance as an object is as a sister to both Simeon and Levi. When Jacob reprimands them, claiming they have brought trouble on him, making him odious among the people of the land, their response is, "Should our sister be treated like a whore?" (34:31). The reference is not to the rape but to Jacob's agreement, never actualized, that Shechem is a legitimate marriage partner for Dinah.

The cases where Dinah appears as an object are the most complex because they concern her rape and the death of an entire city as a result of her brothers' actions in response. Many have focused on whether Shechem rapes Dinah and whether her brothers respond overzealously in their reaction to the crime. Bellis best summarizes what is so distressing about the story and responds with this insight: "From a modern Western individualistic perspective the story of Dinah is disturbing because no one seems to be concerned with Dinah's rights, including what we would view as her right to have a voice in decisions that affect her life."[32]

Dinah's Relationships

There is little information to determine how Dinah feels about anyone. All Dinah's descriptions, with the exception of *na'arah*[33] and *yeldah*, are kinship terms: she is a daughter and sister. In the beginning she has a mother. It is not clear if Leah is still alive when the rape happens. Because Rachel is still alive, dying in the next chapter, it is likely that Leah is also alive. The narrator makes a big statement about Rachel's death, noting how it happens, where it happens, her last words, and where she is buried, meaning had Leah not been alive some reference might have been made to it. Both Leah and Rachel are alive in the previous chapter and nothing intervenes to indicate that Leah is dead. Dinah's reactions are missing and so are her mother's.

Following the rape, Dinah often appears as "Jacob's daughter." Jacob never has a conversation with her nor does he show any concern for her but instead is interested in the effect her rape will have on him and on his status in the land. When he first hears of it he does nothing, because, the narrator claims, his sons are in the field with his cattle. Jacob reveals little concern for Laban's feelings when he leaves in the middle of the night, not allowing Laban to say good-bye to his daughters. This may relate to Jacob's lack of concern for his own daughter.

It is easy to say that Dinah's brothers' response is heavy-handed. In the Bible there is no immediate response or punishment for any rapist or rapists. In Tamar's case a bloody feud between Amnon and Absalom ensues, leading to Amnon's death (2 Sam. 13:24–29). So too the Levite begins a civil war in Israel because of the gang rape of his *pilegesh* (Judg. 20:4–11).

Their response leads to turmoil, but they do something. How Dinah feels about it and whether it is what she wants are not conveyed. They act. They also take her with them since she is on the list of those who go to Egypt, so she remains with them, presumably, until her death. Whether this is good or bad, even in the eyes of the biblical narrator, is unclear.

Conclusion

Dinah is raped by Shechem, a son of the land. Her father is prepared to marry her to Shechem, something her brothers find problematic. The issues raised here still focus on an issue relevant for the other women in this category: why are they not proper mothers for the heir of the Deity's promise?

32. Bellis, *Helpmates, Harlots, and Heroes*, 90.
33. If a *na'arah* is not being protected by the father's house, even this term refers to kinship, or lack of it.

11

Mrs. Judah

Mrs. Judah is not discussed often, though she is married to the son of a patriarch and matriarch. Mrs. Judah's children do not inherit—she is a Canaanite.

Mrs. Judah's Description

There is discussion whether Judah's wife's name is Bathshua or if she is the daughter (Hebrew *bat* or *bath*) of a man named Shua. In her first reference she is a "daughter" (Gen. 38:2). The text notes that Judah sees the daughter of a Canaanite named Shua. The man is named Shua and she is his daughter.

The connotation of being a daughter reminds the reader of Esau's wives in that they are local women not appropriate as wives for the children who inherit the promise. The narrator emphasizes that the woman is Canaanite by not naming her and by noting that her father is a Canaanite before even naming him, though she is never labeled Canaanite herself.

The confusion over her name arises because of how she is referred to at her death: "the daughter (*bath*) of Shua, wife of Judah, died" (38:12). The phrase could also be translated "Bath-shua, wife of Judah, died." The first case provides little room for her name to be Bath-shua, only the second case opens the possibility. In 1 Chronicles 2:3 she is identified as "the Canaanite woman Bath-shua." In Genesis there is no possibility that Bath-shua is her name because of her first reference.

Mrs. Judah is described as a wife when she dies: "the daughter of Shua, wife of Judah, died" (38:12). It is rare to recount the death of women. Only in Genesis are Sarah, Deborah, and Rachel's deaths recounted. Each of those is more about the plot than the woman. Sarah's death leads to the purchase of land, Deborah's confirms that Jacob would inherit the promise, and Mrs. Judah's may explain why Judah seeks out a prostitute.

Like Esau's wives, Mrs. Judah is only a wife and a daughter. Also like Esau's wives, being a "daughter" means that she is Canaanite.

Mrs. Judah as a Subject

Mrs. Judah carries out few actions. In 38:3 she conceives and bears a son. All of the matriarchs name their children, yet here the narrator states that "he," presumably Judah, names him. Mrs. Judah again conceives and bears a son (38:4). This time she names the child. Mrs. Judah bears a third time, without reference to conception, and again she names him.

Mrs. Judah's next action is to die (38:12). Little is said about her death except that Judah is consoled afterward.

Mrs. Judah's actions do not differ from those of Esau's wives, with the exception that she names two of her children and her death is noted. These extra actions are focused more on Mrs. Judah as a mother than as a wife. Mrs. Judah's death pertains to mothering because it is as a result of her death that Judah is interested in sleeping with another, leading to Tamar becoming a mother.

Mrs. Judah as an Object

The places where Mrs. Judah is an object do not vary from those of the wives of Esau, yet because of the story's placement there may be added nuances.

Mrs. Judah first is an object when Judah "sees" her (38:20). Judah's father sees Rachel (29:10), not Leah, Judah's mother. The phrasing is not identical but is similar. Because Mrs. Judah does not have a name, inserted into the position where "Jacob sees Rachel" is "Judah sees the daughter of a Canaanite man." Jacob sees a woman who is a correct wife, according to the parameters laid out by his father, Isaac. In contrast, Judah sees what Jacob is sent away to not marry. Again the issue arises that the family is in Canaan and is not welcome back in Paddan-aram. Who should the sons of this generation marry?

The next verb recalls Dinah because Judah sees and "takes" Mrs. Judah. The difference is that Shechem sees, takes, lays with, and abuses Dinah (34:2). Judah only sees, takes, and comes to Mrs. Judah (38:2). The verb "to come" is used for marriage, and Judah's sight leads to different conclusions—or does it?

149

Shechem first "oppresses" Dinah but then he too tries to marry her. Judah does to the daughter of a Canaanite what a Canaanite recently did to Dinah.

Mrs. Judah's Relationships

Mrs. Judah, following the birth and naming of her first son, gives birth to and names her next two sons. The only relationship Mrs. Judah has is with Judah. Nowhere does Judah say anything negative about her. He needs time to console himself after her death (38:12), implying that he is upset by her death.

That Judah is interested in a sexual liaison only following his wife's death indicates a positive relationship between the two. If nothing else, Mrs. Judah's death does affect him.

Conclusion

Mrs. Judah is a Canaanite who bears three sons to a son of a patriarch and matriarch. Two of her children die, but one appears on the list of those going to Egypt, though he does not have any children. Mrs. Judah's role in the story is to set up a contrast with Tamar. Mrs. Judah is treated in a way similar to Esau's wives.

12

Tamar

Tamar is not a matriarch but she is a mother tied to the patriarchal line, especially concerning inheritance. With Tamar there is little debate about the role her children play in Israel's history, through the line of David. Here we will consider where and how Tamar fits the pattern of other women in this category while highlighting how she differs.

Tamar's Description

Tamar is first introduced after Judah marries and has three sons (38:1–5). Judah "takes" a wife for Er (38:6). In this context, because of Judah's later efforts to procure sons from her for Er, this is a case where marriage is a safe implication. It means she is introduced as a legal wife.

Reference to Tamar as a wife is consistent. When Judah suggests that Onan "come to her" to provide offspring for his brother, Tamar is the "wife of his brother" (38:8). When Onan would spill his seed, the narrator continues to refer to her as "the wife of his brother" (38:9).

Tamar appears as "the wife of his brother" despite being named in the first verse where she is introduced (38:6). This contrasts with Mrs. Judah, who is mother to the sons Tamar marries and sleeps with, but who has no name.

Again in contrast with Judah's wife, Tamar has no ethnic affiliation. She is never labeled Canaanite. The narrator hints that she is Canaanite, leading some scholars to state that "fact" categorically,[1] but the narrator never states it. The absence of such a label for Tamar is more obvious because of its presence with Mrs. Judah and Esau's wives.

Tamar is later labeled a "woman" when Judah sends a kid by his friend to redeem the pledge from the "woman" (38:20). Here the narrator could be playing with the word 'ishah ("wife/woman"), because Judah and his Adullamite friend seek a "woman" who is, or should be, Judah's or his son's "wife."

Tamar's next description is as a daughter-in-law when the narrator notes what Judah says to her (38:11). This description does not provide anything new since the reader knows she is married to Judah's son. Its usage here is notable because he is about to tell her to be something else, a widow. The narrator emphasizes that she is still a daughter-in-law because Judah still owes her a son when he suggests a different state for her.

Tamar is described as a daughter-in-law when Judah propositions the "prostitute" (38:15). The narrator notes that Judah does not know she is his daughter-in-law (38:16). Just as the last reference to her being a daughter-in-law ushers in her term as a widow, this reference occurs when Judah casts her in the role of a prostitute.

The last reference to her as a daughter-in-law appears immediately before someone insinuates that she does something else: prostitution (38:24). Judah is told his daughter-in-law Tamar has prostituted herself. The last time Tamar is called a daughter-in-law Judah thinks she is a prostitute.

Tamar is identified by name and by her relationship to Judah, meaning there is no confusion as to who is concerned or what their relationship is: she is his daughter-in-law. This contrasts to the last time she is a daughter-in-law, when Judah thinks she is a prostitute, and the first reference, when the term initiates her stay as a widow. The first and last references frame Judah's imposition of status on her, and the middle reference is her means out of childless widow status. In none of these cases is reference to Tamar as a daughter-in-law in Judah's words.

In the verse where Tamar is labeled a daughter-in-law Judah tells her to stay as a widow in her father's house until his younger son is old enough to marry her (38:11). Tamar is a widow because her husband is dead. The question is, what should happen to her? According to Deuteronomy, when a man dies without leaving a son, his widow is forbidden to marry outside the family (Deut. 25:5–10). If she has no sons to protect her, is she safer in her father's house? The problem is there is no discussion of a bride price, what happens to any dowry she has, or whose responsibility it is to care for her. Most would agree she is Canaanite, and there is no indication Canaanites would be expected to follow Israelite custom, so whose custom is this? The rest of the verse relates Judah's thought to himself that he has no intention of giving her his son.

1. Fewell and Gunn, *Gender, Power, and Promise*, 87; von Rad, *Genesis*, 358.

The next time Tamar is described is as a prostitute (Gen. 38:15). Most assume she is intentionally dressing as a prostitute, though recent scholarship shows this not to be the case (see below). The text is clear that this is how Judah perceives her: she is not labeled "prostitute" by the narrator. This description is how one person, Judah, perceives her.

Judah's Adullamite friend looks for the "woman" and names her a "cult prostitute" (38:21). The term used, *qedeshah*, has a cultic element that shifts the office from one of mere prostitution to something a bit less raunchy. Frymer-Kensky claims that the term identifies one not as a sacred prostitute but as "a public woman, who might be found along the roadway (as virgins and married women should not be). She could engage in sex, but might also be sought out for lactation, midwifery, and other female concerns."[2] The term's use here could mean that Judah's friend is placing the woman, and Judah, in a more respectable category.

Tamar is described as "more righteous" than Judah (38:26). The word "righteous" translates Hebrew *tsedaqah*, and this root is used in the sense of justice.[3] This is quite an admission by Judah. Prior to his seeing the evidence implicating him as her child's father, he is prepared to burn her; now she is more right than he. Such an admission by a male in the Hebrew Bible is rare.

Tamar is described uniquely. She is a wife, she is a brother's wife, and she is a daughter-in-law. She is described as two different kinds of prostitute, and as more righteous than Judah.

Tamar as a Subject

Tamar is married to Judah's first son, and he dies; she is joined by Judah's second son, who has sexual relations with her that do not result in children, and he dies; she is sent to her father's house as a widow; Judah's wife dies; and Judah goes to Timnah for the sheepshearing—all before Tamar carries out a single action. Thus far she has been acted upon and does everything expected of her. Some of Tamar's actions are unusual compared to women analyzed thus far, but they must be viewed through the lens of her having been dutiful for a long portion of her story with Judah and family.

Only in 38:11 is Tamar the subject of any verbs. In 38:11 Tamar is the subject of two verbs that are a direct reaction to Judah's command to dwell as a widow with her father: she goes and sits. Thus far she has been acted upon and does everything expected of her, and her first two actions further this dutiful image.

In 38:14 she is the subject of five verbs. She first "takes off her widow's garb." There is discussion about why Tamar veils but little discussion as to

2. Tikva Frymer-Kensky, "Tamar 1," in Meyers, *Women in Scripture*, 162.
3. Brown, Driver, and Briggs, *Lexicon*, 841–43.

how a widow dresses. What constitutes a "widow" in the ancient Near Eastern world is different than in the modern, and so it is unclear what a widow should wear. The implication is that a widow wears identifying garb.

Next Tamar "covers her face with a veil." Despite few references to veiling in the Hebrew Bible, scholars have made a number of assumptions about what she does, mostly because of what Judah assumes she is doing, and they translate Tamar's actions based on Judah's perceptions. "The veil appears to be used on special occasions to identify the status or character of women. Women used veils, ṣā'ip, or part of their outer garment to cover their faces on wedding days (Gen. 24:65) or if they were prostitutes (Gen. 38:14, 15, 19)."[4] There is only one case for the use of each of these, and these cases may be extraordinary and not represent the norm.

Tamar's reference to veiling as a mark of a prostitute is not supported by evidence in the biblical text or in the Middle Assyrian Laws. Thus the veil may function differently in this story. The extrabiblical information contrasts with the assumption that a prostitute veils. These laws reflect one opinion from the ancient Near East as to how an issue should be adjudicated. Paragraph 40 of the Middle Assyrian Laws proclaims,

> Wives of a man, or [widows], or any [Assyrian] women who go out into the main thoroughfare [shall not have] their heads [bare]. . . . A concubine who goes about in the main thoroughfare with her mistress is to be veiled. A married qadiltu-woman is to be veiled (when she goes about) in the main thoroughfare. . . . A prostitute shall not be veiled, her head shall be bare. (v. 68) Whoever sees a veiled prostitute shall seize her, secure witnesses, and bring her to the palace entrance. They shall not take away her jewelry, but he who has seized her takes her clothing; they shall strike her 50 blows with rods; they shall pour hot pitch over her head. And if a man should see a veiled prostitute and release her, and does not bring her to the palace entrance, they shall strike that man 50 blows with rods.[5]

In Assyria, wives, widows, and concubines veiled, and the penalty for a prostitute who veiled was severe.

Internal biblical evidence militates against veiling as a sign of a prostitute. Rebekah veils before seeing Isaac (24:65). If one veils before marriage, how can one differentiate between a bride and a prostitute? If royalty veil, are they too prostitutes? How should one categorize Moses, who veils to hide his shining face after speaking with the Deity (Exod. 34:33–35)?

The text never states what Tamar's goal is in putting on the veil or that her intention is to be viewed as a prostitute. The rest of the text could prove that she never functions as a prostitute, if a prostitute is one who has sex for

---

4. Edwards, "Dress and Ornamentation," in Freedman, *Anchor Bible Dictionary*, 2:235.
5. Roth, *Law Collections*, 167–68.

financial remuneration, since she never intends to receive payment. Taking off her widow's garb reveals that she does not want to be seen as a widow, which, as will be discussed below, it is not clear she is according to ancient Near Eastern and biblical definitions of the term. Frymer-Kensky suggests that the veil is not the mark of a prostitute but that it will prevent Judah from seeing Tamar's face.[6]

The narrator notes that she "wrapped herself" (Gen. 38:14). Speiser translates "to disguise herself," though he admits in his notes that the phrase literally translates as "she covered up."[7] The difference between the two translations reveals that Speiser knows what the term means but in order to stress the interpretation that Judah is being set up and Tamar is manipulating the situation, he translates "disguise." Later he states, "she tricked him into leaving her with child, by waylaying him in the disguise of a harlot."[8] Judah is never accused of misinterpreting what she says, forcing Tamar to live as a widow when according to biblical and ancient Near Eastern practice she may not be one, keeping her from having a child and fulfilling her role to her husband and his family.

Tamar's next verb is "sat" (38:14). Tamar is deliberate in her actions by sitting at the entrance to Enaim, which is on the way to Timnah, where her father-in-law Judah is. She knows he will be passing by at some point. With her veil on and no widow's garb, she knows he will not immediately recognize her. Frymer-Kensky suggests that Tamar knows that Judah will be "happy and horny (and maybe tipsy)."[9] Tamar creates a scenario where Judah is likely to act a certain way, but Tamar herself does not have to do or say much. The usual depiction of Tamar is that she is manipulative and is intentionally acting like a prostitute.

The question is, does a mysterious woman sitting by the gate entrance, wearing a veil that does not indicate a prostitute but someone to be protected and shielded, mean she wants sexual advances, or is she just waiting to see Judah and to respond accordingly? If one follows the idea that a woman veils herself on her wedding day, it is possible that Tamar veils and rids herself of her widow's garments because she plans on Judah taking her back to marry Shelah. Assuming she is a prostitute legitimates Judah's perception of the situation, even though the text does not provide enough information to prove that she plans on Judah treating her like a prostitute.

Tamar's next action is that she "saw" (38:14). The reference explains Tamar's actions: she sees that Shelah is grown up and she has not been given to him as a wife. If one assumes she is dressing like a prostitute, this verse proves that she knows Judah is not going to give Shelah to her. When Judah claims he will not give her to Shelah, he thinks the comment; he does not say it. Tamar does not know that Judah never intends to give her to him. It is possible she is going to

6. Frymer-Kensky, "Tamar 1," 162.
7. Speiser, *Genesis*, 298.
8. Ibid., 300.
9. Frymer-Kensky, "Tamar 1," 162.

force his hand and embarrass him into taking her home to marry Shelah. Reinforcement that Tamar never intends to be treated like a prostitute is that the next verse claims that Judah "thought her a prostitute" (38:15). The narrator implies that Judah thinks she is a prostitute, but the narrator knows better.

Tamar's next verb appears in the context of Judah's perception of her as a prostitute. The narrator comments that he thought her a prostitute because she "had covered her face." The standard assumption is that if her face is covered she is a prostitute because all prostitutes cover their faces. Yet none of the other prostitutes or scenes with them in the Hebrew Bible mention them as veiled, and the opposite situation—prostitutes cannot veil—is true of other places in the ancient Near East (Middle Assyrian Laws). Another way of reading this reference is that he does not know it is Tamar because he cannot see her face. It reinforces Frymer-Kensky's idea that Judah, now widowed, is drunk and horny and makes an assumption. The whole point of the story is that he is wrong, or Tamar is more right; it is not hard to imagine the narrator playing with the roles in that she is just a covered mysterious woman and Judah assumes the worst, because of where she sits, precisely as he does later in the story when he assumes that she is with child through harlotry and suggests burning her.

Tamar next is the subject of "says" (38:16). She does not initiate conversation but responds to Judah's suggestion. Her question is, "What will you give me to come to me?" Irony abounds because what he should give her is his son Shelah. What is not clear is if she is sitting on the roadside waiting for Judah to give Shelah to her or if she is waiting for Judah to ask to do so himself. Both propositions fill her need to provide a son to Judah's family, and apparently any seed will do.

Tamar again speaks when she explains that she needs a pledge from him (38:17). He is prepared to pay her a kid, something in which she is not interested, and she wants the pledge, not so she can get the kid but as proof of paternity. When she is again the subject of the verb "say" in the next verse, she details what his pledge should be: his seal, cord, and the staff he carries (38:18). These objects are personal items that would be readily recognized, at least by Judah. Throughout this exchange Tamar only speaks in response to Judah's suggestions. She does not initiate or lead the conversation but responds to his queries.

The outcome of their encounter results in the next verb for which Tamar is the subject: she "conceives" (38:18). The narrator notes this in the very verse where Judah gives his seal and cord to her and "goes in to" her. The text is explicit that she conceives by him. In other instances where the text notes that the woman conceives, the narrator does not refer to the man by whom the woman conceives.[10] In these cases no other sexual partner is considered.

10. See Hagar (16:4), Sarah (21:2), Rebekah (25:21), Leah (29:32, 33, 34, 35; 30:17, 19), Bilhah (30:5, 7), and Rachel (30:23). Some cases refer to whom the woman bears but not with the word conceives.

Because Tamar is accused of prostituting and the paternity issue is later raised, the text is explicit as to who the father is as soon as conception occurs. The outcome of their encounter is communicated to the reader immediately. Judah must wait three months (38:24) to learn the results of his stop on the way home from Timnah.

In the next verse Tamar is the subject of four verbs that allow her to go back to how everything was before she left her father's house. She gets up, she goes, she takes off her veil, and she puts on her widow's clothes (38:19). How long she is gone is not clear, but with this verse she replaces and undoes everything she had done earlier (38:14). The one difference is probably not even known to her: she is pregnant.

The next verbs for which Tamar is the subject are hearsay. The text notes that about three months later Judah is told that Tamar, labeled as his daughter-in-law, has prostituted herself (38:24). She is labeled Judah's daughter-in-law when she is living as a widow in her father's house. The reason for suggesting that she has prostituted herself is that she is pregnant, according to Judah's informant. Since she is living as a widow in her father's house, the assumption is that she must have prostituted herself.

Tamar sends a message to her father-in-law (38:25). Judah demands she be burned because of actions he assumes that she does. Tamar's action is a reaction to Judah's assumptions. Her message is that she is pregnant by the man to whom the seal, staff, and cord belong (38:25).

When Judah sees Tamar's evidence of paternity he states, "She is more right than I" (38:26). Judah recognizes Tamar's innocence and where he is wrong. Frymer-Kensky suggests a different reading of the phrase: "she is innocent—it [the child] is from me. Judah has now performed the levirate."[11]

Tamar carries out actions at two points in the story. In the rest of the story Tamar is a dutiful daughter, wife, daughter-in-law, and widow. Prior to her actions she does what is expected without comment. When she is the subject of verbs, she is methodical in her actions. It is unclear whether her original intent is to be viewed as a prostitute and conceive through Judah, or whether she is preparing for Judah to marry her to Shelah and to fulfill her levirate duty that way. In either case she is committed to providing a child to the family into which she has married.

Tamar as an Object

Tamar's actions are bold and decisive, in stark contrast to the person who is acted upon by the family of Judah. The text notes that Judah takes a wife for his son Er (38:6). There is no consistent pattern by which spouses are

11. Frymer-Kensky, "Tamar 1," 162.

determined in Genesis. Hagar finds a wife for Ishmael (21:21), Abraham's servant finds a wife for Isaac (Gen. 24), Esau finds his own spouses (26:34; 28:9), as does Jacob (29:18, 21, 23, 28), with input from his father (28:2), and Judah finds his own wife (38:1).

Tamar is again an object when Judah tells Onan to join with his "brother's wife" and do his duty as a brother-in-law, providing offspring for his brother (38:8). Tamar is not named and is treated as an obligation and burden on the family, though she is the only means of providing an heir for Er. She continues to be identified only as "his brother's wife" when he wastes his seed so as not to provide offspring for his brother (38:9).

When Judah speaks to his daughter-in-law she is named Tamar (38:11). He tells her to stay as a widow in her father's house until his son Shelah grows up, though Judah's thoughts to the reader indicate that he has no intention of giving Tamar to his son Shelah.

At issue is whether Tamar is a widow according to biblical and ancient Near Eastern custom. Tamar's husband is dead (38:7), but it is not clear that the Hebrew term 'almanah matches the meaning of English "widow." Based on the Akkadian cognate almattu in Middle Assyrian Law 33, scholars argue that in ancient Israel a widow was a woman whose husband and father-in-law were both dead and who had no son.[12] Nash notes that Tamar is labeled an 'almanah only when she is deprived of her father-in-law's support, thus presuming that withdrawal of the father-in-law's material support is the functional equivalent of his death.[13] It also means that sending her to live as a widow in her father's house signals a dismissal of her.

The next time Tamar appears as an object she is told her father-in-law is coming up to Timnah for the sheepshearing (38:13). This information sets Tamar in motion to carry out the bulk of the verbs of which she is the subject. Judah identifies Tamar as a daughter-in-law precisely when he breaks off his relationship to her as a father-in-law by identifying her as a widow and sending her to her father's house. By identifying Judah again as her father-in-law, is the narrator subtly reminding the reader that Tamar is not a widow, if the expanded meaning of "widow" is what is intended? Is the narrator legitimating her actions by reminding the reader that Judah is a father-in-law and has a responsibility to Tamar because she is not a widow?

She next appears when Judah "sees" her (38:15), though he does not see Tamar but sees a prostitute. Previously, Judah seeing a woman leads to descendants: Judah marries Mrs. Judah after he sees her. Earlier he takes Tamar for Er and he speaks to her, but this is the first time Judah "sees" her. And he does not see Tamar but a prostitute, and the result is heirs.

12. Kathleen S. Nash, "Widow," in Freedman, Eerdman's Dictionary of the Bible, 1377.
13. Ibid.

Judah says, "Here, please, let me come to you" (38:16), leading her to ask what he will give her. Judah asks nicely, using *na'*, the sign of entreaty, thus asking, not demanding. Judah, after agreeing to the price set by Tamar, gives them to her and comes to her (38:18).

Throughout the proposal for services and negotiating, Judah is polite and respectful. He carries through with payment, sending his friend the Adullamite to redeem his pledge (38:20). His next action where Tamar is the object contrasts vividly. When Judah learns that Tamar has prostituted herself and is pregnant, he demands they bring her out and burn her (38:25). Leviticus recognizes burning because of prostitution only in cases of a priest's daughter (Lev. 21:9), whereas if a man lies with his daughter-in-law Leviticus recommends they both be put to death (20:12).

At issue here is what the offense is and how the participants are related. Von Rad questions on what basis the complaint is made, prostitution by a widow or by an engaged girl.[14] He considers Judah taking on the role of judge as indicating that he views the matter as Tamar being an engaged girl and part of his family.[15] Judah plays both sides of the father-in-law game. He does not want responsibility for Tamar and sends her to her father's house as a widow, yet when he finds out she is pregnant, he treats her as a daughter-in-law, asserting rights over her when he is not willing to take responsibility for her, something even he will eventually recognize.

Tamar is again an object as she is brought out to be burned (Gen. 38:25). After seeing the objects she holds and recognizing them, Judah claims she is more right than he but explains why: "I did not give her to my son Shelah" (38:26). Immediately thereafter, the text notes that he does not know her again. According to Leviticus 20:12, touching a daughter-in-law is an incest violation and Judah would be guilty. Whether because of Leviticus or not, following Judah's admission he does not touch her again.

Tamar is last an object in relation to childbearing. The narrator notes that there are twins in her womb (Gen. 38:27). When she is in labor one puts out his hand to come out first, but then withdraws his hand and the other one comes out first. Finally Tamar is a mother.

The Tamar depicted as an object is docile and does what she is told. When she is in her father-in-law's house she is handed from son to son. Her father-in-law sends her to her father's house as a "widow," a status she may not hold. When Judah speaks to her he is polite but he thinks she is a prostitute. When he learns she is pregnant he metes out the harshest judgment possible. Despite this, Tamar fulfills her levirate duty and becomes a mother, David's ancestor.

14. Von Rad, *Genesis,* 360.
15. Ibid.

Tamar's Relationships

The text provides no information on Tamar's relationship with her husband, Er, or his brother Onan. Onan does not miss his brother nor does he care about his brother's name, but that does not concern Tamar. He maintains a sexual relationship with her but ensures that pregnancy does not result. From his comment that Shelah too might die if he sleeps with Tamar, Judah is nervous about her. Tamar does not interact with Mrs. Judah.

No relationship between Tamar and the Deity is expressed. The only thing the Israelite Deity does is take the lives of Er and Onan (38:7, 10).

Tamar expresses a duty toward Judah's family and an heir. She creates a scenario, either posing as a prostitute or seeking to marry Shelah, whereby she bears children to Judah's family. Judah recognizes this and praises her: she is more right than he.

Conclusion

Tamar is not a dazzling character; in most of her story she is passive. When she acts, it is to fulfill a responsibility to Judah's family. She is rewarded by becoming the ancestor to the most important family in Israel and the Hebrew Bible.

13

Asenath

Asenath, the wife of Joseph, is Egyptian. This raises the question, what does Asenath being Egyptian mean for her character and her children?

Asenath's Description

Asenath is first identified as the daughter of Potiphera, a priest of On (41:45). The reference is almost an aside since it occurs in a verse where Pharaoh "names" Joseph Zaphenath-paneah,[1] gives him Asenath, and refers to Joseph emerging in charge of the land of Egypt. The verse showcases the various activities Pharaoh carries out to put Joseph in charge of Egypt. The steps include: removing the signet ring from his hand, putting it on Joseph's hand, dressing him in robes of fine linen, putting a gold chain about his neck, having him ride in the chariot as his second-in-command, and having people yell "Abrek!" before him (41:42–43).[2] Asenath is treated as another item Joseph needs in order to command Egypt.

Asenath is again identified as the daughter of Potiphera, priest of On, when the narrator discusses Joseph's children by her (41:50). Here too reference to

1. Pharaoh does not "change" his name but "calls him," using the terminology Rachel uses at his birth (30:24).
2. It is not clear what the word "Abrek" means. It is connected to the Semitic verb for bowing, see Brown, Driver, and Briggs, *Lexicon*, 7–8.

Asenath is an aside since the verse dates the episode by noting that it is before the years of famine and is followed by the names of his children, described as having meaning for what happens in Joseph's life (41:51–52).

Finally, Asenath is identified as the daughter of Potiphera, priest of On, when the text lists the names of the Israelites, Jacob and his descendants, who come to Egypt. Contrary to the rest of the list, Manasseh and Ephraim are born in the land of Egypt (46:20).

It is not clear why Asenath is repeatedly labeled Potiphera's daughter rather than Joseph's wife. It is unusual for a woman to be labeled someone's daughter after she is married. When women are labeled daughters it carries the connotation that someone protects them, or should (see chapters 2, 4, and 10 above on Rebekah, Rachel, and Dinah), or that they are foreign and inappropriate (see chapter 7 above on Esau's wives). Mrs. Judah is a Canaanite, as indicated by her being the daughter of a Canaanite, in contrast to Tamar, who never receives this designation. The reader learns that Tamar has a father because she is sent to live in his house, and yet she is never labeled his daughter.

The reason for constantly referring to Asenath as the daughter of an Egyptian priest relates to the narrator never labeling her as Egyptian. She has an Egyptian name, she is given to Joseph in Pharaoh's effort to make Joseph more Egyptian, and her father is identified as a priest of On, an Egyptian deity, yet she is never so labeled. This contrasts with Hagar, who is identified as Egyptian at a number of different points in the text. Instead, the text always refers to Asenath as "the daughter of Potiphera, priest of On." Does this make her children more or less acceptable?

The only time Asenath is identified as a wife is when Pharaoh gives her to Joseph as a wife (41:45). This reference is odd since a woman who is only referred to as the daughter of someone, never Joseph's wife, is not given to him by her father but by Pharaoh. Sarah's visit to Egypt reveals that Pharaoh or his courtiers feel any pretty woman may be of interest to Pharaoh, hence she is taken into his house (12:15). Here Pharaoh has the power to decide what woman goes with whom, though in this case Pharaoh is not interested in her for himself but for Joseph. This is the only time Asenath is labeled a wife.

Asenath is a daughter more than a wife. Joseph receives her from Pharaoh as part of the attempt to make Joseph Egyptian. Despite her role in making Joseph Egyptian, she is never labeled Egyptian herself.

Asenath as a Subject

Asenath carries out one action: she bears children. This happens before the years of famine (41:50). As with Esau's wives, the text does not recount each incident when she bears but summarizes that two sons are born to Joseph, and repeats that Asenath, labeled the daughter of Potiphera, priest of On, "bears."

When listing Jacob's children who are in Egypt, the text refers to Ephraim and Manasseh as sons that Asenath, daughter of Potiphera, priest of On, bears to Joseph. Asenath's only action is to produce offspring for Joseph.

Asenath as an Object

Asenath carries out one action and one action is carried out toward her: "he [Pharaoh] gives him [Joseph] for a wife, Asenath, daughter of Potiphera, priest of On" (41:45).

Asenath's Relationships

Asenath is a flat character. She is identified more as the daughter of Potiphera, the priest of On, than as Joseph's wife. She is identified with her children two times, both in passing. Her father-in-law, Jacob, "adopts" her children as his own, opening the door for their descendants to inherit land after the exodus. Does Jacob adopt the boys because of their mother? Tamar too is likely Canaanite, though the text does not label her as such, but she carries out actions proving her to be special and a legitimate mother of the promise. Asenath never does anything, positive or negative. Is part of the problem of Ephraim and Manasseh and their role in the later exile to be traced back to their mother?

Conclusion

There is little data about Asenath. She is Egyptian yet not labeled that way. She is the wife of Joseph, who brings the Israelites down to Egypt. She too highlights how women as wives are less important than their role in bearing children, especially males.

14

Review of Part 2

Mothers of Potential Heirs (or Slaves, Concubines, Daughters, and Daughters-in-Law)

This section is an odd mix of characters, but important factors are highlighted by grouping these women together.

Descriptions of Mothers of Potential Heirs

There are no common descriptors in this category. Many of the women are foreign. Hagar is Egyptian, hence not only foreign but from the country where Sarah is taken into Pharaoh's house (12:15) and the Israelites are enslaved. Esau's wives are Hittites (26:34; 36:2), Ishmaelites (28:9; 36:3), and summarized as Canaanites (36:2). Their foreign background is a problem, at least to Esau's parents (26:35; 27:46; 28:8). Mrs. Judah is the daughter of a Canaanite (38:22). Asenath, though never labeled Egyptian, is the daughter of Potiphera, priest of On (41:45, 50; 46:20), more than she is Joseph's wife.

Other women in this unit are not foreign. Bilhah and Zilpah are from the area where Rachel and Leah live, and no ethnic affiliation is listed for them. Dinah, the daughter of Leah and Jacob, born in Paddan-aram, is not Canaanite. Tamar's situation is more like Bilhah and Zilpah's since she is probably a Canaanite but is never connected to an ethnic group.

Except Dinah, all the women are given as a wife at some point, though it is not clear that this is a title, position, or rank they maintain. Hagar carries this title only when she is given to Abraham for procreative purposes (16:3). Esau's wives all carry this title. Zilpah and Bilhah are so labeled when they are given to Jacob for procreative purposes (30:4, 9) but later achieve this status without producing more children (37:2). This is one of Mrs. Judah's few descriptions (38:12). Even Tamar carries this title, though it is often modified as a "brother's wife" (38:9). Asenath, though there is no suggestion she is not Joseph's true wife, receives this title only when she is first given to Joseph (41:45). Arrangements are made for Dinah to become a wife, but this event never happens and she is never so identified.

These women are not consistently in any kinship relationship. Hagar is only a mother, and that happens late in her story (21:21). Esau's wives are all daughters. Zilpah and Bilhah have no family and are never labeled "mothers." Dinah is a daughter and sister, and these relationships keep her from becoming a wife and mother. Mrs. Judah is a daughter. Tamar is a daughter sent to live with her father after being a wife. Asenath is a daughter more times than she is a wife.

The status of these women not only differs among them but, for some, changes within their own story. Hagar, Bilhah, and Zilpah are in servitude that changes throughout the story. The other women are not servile. The mother's free or slave status does not affect whether the children inherit. This group has no common descriptors. Some have family, some are foreign, some are servile.

Mothers of Potential Heirs as Subjects

In this category there are no consistent verbs. With the exception of Dinah, all the women bear children. Dinah's brothers' actions, the brothers' comment to their father (34:31), and the lack of a spouse when Dinah goes down to Egypt with the rest of the family (46:15) suggest there is no worthy spouse for her.

Mothers of Potential Heirs as Objects

Here too there are no places where the women are consistently the object of the same verb or prepositional phrase. All of the women are "taken" at some point in their story, though not always in a sexual sense. Sarah takes Hagar and gives her to Abraham (16:3). Esau takes all his wives in marriage (26:34; 28:9). Bilhah and Zilpah are both taken but with the other wives of Jacob when he crosses the Jabbok (32:23). This is one of the verbs used to describe Dinah's rape (34:2). Mrs. Judah is taken by Judah and so is Tamar (38:6). Asenath is taken by Pharaoh (41:45).

165

Mothers of Potential Heirs' Relationships

This category contains the least amount of data for any of the women in this category. None of these women has the same kin described in the text and there is no common marital status, nor do they all have children.

Conclusion

There are few similarities among these women, but this does not mean that comparing them is not meaningful. Zilpah and Bilhah are often treated as a unit and yet never compared with Hagar, with whom they share many similarities. Examining them as separate entities reveals how they are the same and different, especially when compared to Hagar and to Esau's wives, with whom they are compared by the narrator, in Abraham's and Isaac's instructions, and with regard to the status of their children. How Bilhah differs from Zilpah emphasizes the problem that the children of Jacob have of not being able to return to Paddan-aram to find legitimate wives. This unique situation places the status and issues related to Dinah, Mrs. Judah, Tamar, and Asenath in a different perspective.

The women in this category emphasize elements revealed in the evaluation of the matriarchs. The role of women as mothers is more important than their role as wives, slaves, or daughters. Also at issue is the mother's background. Zilpah and Bilhah emphasize that the status of the women, free or servile, is not as much an issue as their background. Tamar's situation reveals that a foreign woman's children can be legitimate. Dinah's case reveals that a woman with the right family, without the backing of her brothers or the correct partner, is not enough either.

PART 3

Mothers Who Predate the Promise

This unit considers the women with children who predate the promise. The definition of this category is unusual in biblical scholarship. This category relates to the matriarchs because these women predate the promise and some of their children inherit on some level.

This group is complicated because some of them either do not have names or the boundaries of their character are not well established. For example, most studies of Eve assume that she is the woman in the garden; in this study I do not—Eve is separated from the woman in the garden. Keeping these women in one unit allows easier comparison with the other women who are in a similar situation. So too, because of certain themes that have emerged from the previous two sections, how these women and their roles differ, if at all, from the other categories of women is more easily determined.

15

Eve

ve is complicated because of how she has been treated through the ages,
including in modern scholarship.[1] In this treatment I will differentiate
Eve from the woman in the garden.

I have methodological reasons for making this distinction. When Eve is
discussed the focus is on the story concerning her creation and her conversation with the serpent. Few scholars focus on Eve's actions surrounding her
role as a mother, which occur after she is named.

I also have textual reasons for separating Eve from the woman in the garden.
Eve is not named until Genesis 3:20. Most issues for which Eve is judged harshly
occur prior to this event. The text recounts how the "woman" is "built" in
2:21, but she is only named "woman" in Adam's song (2:22). In the first three
phases of creation—day and night, the expanse above and water, dry land and
water—creation is not complete until Elohim names it (1:5, 8, 10). Later the
man names all the animals (1:19), yet this never happens for the woman.[2] Is
"woman" created when the man "calls" her? If so, who is this other individual
he names and who comes at the end of the process of creating?

Most discussions assume that the woman in the garden is the same as the
man's wife. The new attribute added to her responsibilities, bearing children

1. For a sample of some of those views, see Carol Meyers, "Eve," in Meyers, *Women in Scripture*, 79–80.
2. The word for "man" and "Adam" is the same in Hebrew, *'adam*. The text differentiates
between the two more clearly than between "wife" and "woman" (both Hebrew *'ishah*) by not
using the definite article before the term *'adam* when it means "Adam." I will differentiate the
two by referring to the character with the definite article as "the man" and the character without
the definite article as "Adam."

169

in pain, raises the issue as to whether the woman is the same prior to Elohim's comments to the woman as after, and if she is the same individual previously named "woman" because she comes from man.[3]

For these reasons I will treat Eve separately from the woman in the garden. Eve is treated in this unit because she bears children. Her children populate the world and no promise has yet been made. The woman in the garden does not bear children and will be treated in part 4.

Separating Eve from the woman in the garden highlights issues lost when she is coupled with the woman in the garden, especially concerning her role as a woman who bears children. Eve's relationship to the woman in the garden will be discussed in the section "Relationships of the Woman in the Garden." Treating Eve as a separate figure highlights how Eve is similar to many other women examined thus far in Genesis.

Eve's Description

Eve is described at only one point in her story, when she is labeled "the mother of all living things" (3:20). This appears in the context of the man naming her. The Hebrew name Eve, "life giver," derives from the same root as the verb "to live," and thus the description is an explanation of her name.[4] It follows immediately the cursing of the serpent (3:14–15), women bearing children in pain, and cursing the ground because of Adam (3:17–18).

Eve is not yet a mother. She does not become a mother until after they are out of the garden. Someone, either Eve or the woman in the garden, has just learned that she will bear children and it will be painful (3:16). The man's explanation provides an etymological reason for her name, but the timing seems premature.

When she is labeled "the mother of all living things," she is also identified as the man's 'ishah (3:20). The narrator plays with the idea that 'ishah can mean "woman" or "wife." Is this the first reference to Eve as a wife, or is it the status she has since she is first created, because the first thing the man does upon seeing her is to claim her as his woman (2:23)? In either case the role of wife fits neatly since this is the first reference to her procreative functions by the man.

Eve is labeled a "woman/wife," without using her newly applied name, when the Deity clothes both Eve and Adam (3:21). This reference is one that may assume a connection between Eve and the woman in the garden, because the sign that both the woman and Adam have eaten from the forbidden tree is the opening of their eyes and the knowledge that they are naked (3:7), leading them to hide from the Deity (3:8), who figures out what must have happened (3:11). Verse 22 focuses on the man being like Elohim, knowing good and bad, without

3. The Hebrew text never claims the woman is cursed. See Adrien Janis Bledstein, "Are Women Cursed in Genesis 3.16?" in Brenner, *Feminist Companion to Genesis*, 142–45.
4. Meyers, "Eve," 79. See also Brown, Driver, and Briggs, *Lexicon*, 310.

reference to the woman. Since the woman in the garden also eats the fruit, and is the one who suggests that her man eat it (3:6), her absence from verse 22 suggests that the woman in the garden and Eve are separate entities.

Eve, identified by name, is later labeled a wife when she conceives and bears Cain (4:1). She is described as a wife, without her name, when Adam "knows" her, leading to the conception of Seth (4:25). Reference to Eve as a wife sets the pattern of the matriarchs and the women who bear potential heirs, most of whom are labeled a "woman/wife" prior to conception.[5] Eve is not an exception to other women in Genesis in this regard.

Eve as a Subject

Like Eve's descriptions, Eve's actions do not vary from those associated with other women considered thus far, especially the women of potential heirs. In 4:1 Eve conceives the son who will be named Cain. It is the only time she "conceives"; with her other children she only "bears" (4:2, 25). Reference to women conceiving in Genesis is not consistent, and so Cain's conception does not suggest any significant difference between this child, who commits fratricide, and Eve's other children.

Three times Eve is the subject of "bearing." The first is for Cain (4:1). The second is for Abel, though her name is not given (4:2). A more significant difference between these birth narratives is the absence of an explanation for Abel's name.[6] This is particularly glaring as there is one for Eve's third child, whom she "bears" (4:25). Both conceiving and bearing are standard actions carried out by many women in Genesis.

Eve is the subject of verbs in the naming process. With Cain, her first child, she speaks prior to the explanation of the name (4:1). This is the first time Eve's voice, distinct from the woman in the garden, is heard. The implication is that she names the child.

Eve's comment translates, "I have created a man with the Deity" (4:1). The creation verb Eve uses, *qanah*, has as a base meaning, "get, acquire."[7] Here the verb used forms a wordplay with the name given to the child, Cain.[8] The term is complex. Von Rad claims, "the verb *qānā* ('get,' 'acquire') is just as unusual for the birth of a child as is the use of *'īš* ('man') for a newborn boy."[9]

Eve's statement highlights that she considers herself involved in the process of creation, working with the Deity. The creation verb Eve uses is one

5. The only exceptions to this are Leah and Dinah.
6. Finlay thinks that the lack of an etymology for Abel suggests that something will happen to his line (*Birth Report Genre*, 79).
7. Brown, Driver, and Briggs, *Lexicon*, 888.
8. Speiser, *Genesis*, 29.
9. Von Rad, *Genesis*, 103.

of the verbs used to refer to the Divine's role in creation (14:19, 22; Deut. 32:6), and of the Deity redeeming the people (Exod. 15:16; Isa. 11:11). The unusual reference to a newly born child as a "man," *'ish*, may relate to Eve's ideas about her role in creation. When the Deity fashions the man's "side beam" into a woman, the man argues, "from man she was taken" (Gen. 2:23). Eve, with the birth of Cain, argues for her role in creation not only of the first human child but of human beings in general that will flow from him. Without reference to Eve conceiving immediately after the man sleeps with his wife, the text could be construed as Eve bearing children on her own. The narrator is explicit that the Israelite Deity is responsible for each of the matriarchs conceiving. In the conception of the first human child, Eve articulates the same idea.

Eve "calls the name" of her third son Seth (4:25). The terminology she uses is that used by other mothers considered in this volume. Its appearance here is different because this is the first time a human applies this terminology to a newborn child. The reference to Seth's birth follows that of other people who are born in the interim. Despite this, no other individual uses this terminology. This is creation terminology employed by the Deity in the first three acts of creation. It is also the terminology the man uses to name Eve. Only in the naming process of her third son does Eve "call his name."

Eve's explanation of her son's name distinguishes her as the first mother to lose a child. Her explanation of Seth's name is, "Elohim established for me another seed, underneath Abel, for Cain killed him." As with Cain's name, the root of the verb "establish" is in assonance with "Seth" and explains the name.[10] Yet this misses the point that Eve, who does not appear in the scene of Abel's murder, is also a mother mourning. The reference reveals Eve's recognition of the role of the Divine in her ability to bear children.

The verbs of which Eve is the subject are in line with the roles of other mothers. Eve "conceives" and "bears." When naming her children she recognizes the role of the Deity. The names of her children reflect issues relevant to the mother, in this case her ability to bear and the loss of Abel. Eve, despite being the first woman to bear, is not different from other mothers in Genesis.

Eve as an Object

Eve is first identified as an object when she is named by the man (3:20). The man names her when he is still "the man" rather than Adam. This verse is treated as Eve's beginning because prior to this she has been "the man's wife/woman." Only here does she emerge as a named woman. She is named "the mother of all living things" prior to becoming a mother.

10. Speiser, *Genesis*, 35.

Immediately after Adam names Eve, the Deity makes garments of skin for them (3:21). Eve and Adam are objects together here with the Deity as the subject, though Adam is identified by name and Eve is not. The reason the two need to be clothed is that after eating from the tree of knowledge they realize that they are naked (3:7). Between the Deity realizing that the woman in the garden and the man have eaten from the tree and the Deity's making clothes for Adam and his wife, the Deity has been busy meting out punishments. Clothing the two here is the first time the Deity addresses the problem of their naked state. The act appears immediately before the man is driven out of the garden. It provides closure to the fruit incident and readies the couple for living outside the garden.

The narrator does not state that Eve is driven out of the garden; the Deity only comments, "the man has become like one of us, knowing good and bad," and notes the fear that he will eat from the tree of life and live forever (3:22). The text is explicit that the man is driven from the garden of Eden to till the soil (3:23–24). Eve apparently goes with him since she is identified by name in the next verse (4:1), but only a singular male is the object of the Deity ridding the garden of occupants.

Eve is next the object of the man "knowing" her (4:1). The reason the man is driven out of the garden is because he has become godlike, "knowing good and bad," and as soon as he is out of the garden he "knows" his wife. Later Adam "knows" his wife, not identified by name, and this "knowing" leads to Seth's birth (4:25). In the interim Abel is born, and the text does not note that Adam knows Eve, that she conceives by him, or why Abel receives his name. The text mentions only that "she" bears him. Seth's birth, a mere 24 verses later, follows a number of events: Cain's murder of Abel, Cain having a wife and bearing children, and information about what happens to some of those children (4:25). Seth's birth appears immediately before the line of Adam is presented. In this birthing sequence, Eve is not named but she names the child, and her name reflects her role as the first mother in history and the first mother who loses a child.

The places where Eve appears as an object do not differ from the cases of other women. Adam knows her sexually, leading to the birth of two of her children. The only verb unique to her is used where the Deity "clothes" her. Presumably Eve, though unnamed, is grouped with Adam in the clothing context, highlighting that it is not about her but about them. While the verb is unusual, because of the placement of the story it is not shocking nor is it a comment on Eve, but on the couple.

Eve's Relationships

Despite the little difference between Eve and the other female characters examined, there is more information about her relationships than others. One critical piece in her story, her relationship to the woman in the garden, I will not evaluate here (see chapter 21).

Eve is connected to Adam through marriage. Her feelings are never labeled, but, possibly following the theme of urges being for one's husband (3:16), she follows him out of the garden. Her comments upon the birth of her first and third sons address her relationship not with her husband but with the Deity (4:1, 25). The matriarchs too highlight the role of the Deity in their lives. This is the first appearance of that theme, which likens Eve to the matriarchs.

Eve establishes a relationship with the Deity. If Eve is the woman in the garden, then her relationship with the Deity begins in 3:13. If Eve and the woman in the garden are different, then the relationship between the two begins in 3:21 when the Deity likely clothes her, though she is not named. There the Deity does not speak with her. Her situation is similar to the matriarchs in that the Deity does not establish a relationship with her but she brings the Deity into the situation, at least verbally, since the Deity does not speak when the couple is clothed. Even after losing her second son, Eve continues to refer to Elohim when she bears Seth. There she refers to the role Elohim plays in providing her another offspring to take the place of Abel (4:25). The first mourning mother highlights the role the Deity plays in her ability to bear children.

There is little contact between Eve and her children. Cain is mentioned when Eve names Seth, but the reference, "because Cain killed him," could be in the mouth of Eve or an aside by the narrator. There is no accusation in the reference indicating that Eve or the narrator judges Cain harshly, but it explains why Eve misses a son. Eve hints that she misses Abel, discussing it in the birth of her third son, viewing him as a replacement, yet she never criticizes Cain.

No relationship between Eve and Adam or the man is expressed other than a sexual union leading to children. Eve expresses an awareness of the Deity, whom she associates with her ability to bear children. There is no evidence that Eve judges her children, even though one commits the first murder. She does express a feeling of loss as he is being replaced with the birth of Seth.

Conclusion

Throughout time many comments have been made about Eve. When she is separated from the woman in the garden, a different character emerges. The verses where Eve appears reveal a woman who carries out many of the same actions as other women in Genesis: she bears children, calls (names), and speaks. Eve plays almost no role as a wife; her primary purpose is to be a mother. Like the matriarchs, she is mindful and respectful of the role that the Deity plays in her ability to bear children.

16

Adah and Zillah

I will treat Adah and Zillah together for methodological reasons. They are
married to the same person, treated together in the section where they appear, and are the subject of the same verb; and their children serve similar
functions.

These two women appear at a sensitive point in the narrative about populat-
ing the world and dealing with the crisis of Abel's murder. Being the second
and third named women in the book, and appearing before Eve bears for the
last time, how they compare to Eve is critical to understanding Eve and the
role of the early women in Genesis.

Description of Adah and Zillah

Adah and Zillah are introduced together as the wives of Lamech (4:19). In
that same verse both of their names are identified. Cain, the firstborn human,
has already killed Abel, no female births have been recorded, and Cain has
a wife, whom he "knows" and who bears Enoch, who bears Irad, who bears
Mehujael, who bears Methushael, who bears Lamech (4:17–18). How these
other people suddenly appear and to whom they are related are matters that
are never explained. Thus one cannot evaluate their family or background.

The second and third time they are referred to as wives is prior to and at
the beginning of Lamech's "song" (4:23). In the first case, the narrator notes
that this is what Lamech says to his wives (4:23). In the second, he exhorts

his wives to "listen to his words." It is not clear why they are labeled "wives" in the second case since it is clear to whom he is speaking. It is also not clear why he addresses them since there is little in his statement that concerns the women.

To understand these women, all scholars have to work with are their names and what their children do. Adah's name comes from Hebrew 'adah, "to adorn, ornament oneself."[1] Meyers posits that the reference may point to the idea that female beauty was deemed important, though she notes that men's names in the Hebrew Bible are based on the same root.[2]

The meaning of Zillah's name is less certain than Adah's. "Zillah" may come from Hebrew tsel, meaning "shadow, protection," or Hebrew tsalal, "to shrill, tinkle," related to tseltselim, "cymbals."[3] Meyers hypothesizes that if one takes Zillah from the musical meaning and Adah relates to ornamentation, then with the inclusion of Naamah, Zillah's daughter, all the females are linked "with aspects of aesthetic expression."[4]

Meyers's argument is rooted in the placement of the story of Lamech and his wives. They appear in the seventh generation of humans. Adah and Zillah are the only females, along with Naamah, Zillah's daughter, who appear in the list of the otherwise all-male genealogies of Genesis 1 through 10.[5] Adah and Zillah's children, the eighth generation, represent four civilized arts in human society: pastoralists (4:21), instrumentalists (4:21), metallurgists (4:22), and vocalists (4:21).[6] The inclusion of these women in the seventh generation is unique and "acknowledges that human creativity is inextricably linked to female parentage."[7]

The appearance of Adah and Zillah, the roles their children play, and the meaning of their names combine to highlight these women as factors in the development of society and, even with the first mothers, how important a role they play in civilization. This case too indicates that their role as mothers is at least as important as their role as wives.

Adah and Zillah as Subjects

The only action for which they are subjects is that they "bear." Adah bears Jabal, the ancestor of pastoralists (4:20). The text does not state that Adah bears Jubal, but notes his name and that he is Jabal's brother. Jubal is the

---

1. Brown, Driver, and Briggs, Lexicon, 725; Carol Meyers, "Adah 1," in Meyers, Women in Scripture, 46.
2. Meyers, "Adah 1," 46.
3. Carol Meyers, "Zillah," in Meyers, Women in Scripture, 169.
4. Ibid.
5. Ibid.
6. Ibid.
7. Ibid.

ancestor of those who play the lyre and pipe (4:21). No other woman is recorded, so Adah is likely his mother, though she is the subject of "to bear" only one time.

Zillah is also the subject of "to bear": she bears Tubal-cain, who forged all implements of copper and iron (4:22). Tubal-cain's sister is Naamah (4:22). Unlike her brother, Naamah is not linked with the founding of any aspect of human culture.[8] Like Adah's situation, Zillah is treated as the mother, but again the text does not state this explicitly, so Zillah too is the subject of the verb "to bear" only one time.

Zillah's case is unique because she has a daughter. This is the only generation in Genesis 1 through 10 where women appear in the genealogy, and they are mother and daughter.

The verb for which both Adah and Zillah are subject is one often associated with women in Genesis and focuses on their role in childbearing. With no promise yet designated and no background available for either one, their importance is highlighted by their appearing on the list.

Adah and Zillah as Objects

Adah and Zillah are grouped together where they appear as objects. Lamech takes to himself two wives, named Adah and Zillah (4:19). Lamech speaks to his wives at the beginning of his "song" and names them both (4:23). His song addresses them but does not talk about them or their children.

The only comment involving them is his order to "listen to my voice" (4:23). The meaning may be that they should listen, but the use of the phrase in Genesis indicates more. It is used in the garden when the Deity explains that the reason for cursing the ground is because the man "listened to the voice of [his] wife" (3:17). The Deity instructs Abraham to "listen to the voice of Sarah" before banishing Hagar and Ishmael (21:12). Rebekah tells Jacob to listen to her voice when she instructs him to prepare for his father's blessing (27:8, 13). Rebekah again tells Jacob to listen to her voice when she instructs him to leave town lest his brother kill him (27:43). In all these texts the man listens to the woman. Elohim rewards Abraham for listening to Elohim's voice to sacrifice Isaac (22:18). Lamech's is the only case where a man says it to women.

Adah and Zillah do not appear as objects of anything extraordinary compared to other women in Genesis. They are "taken" as wives and their husband "speaks" to them. The unique element is that Lamech tells them to "listen" to his voice, something women in Genesis do to men or the Deity does to humans. Adah and Zillah are legal wives who bear children.

8. Naamah's name may link her to song. See Carol Meyers, "Naamah 1," in Meyers, *Women in Scripture*, 129.

Relationships of Adah and Zillah

Little can be said regarding the relationships among Adah, Zillah, Lamech, and their children. One point highlighted by the text is that Lamech treats Adah and Zillah as a unit.

Conclusion

Adah and Zillah are proper wives who bear children. Their husband speaks to them, exhorting them to listen. Their importance is that they are even mentioned. The seventh generation is treated differently by labeling the mothers in that generation and their children's accomplishments. Their appearance so early already suggests the important role of the mother.

17

Milcah

Milcah is introduced with and as a counterbalance to Sarah (11:29), predating the Deity's promise. Milcah disappears shortly thereafter only to reappear before Sarah's death (22:20). Despite her absence for much of the story, her descendant, Rebekah, becomes as important to the promise as Sarah's son Isaac. Thus, despite the limited amount of material on Milcah, she is significant to the story.

Milcah's Description

Milcah is introduced at the same time as Sarah, and both are first identified as wives (11:29). The introduction appears in the discussion of Terah's line, where all his sons appear equal in terms of their importance in that generation. The text first notes that Abraham and Nahor took wives. In the same verse each woman is introduced individually (11:29). Milcah is introduced as a wife like Sarah, and then the way the two differ is identified.

Milcah is not named a wife again until Rebekah's story. When the narrator reveals that she has borne children (22:20–24), she is not labeled "the wife of Nahor" (the father of the children). In that reference, Nahor's *pilegesh* Reumah is named, but Milcah's specific relationship to Nahor is not included; she apparently does not need further description.

When Rebekah appears at the well, Milcah is described as a wife. This appears after Abraham's servant defines the criteria so he will know that the woman is the correct one. Abraham's criteria do not address the woman's parents, only the location. The narrator identifies Rebekah as born to Bethuel, son of Milcah, wife of Abraham's brother Nahor (24:15). Milcah and Bethuel are legitimated as parents. The sentence identifies Milcah first and then how Nahor relates to Abraham.

Right after her introduction, Milcah's next description is as a daughter of Haran (11:29). This verse follows the death notice of Haran, Abraham's brother and Terah's son. The text nowhere states that Abraham's brother Haran is the same as Milcah's father, who is also Iscah's father. The text states that Lot is Haran's son (11:27). When Milcah's father Haran is identified, Lot is not. Is Milcah's father the same Haran and therefore Milcah and Lot are brother and sister?[1] Does Abraham take Lot with him just as Nahor takes Milcah after Haran's death? If so, Milcah is Nahor's wife and Haran's daughter, so in Isaac's generation all of Terah's descendants merge.

Reference to Milcah's family emphasizes its absence for Sarah. Milcah and Sarah's introduction demands they be compared. Milcah is introduced with family, possibly the most important family, Terah's. The next verse emphasizes by redundancy that Sarah is barren; she has no children (11:30).

Milcah has a name, is a legitimate wife, and has family, possibly the only family that matters. From the beginning the narrator points out that Milcah is as legitimate, if not more so, than Sarah. Her status is so secure that when she bears children, she needs no introduction.

Milcah as a Subject

Milcah is the subject of one action: she "bears." After Genesis 11 the narrator ignores her until Genesis 22. Neither Nahor nor Milcah appears on the list of people Terah sets out to take to Canaan before they stop in Haran (11:31). When Milcah again appears, where they live is not named, but their children live in Abraham's "native land," which, if Abraham's servant is correct, is Aram-naharaim, specifically the city of Nahor (24:10). Either Nahor and his family go with Terah and the text does not include them, or they leave Ur of the Chaldeans at some later date.

Abraham is told that Milcah has borne children to his brother Nahor (22:20). After listing the children Milcah bears, they are grouped as the eight Milcah bears to Nahor. Because of the sentence structure, Milcah, not Nahor, is the subject of this verb twice. Nahor is labeled Abraham's brother and his importance is qualified; Milcah's status needs no explanation.

These verses appear immediately following the near sacrifice of Isaac. After the Deity saves Isaac, Abraham returns to his servants and they depart together

1. Speiser states this categorically (*Genesis*, 78).

for Beer-sheba, where Abraham stays (22:19). The text notes that some time later Abraham hears the news about Milcah. Both Abraham and the reader hear about the birth of Milcah's children after Isaac's life is secure.

In the next chapter Sarah dies (23:2). In the discussion of Milcah's children the narrator identifies Rebekah as her granddaughter, daughter of Bethuel (22:23). She is the only child from that generation identified in this passage. It is unusual for women to appear in these lists, and for a woman to be the only person so identified is striking. The narrator emphasizes, before the last matriarch dies, that a new matriarch is born. It appears in the context of Milcah because Milcah is a legitimate wife and the daughter of a key person.

Milcah bears to Nahor three times in Genesis 24: when Rebekah first arrives at the well (24:15, though here the verb is passive), when Rebekah tells Abraham's servant who she is (24:24), and when the servant recounts who Rebekah claims she is (24:47). Two of these contexts highlight Milcah's role. The third, in the mouth of Abraham's servant who is negotiating with her male relatives to take Rebekah to Isaac as a bride, highlights Nahor's role above Milcah's.

The narrator considers Milcah important and legitimate but does not use much space to convey this information. She is the subject of only one verb: she "bears." Because of her background and the ease with which she bears children, no more text is necessary. The text identifies Reumah, a *pilegesh* for Nahor, Abraham's brother and Milcah's husband, but no inheritance issues arise.

Milcah as an Object

Milcah does not appear often as an object. She is first so identified when the text notes that Abraham and Nahor take wives (11:28). The next place she is an object is because someone is her son. When the narrator first identifies Rebekah, she is born to Bethuel, the son of Milcah (24:15). Because of the sentence construction she is also the wife of Abraham's brother, but she is not named nor is she the object of a preposition. This is also the case when Rebekah introduces herself to Abraham's servant (24:24). Only in the words of Abraham's servant does Bethuel become the son of Nahor rather than the son of Milcah. Here Bethuel's status or key identifier, according to his daughter Rebekah, is first through his mother, Milcah. Because of the sentence structure used in referring to Milcah as the one who bears to Nahor, she is a subject of a verb and rarely appears as an object.

Milcah's Relationships

The text never depicts Milcah with anyone. The narrator and Rebekah identify Rebekah's key relationships through Milcah, not Nahor. Support that this is intentional appears when Abraham's servant recounts Rebekah identifying herself, and he changes the sentence structure to highlight the men in Rebekah's line rather than Milcah. Rebekah and the narrator identify her as the daughter of Bethuel, son of Milcah.

Conclusion

Milcah is important enough to be introduced at the same time as Abraham and Sarah. She is a legitimate wife. She does not carry out any actions different from other women and she creates a place for herself: she bears children. She is a rare case of a woman seldom appearing as an object. The sentence structure in which she "bears" highlights her and keeps her name from appearing as an object. Her key descendant is a female who becomes a matriarch, the only one depicted as having at least as much authority as, if not more than, her husband.

18

Mrs. Lot

Mrs. Lot has offspring who bear and create groups with whom the Israelites will be in contact and, through the book of Ruth, become part of the line that inherits the promise (Ruth 4:22). When Mrs. Lot appears, the promise has been made (Gen. 12:7; 15:13–18) and a potential heir identified (17:19), though he has not yet been conceived (21:2).

Mrs. Lot's Description

Lot's wife is never named. The only way she is described is as a wife, though she has a transformation that will count as a description. Her limited role is highlighted by her appearance only halfway into her family's story.

Genesis 19 focuses on what happens in Sodom, where Lot and his family live. Mrs. Lot does not appear until 19:15, after the messengers have been invited to Lot's house (19:2), the house is surrounded by the mob (19:4), and Lot has offered his two virgin daughters to the mob (19:8). Lot does not mention having a wife, but the messengers refer to her when they urge Lot to take his wife and his remaining daughters lest he be swept away because of the iniquity of the city (19:15). The reader knows that Lot has a wife, but she is so inconsequential to him that she is referred to only in passing. In contrast to Mrs. Lot are Lot's daughters, who are referred to earlier in the story.

Despite the messengers' warnings, Lot continues to delay, so the messengers seize his hand and that of his wife and his two daughters, bring him out, and leave him outside the city (19:16). Lot has not yet paid any attention to her, and he appears not to fully grasp the situation.[1]

Mrs. Lot is referred to one more time as "Lot's wife" when she looks behind and turns into a pillar of salt. After being led out of the city by the messengers and witnessing the destruction of the cities of the plain, "she looked, his wife, behind him," and turned into a pillar of salt (19:26). Few commentators bother addressing the transformation of Mrs. Lot. Von Rad recognizes an etiological motif present in her strange death.[2]

An alternative explanation may stem from a pattern that begins with the woman in the garden: men do not fully inform women. It is not clear that the man provides the woman in the garden with all the correct information regarding the various trees in the center of the garden. In this case, Mrs. Lot might not have all the information Lot has.

Despite the obvious danger in which Lot's family finds itself and the straight-forward instruction from the messengers to Lot that he should leave the city, the messengers must take Lot and his family out personally. The messengers direct their commands to a singular male object, presumably Lot, since the only people with him are his wife and his two female daughters (19:16). In 19:17 the messengers tell Lot he needs to flee for his life and not to look behind him or stop. Nowhere is this information conveyed to Lot's wife or daughters. When the city and the plain are destroyed, it is not clear that Mrs. Lot knows that she is not allowed to look back. Does the pillar of salt represent a woman who does not follow the Deity's instructions or a woman whose husband is so ill prepared to protect her that he does not provide her with the information she needs? How one answers the previous question affects how one evaluates the later behavior of Lot's daughters (see chapter 19 below).

Mrs. Lot is a wife and a pillar of salt. There is no comment about her background prior to being the wife of Lot or any connection she may have to her children. Mrs. Lot is one of the rare women in Genesis whose role as a wife is more important than her role as a mother.

Mrs. Lot as a Subject

Mrs. Lot is the subject of two verbs, though they are different from those used with other women. Lot's wife is the subject of "to look" (19:26). Her action leads to her second verb, she "becomes" a pillar of salt. Because it serves an etiological purpose, explaining the odd formations around the area of the Dead Sea, she becomes a symbol. The answer to whether Lot tells her not to

---

1. For other reasons why Lot delays see Heard, *Dynamics of Diselection,* 56–57.
2. Von Rad, *Genesis,* 221.

look back is at the heart of whether she is the symbol of a woman whose husband does not protect her, or a woman who defies the Deity's messengers.

Mrs. Lot never "bears," despite having children, if Lot's daughters are hers. The verb "to look" for which she is a subject is an action that no other woman does in the Hebrew Bible and leads her to become a pillar of salt, also unique in the text.

Mrs. Lot as an Object

Mrs. Lot is the object of two verbs. The first time Mrs. Lot appears is in the context of the messengers telling Lot to leave (19:15). The messengers tell Lot to "take" his wife and his two daughters. The verb is the same used for "taking" a wife and is used with many women in Genesis. Here Lot is commanded to take her and to lead her and his daughters to safety. He is commanded by the messengers of the Deity but neglects to do so.

Mrs. Lot is again the object of a verb because her husband delays leaving the city. The messengers must seize Lot's hand and the hands of his wife and his two daughters (19:16). Her husband does not inform her of the urgency facing the family nor does he do anything about it. It is up to the Deity's messengers to protect Lot's family.

Mrs. Lot's Relationships

The only person who has a relationship with Mrs. Lot is Lot. She is never named a daughter or mother. No communication is represented in the relationship between Mrs. Lot and Lot. Lot never speaks to her, not when he suggests a mob take his daughters, when they leave the city, or when the Deity's messengers command Lot not to look at the city.

Conclusion

Mrs. Lot is never identified as anything but a wife, and so she is the only woman examined thus far whose primary role is as a wife. Even Judah's wife, who has no name, is described as a daughter and bears children. Mrs. Lot is never identified as the mother of the daughters who leave Sodom with Lot and his wife, and she is never listed as bearing children. The text never explains why she "looks behind." She is simply a wife. If this presentation of Lot's actions is correct, she is a wife whose husband does nothing to protect her or her family.

19

Lot's Daughters

Lot's daughters are treated together because, like Esau's wives, there is little data on either one separately and they function as a unit in most references to them. Only toward the end of their story, when they act, are they separated.

The daughters, like their mother, appear in the text after the promise has been made (12:7; 15:13–18) but before the person identified as inheriting the promise from Abraham (17:19) is conceived (21:2). They are like other women in Genesis because their primary function is bearing children. Their offspring are more complicated than some because their line merges with Judah's in the book of Ruth to form the line of David (Ruth 4:22).

Description of Lot's Daughters

Lot's daughters are never named in the text. Their primary description is as daughters. Issues concern whether they are the same daughters offered to the crowd in Sodom, and what their relationship is to the sons-in-law of Lot within the city of Sodom. I will consider each of these issues and allow the reader to make the final decision.

The reader is first introduced to Lot's daughters in 19:7 when Lot begs the people of Sodom, who have asked for the Deity's messengers so they can be intimate with them (Gen. 19:5), not to commit such a wrong and suggests that they do what they please with his two daughters who have not known a man (19:8). Being a daughter of Lot offers no protection.

The next reference to daughters is in the mouth of the messengers of the Deity, who ask Lot who else he has in the city, suggesting he consider such people as sons-in-law, sons, and daughters (19:12). That the men ask a question implies that he does not necessarily have these relatives.

Lot takes the messengers up on their offer and goes to speak to his sons-in-law, the "takers" of his daughters (19:14). Stone takes this reference to mean that the daughters earlier referred to as not having known a man are these daughters and they are betrothed.[1] Another option is that Lot has at least two older daughters who are already married but will be left behind with their husbands.[2] Lot either has two daughters who are engaged to be married but have not yet consummated their marriage, or he has at least four daughters, two living at home and at least two already married off to and living with their husbands elsewhere in Sodom.

The next reference may serve to elucidate the difference, since the messengers urge Lot to take his wife and his two remaining daughters (19:15). Describing the daughters as "the ones remaining" implies there are others, but he now can be concerned only with the two still under his control.

Lot continues to delay, so the messengers seize his hand and the hands of his wife and two daughters to get them out of the city (19:16). The reference to the two here, as well as in the previous verse and in the original reference, points to the idea that regardless of how many daughters Lot may have had in total, it is these two who are the focus of the story.

The daughters are again mentioned after Elohim destroys the cities of the plain and annihilates the cities where Lot dwells (19:29). Lot goes up from Zoar and settles in the hill country with his two daughters because he is afraid to dwell in Zoar (19:30). It is not clear why Lot is afraid to dwell in Zoar, and whether other people still live there.[3] Lot and his two daughters live in a cave (19:30).

Up to this point the two daughters have been treated as one unit. The only description of the daughters is that they are the "remaining ones." They have not spoken or taken any action in the text. Only when their world has been destroyed, their mother turned into a pillar of salt, and they are living in a cave does the narrator separate them. Even then, there are still references to them as a unit that we must consider.

The narrator differentiates between the two daughters in terms of age to lay out the scenario as they understand it, and to make a suggestion as to how to alleviate the situation. The text notes that "they" make their father drink

1. Ken Stone, "Daughters of Lot," in Meyers, *Women in Scripture*, 179.
2. Speiser, *Genesis,* 140.
3. Heard, *Dynamics of Diselection,* 59.

wine (19:33). The idea comes from the firstborn daughter, and they work together to make their father drunk. So too when the younger sleeps with Lot, they both make their father drink wine (19:35). The text summarizes that the two daughters of Lot came to be with child by their father (19:36). Though each one lay with him separately, and different nations result from them, the two are treated as a unit.

The two are described as a unit as "not having known a man" (19:8). The reference appears when the reader first learns of their existence as Lot offers them to the mob that wants to sodomize the messengers of the Deity (19:8). Lot's action insinuates that male rape is worse than the rape of his daughters who "have not known a man." Horrific as Lot's suggestion is, the reference suggests important issues for understanding the daughters and some of their later actions. The daughters are taught that they are less important to their father than the messengers of the Deity. Lot's action indicates that there are issues more important to him than preserving a daughter for marriage or determining who fathers their children.

When Lot's daughters are treated as separate entities, the titles of the daughters clarifies that for the narrator the major distinction between them is that one is the firstborn, since no names are used. The firstborn is the first to speak, and in the first reference to her as separate from her sister she provides the analysis of both sisters' situation: their father is old and there is not a man on earth for them to consort with (19:31). Since no change in subject is noted, she is the one who suggests that they lie with their father and maintain life (19:32). The narrator separates the firstborn when she goes in to lay with her father (19:33). It is the firstborn who reminds the younger what she does and suggests that the younger do the same on the next night (19:34). The firstborn is so designated when she bears Moab (19:37).

The firstborn daughter analyzes the situation and determines a plan of action. It is unclear if this is because there is no other way to separate the daughters, so one daughter has to speak first, or if this is a comment about the primogenitor. Many stories in Genesis about the men concern how the primogenitor is not the one who inherits. The firstborn daughter is the mother of Moab, one of Israel's enemies but the background of Ruth, David's ancestor (Ruth 4:22).

The younger is so designated fewer times than her firstborn sister. She is described when the firstborn speaks to her, suggesting she lay with her father (Gen. 19:34), and when she carries it out (19:35). She is also described as the younger when she bears her son, Ben-ammi, the father of the Ammonites (19:38).

Lot's daughters are primarily described as daughters. When they are treated individually, they are distinguished as "older" and "younger," thus using as the basis for comparison their role as daughters. The only other description of them is that they have not known a man, a situation that changes by the end of the chapter.

Lot's Daughters as Subjects

Lot's daughters are the subject of verbs, like their mother, late in their story. The two daughters are treated independently only when one of them is the subject of a verb. The first daughter to be the subject of a verb is the firstborn. She is the one who says to the younger that their father is old and there is no man on earth to consort with them in the way of the world (19:31). This happens after they have been offered sexually to the Sodomites (19:7), the messengers have taken them out of the city (19:16), their mother has turned into a pillar of salt (19:26), and their father has taken them out of Zoar to live in a cave (19:30).

It is not clear why their father's age is at issue. In the previous chapter Sarah is excited about the idea that her husband will perform the necessary task of impregnating her at his age (18:12). The daughter does not question whether her father is able to impregnate anyone but possibly who will take care of them or find them spouses. Speiser suggests that they use the inchoative aspect to point up the urgency of the situation, indicating that they have a timing issue: they need to have children before their father dies. Speiser assumes that the daughters do not know there are men still in the world,[4] though the verse could be read as the daughters not thinking they have access to men.

Following her initial summary of the situation, the firstborn suggests that they give their father wine, lie with him, and maintain life through him (19:32). The verb used for giving their father wine has a "primary meaning . . . 'to irrigate the ground' . . . the scheme is not just to make Lot drink but to get him drunk."[5] The implication is that they need to maintain life on earth and the only way is through their father. This verse provides more support for the idea that the daughters do not know there are still men in the world, something not apparent in the firstborn's initial comment. In this verse the elder's suggestion is not selfish, but as Speiser suggests, "The young women were concerned with the future of the race, and they were resolute enough to adopt the only desperate measure that appeared to be available."[6]

The daughters carry through on the firstborn's suggestion, and the firstborn daughter goes in and lays with her father (19:33). The verbs used for what the firstborn does to the father are those usually reserved for men. She "comes to" him sexually. She also "lays with him," using the same verb, *shakab*, that describes what Shechem will do to Dinah (34:2) and Reuben to Bilhah (35:22), with the preposition *'et* rather than *'im*, "with," as in the case of Jacob and Leah (30:15) or Mrs. Potiphar and Joseph (39:12–14). The firstborn is again the subject of verbs when their father does not know when she lay down or rose up (19:33). Lot is not sure what he is doing and cannot be considered

4. Speiser, *Genesis*, 145.
5. Ibid.
6. Ibid.

a willing partner. This reinforces the use of "lay" with 'et as indicating that the object of the verb is not a willing party to the sexual encounter. As the subject of masculine verbs the elder daughter appears to be taking over masculine roles.

The firstborn is the subject of the standard verb for women in Genesis: she "bears" (19:37). She calls the name of the son Moab (19:37). In order to be able to bear, the firstborn daughter carries out a number of actions normally reserved for men in the story. Prior to 19:31 the firstborn is not the subject of any verb, despite being the object of quite a few. She has been a dutiful daughter in light of horrifying experiences: offered to a mob by her father, witness to the destruction of the plain, and the transformation of her mother into a pillar of salt. The daughter's only goal is to bear children because in her mind there is no one left to do so.

The day after the firstborn sleeps with her drunken father, she again speaks to her sister. This time the elder points out that she lay with their father, they should again make him drunk, and this time the younger should lie with him (19:34). Again the firstborn is the one who reviews the situation and suggests a plan of action.

The younger sister carries out actions similar to her older sibling but she is less forceful. The younger follows her sister's suggestion, coming and laying with her father, and he does not know when she lay down or rose (19:35). This is not her idea, and she does so only at her sister's suggestion and after her sister carries out the same actions. The younger bears a son and calls him Ben-ammi (19:38).

Lot's daughters are dutiful until they end up in a cave with only their father. The firstborn takes the initiative, explains the situation to her sister, and suggests a resolution. Together they get their father drunk, so they both can lay with their father, resulting in both bearing sons.

The firstborn is more active than the younger. The elder suggests a plan. The older sister is the first to lay with Lot and the younger follows her sister's suggestion.

Lot's Daughters as Objects

Lot's daughters first appear as objects. The reader learns of their existence when Lot says, "Please, I have two daughters who have not known a man. Please, I will bring them out to you and you may do to them what is right in your eyes" (19:8). They are treated like objects whose abuse is less an affront than if similar actions were carried out against the men/messengers of the Deity.

The next place the daughters are objects is when Lot speaks to his sons-in-law, the ones married to his daughters (19:14). It is unclear whether this refers to the same daughters offered to the mob or if he has married daughters. This is the one place where Lot shows an effort to protect his daughters, though it may also be the only reference that does not mention the two daughters who survive Sodom's destruction.

The daughters are the objects of the verb "take" when the messengers urge Lot to leave the city (19:15). The goal of the messengers is to get Lot to do something to save his family and make them the object of his concern. Lot is unable either to comprehend what is happening or to act, so his wife and daughters are the next object of the messengers' action when they seize the hands of his wife and daughters to bring them outside the city (19:16). The only thing that protects the daughters from gang rape is that the messengers carry out some action that keeps the Sodomites from being able to find the door, thereby saving Lot's daughters (19:9–11). These verses were not discussed earlier because Lot's daughters do not appear. The daughters are absent from the text, but the messengers' actions protect Lot's daughters, just as they protect them here. The Deity protects the women from men who are not prepared to do so.

The daughters last appear as objects before they act. Genesis 19:30 recounts that Lot settles in the hill country with his daughters. This is one of the last times the daughters are grouped together, and following this verse they are only subjects of verbs, never again objects.

Where the daughters are objects of verbs parallels the analysis of them where they appear as subjects. The daughters are objects through the bulk of the story and only when they are in the cave are they active. Once they become active, they are never again objects in the story.

Relationships of Lot's Daughters

Lot's daughters are active only late in their story, but one can make some suggestions about their relationships. The daughters witness horrifying experiences while they function as dutiful daughters. The town wants to rape their male guests, their father suggests the mob take them instead, and their father does not move to take them out of harm's way. They witness the destruction of the plain and the transformation of their mother into a pillar of salt because their father does not act. It is possible, by the time the firstborn suggests getting her father drunk, that she has little respect for Lot. He has not carried out any actions to protect either of his daughters.

The nature of the relationship between the sisters is rare. There are few cases of sisters in the Hebrew Bible, and the relationship depicted between Leah and Rachel is not great. Lot's daughters have only each other. The elder is the leader. The younger never questions her sister. They witness the same horrors and possibly consider themselves the last women on earth. They work together to inebriate their father. They each have only one child, suggesting that neither is interested in repeating that experience. The only one who speaks is the firstborn, and it is never to their father but only to her sister. Thus their main relationship is with each other.

Conclusion

Lot's daughters function as a unit, but there are distinctions between them. They are never wives or anything like wives. They witness tragic events. Their father is prepared to subject them to a mob intent on rape. The Deity's messengers are the only ones who protect them, first in the thwarted rape scene and then when taking them out of the city. Lot's daughters understand their situation to be such that they are forced to inebriate their father so they may populate the world. The actions they carry out are those normally reserved for the males in Genesis, reinforcing how, because of their perception of an absence of men, they take on those roles to become mothers and repopulate the world.

20

Review of Part 3

Mothers Who Predate the Promise

The material about women whose children predate the promise should not be subject to the same qualifications as the heirs to the promise, and their mothers and their mother's actions might be under less, or different, scrutiny.

Descriptions of Mothers Who Predate the Promise

In this group there is little discussion about the mother's background. Eve, as the first woman to bear children, has no background issues. Where Adah and Zillah come from is problematic and cannot be counted as positive or negative. Milcah is from the right stock through her relationship with Terah. The narrator provides no information as to where Lot finds Mrs. Lot and therefore no information about her daughters' background. And since the text never names Mrs. Lot as the mother of the daughters who procreate with their father, the daughters' background is even more difficult to determine.

There are no common descriptors for the characters in this category. Birth order is relevant for Eve (she is the first), and Lot's daughters are distinguished as the firstborn and the younger. All of these women are called "wives" except Lot's daughters.

Mothers Who Predate the Promise as Subjects

There are no consistent actions for the women in this category. With the exception of Mrs. Lot, all are said to bear children. Mrs. Lot appears to have children, though the text never states this categorically.

Mothers Who Predate the Promise as Objects

Few cases relate these women to one another. Adah and Zillah are spoken to, the one thing Lot never does with Mrs. Lot or his daughters. Because the marriage scenes for these women are not recounted, they are not even the object of the verb "to take."

Relationships of Mothers Who Predate the Promise

The one consistent element in this group is that the narrator considers the children of these characters important. Eve is the mother of all the living. Adah and Zillah's children invent the civilized arts. One of Milcah's descendants becomes the future mother of one who inherits the promise. Mrs. Lot probably bears the daughter who becomes the ancestor of the Davidic line. Lot's firstborn is also an ancestor of the line of David.

Conclusion

Though the similarities of the women in this category are few, all of their attributes direct one to the role of their children. It is not anything these women do but what their children do and become that is brought up by the narrator as their significant contribution. The primary point of a woman's story in Genesis concerns her role as a mother.

PART 4

Women Who Do Not Bear

A small group of women in Genesis are the subject of verbs but do not bear children.[1] The women in this group are seldom treated together because they make up an odd assortment: the woman in the garden, Deborah, and Potiphar's wife. They appear to have little in common. By treating them as a category I highlight how pervasive the role of mother is among the other women in Genesis and how this group of women characters who are not mothers is unique.

Verbing the character with this group is important since the act of bearing is absent for all of them. If the main role of women in the book of Genesis is to bear children, and their evaluation is focused on whether the woman's descendants are worthy of inheriting the promise, then what is the point of women who do not fit into that scheme? Is it possible to still tie into that thesis without bearing children?

1. Dinah, as noted above in chapter 10, falls into another group of women because of her relationship with a patriarch and matriarch, though one might argue that she fits into this section. She is placed in the earlier group for methodological reasons, and after examining her descriptions and places where she is the subject and object, one can say that she continues to fit neatly into that other category.

21

The Woman in the Garden

One of the difficulties in understanding the woman in the garden concerns when her story begins. Is she part of the male/female character originally created by the Deity during the first week of creation, or does she only appear once the Deity takes Adam's "side beam" from him and forms a female? When does the story about the woman in the garden end? This is a more difficult question because of the significant overlay from years of religious tradition.[1]

A number of places that could possibly refer to the woman in the garden will be examined, through verbing the character, so the reader has all the available data. The relationship between Eve and the woman in the garden will be discussed in this chapter under "Relationships of the Woman in the Garden."

Description of the Woman in the Garden

When Elohim first creates humans, the language is complex. The text claims that Elohim creates the man in his image,[2] and then notes that Elohim creates "them": masculine and feminine (1:27). The issue here is, what is the role of

1. Meyers, "Eve," 79–80.
2. Here *'adam* is the Hebrew word for "the man." The problem is that because in this verse it is also identified as being masculine and feminine, "the human" could be more appropriate.

197

the feminine element in the Deity's creation of humans?[3] Does this describe the woman in the garden?

The text suggests that there is one human who has two significant characteristics: masculine and feminine. As the story progresses only the masculine side is addressed (1:29–30; 2:15–17), to the point that the Deity notes it is "not good" the man is alone (2:18) and creates another being (2:21–22). The new creature is made from the original (2:21), making it possible to argue that the original human had the potential for female characteristics, but the idea is too complex for one human and those two sides are separated. One element of the woman in the garden may be described in 1:27, as part of the original human.

The woman in the garden is first identified and described as a woman in 2:22. After checking all the animals as possible "helpmates" for the man, the Deity creates one from man, possibly because the right potential is already there, according to 1:27. The woman is described as and labeled a "woman" at the moment of her creation and/or separation from the man (2:22).[4] The term used, 'ishah, is the word for a wife, so it is possible that the Deity is creating a wife for the man, since the translation of "wife" or "woman" in this chapter and the following is determined by one's theological understanding of what happens in the scene.

The woman is described by the man when he awakens from his deep sleep in the previous verse (2:21). The man declares, "This one will be called woman" (2:23). The verb qara' used for "to call" is one used later by men and women naming children. It is what the man does a few verses earlier when he "names," or "calls," the animals (2:20).

It is not clear if the next reference to a woman/wife is the woman in the garden. Genesis 2:23–24 indicates that a man leaves his father and mother and "clings" to his wife because woman comes from man. Since the same terminology is used for "woman" and "wife" and "woman" is used for the first time in the previous verse, is the woman in the garden now the first wife or is this reference used to explain how these relationships will develop in the future?

The woman in the garden is the focus of the next verse (2:25), where they are both described as naked. Most translations of 2:24 and 25 refer to the woman who is with the man as his "wife," yet in the next episode, though the same word is used and the same individual is the referent, the translators choose "woman" to identify her.

The translation choice is striking since 2:25 is a setup to the next scene, where the woman in the garden is a major focus. She is identified as a woman/

---

3. For bibliography see Phyllis Bird, "'Male and Female He Created Them': Genesis 1:27b in the Context of the Priestly Account of Creation," *Harvard Theological Review* 74 (1981): 129–59.

4. For a brief discussion on separation as an element of meaning see Fewell and Gunn, *Gender, Power, and Promise*, 23.

wife in her conversation with the serpent and labeled "the woman," by most translations, when the serpent initiates conversation with her (3:1), when she responds to the serpent (3:2), when the serpent assures her that if she eats from the tree she will not die (3:4), and when the woman evaluates the tree (3:6). The woman in the garden is the one involved in the fruit-eating episode. Throughout the scene with the serpent, the woman in the garden continues to be referred to as a "woman/wife" in the text, though most translators refer to her only as a "woman," not "wife."

The woman is so labeled again when the Deity asks her what she has done and she replies. This title is applied when the Deity curses the serpent, putting enmity between the serpent and "the woman" (3:15). Woman terminology continues when the Deity speaks to her about childbearing and having urges toward her man (3:16).

Following that episode the text notes that the man named his woman Eve (3:20; the rest of the references are covered in chapter 15 on Eve). A key transition between Eve and the woman in the garden concerns the only other description of the woman in the garden: she is naked. That reference occurs prior to the conversation between the woman in the garden and the serpent. Both the man and the woman are naked (2:25). They are not ashamed of it, an important distinction since that is the telltale sign later used to reveal they have eaten from the tree (3:11). It is not their depiction as naked but their efforts to hide their nakedness that reveal their level of knowledge to the Deity. The first thing the Deity does after laying out their future because of the fruit episode is to clothe them (3:21), though neither is described then as naked.

The only title the woman in the garden receives is "woman," possibly "wife," depending on one's definition of wife and translation methodology. She is described with her husband/man as naked. Her background is not described in the same way the background of other women in Genesis is depicted, but the reason for this is how she is formed.

The Woman in the Garden as a Subject

The woman in the garden by herself is the subject of verbs, and the woman and her man/husband together are subjects of verbs. I will first treat places where the woman alone is the subject of verbs, followed by the places where the two together are subjects of verbs.

The woman in the garden does not appear as the subject of a verb until she "says" to the serpent that "we," referring to the man and herself, may eat of the fruit of the other trees of the garden (3:2), but only the fruit of the tree in the middle of the garden Elohim said not to eat "lest you die" (3:3). She does not initiate conversation but answers the serpent.

The woman in the garden repeats information given to the man (2:16–17) prior to her appearance in the garden as a separate entity (2:22). This raises the issue of the relationship of the male/female human to the man who needs to have a woman formed from him. If the two are one, then it is possible to argue that the woman in the garden receives the same instructions from Elohim as the man. If one considers the woman in the garden a separate entity, there is no communication between the woman in the garden and the Deity or Elohim, and the woman in the garden receives her information from the man. There are two trees in the middle of the garden, the tree of life and the tree of knowledge of good and bad (2:9). The Deity instructs the man not to eat from the tree of knowledge of good and bad (2:17). The issue raised here is similar to that raised with Mrs. Lot: Is the man providing the woman with the proper information to make evaluations that concern life and death?

The woman in the garden "says" to the Deity that the serpent duped her and she ate (3:13). This too is in response to a question asked her. The question is posed by the Deity following the fruit-eating episode, "What is this you have done?"[5]

The woman in the garden next "sees" (3:6). Seeing with one's eyes is not necessarily a good thing, and the woman sees that the tree is good for eating and a delight to the eyes (3:6). The text notes that the tree is desirable as a source of wisdom.

The result of the analysis by the woman in the garden based on sight is that she "takes" the fruit (3:6). The verb "to take" is one that appears a number of times in Genesis, usually with women as the object of the verb being taken, sexually or physically.

After the woman in the garden takes, she "eats" (3:6). She is both the first person in the Bible to eat and the only woman in Genesis to do so. This reference emphasizes the kinds of situations in which women do, and do not, appear in Genesis.

The woman in the garden, after eating, "gives" some to her man/husband, who eats. There is nothing odd about men eating in Genesis. The idea of the woman giving the man to eat is reiterated by the man later when the Deity realizes the man has eaten (3:13). The reference to her giving to him and his eating is an accusation.

The woman's last action is to speak to the Deity. The rest of her actions are carried out with her man/husband. The woman in the garden is the subject of only a few verbs, none related to bearing children. The first two verbs concern speech. Like Tamar, the woman in the garden does not initiate conversation but responds to questions. The verb used with the woman in the garden, from

5. This phrase is the same used in all the wife/sister episodes by the ruler who has unknowingly taken a wife of a patriarch who the ruler thought was the patriarch's sister: Pharaoh to Abraham (12:18), Abimelech in Gerar to Abraham (20:9), and Abimelech in Gerar to Isaac (26:10).

which so much discussion flows, is "eats." The issue is not *that* she eats but *what* she eats. This too suggests the question I raised in chapter 18 on Mrs. Lot, whether women are given the correct information by the males who are the recipients of information that could protect the women's lives.

The woman in the garden and the man together are the subject of verbs. The first is that they are not ashamed (2:25). This is a verbal construction. The point is to highlight how, despite their naked state, because they are in the garden and have not yet eaten the forbidden fruit, they are ignorant. After the fruit episode, their knowledge of their naked state and their reaction to it are the signs to the Deity that they have eaten from the forbidden tree.

The naked state of the two is the focus the next time they are the subject of a verb together, following the fruit episode, when they both know they are naked (3:7). The first thing they do, after eating of the tree of knowledge, is to "know" they are naked, the marker used earlier to generalize their ignorance, or lack of knowledge, in the garden.

The knowledge leads them to another joint action: they sew together leaves and make loincloths (3:7). The couple's reaction to knowledge leads them to actions. In the next verse they hear the sound of the Deity moving in the garden, leading them to act again together: they hide (3:8). This indicates to the Deity that they have eaten from the tree, for how else would they know they were naked (3:10)?

Hiding is the last action the two do together. Following this, the Deity asks them questions individually and they answer separately. In the process they turn on each other. The man and the woman in the garden take actions together only to hide what they have done from the Deity. The actions they take reveal what they do.

The Woman in the Garden as an Object

This category is complex because it is not clear when the woman in the garden begins, nor is it clear where the man and the woman in the garden are both addressed. If the original human contains the woman in the garden, then she is first the object in a sentence when Elohim creates this entity (1:27). The verb used is *bara'*, the same one used by Elohim to create the heavens and the earth (1:1), sea creatures and birds (1:21), and all the work of creation (2:3). This is not the verb used for other parts of creation or for women bearing children.

What will eventually be the woman appears as an object when the Deity decides that the man needs a "helpmate" (2:18). The Deity determines it is not good for the man to be by himself and so the Deity makes a "fitting helper." The right entity for this task ends up being the woman in the garden. It is not clear when the Deity considers this alternative. First the Deity brings all the animals and birds out for the man to name (2:19). When no "fitting helper" is found in that group, the Deity resorts to fashioning one (2:22). It is not clear that the "fitting helper" is originally a direct reference to the woman. She is fashioned so the man has one, but whether to equate her with the reference in 2:18 is unclear.

Also problematic is what a "fitting helper" means. Von Rad argues that the Hebrew literally means "a helper against him," and one cannot translate "helpmate" with reference to the later creation of woman.[6] He understands the term as referring to an assistant.[7] Speiser notes that it is subject to confusion as the phrase becomes "helpmate."[8] He prefers "an aid fit for him," since the Hebrew complement means "alongside him."[9] Meyers notes that the noun "helper" can mean "an assistant" (subordinate) or "an expert" (superior).[10] She points out that the prepositional phrase, used only here, apparently means "equal to."[11] Her more literal translation is "an equal helper."[12]

The woman in the garden is formed by the Deity in 2:22. The Deity takes a "side beam" from the man while he sleeps and builds it into a woman.[13] The term used for the man's "side" is *tsela'*, which is used primarily in building contexts. This would be the only place where the term could refer to a human "rib." It means "rib" only in the sense of the "rib" of a hill (i.e., ridge or terrace), side chambers, ribs of cedar (i.e., planks and boards), and leaves of a door.[14] This terminology fits this context because the verb used by the Deity to "create" the woman in the garden is *banah*, a verb whose primary meaning is "to build."[15] The creation of the woman in the garden is different from the process used to create the man and the other elements of the world.

In the same verse where the Deity builds the woman, the Deity brings her to the man (2:22). This leads the man to call her "woman," explaining that from man she is taken (2:23). The narrator summarizes that it is because of this that a man leaves his father and mother and clings to his wife/woman (2:24). This appears to be a principle that does not relate directly to this specific woman in the garden but to women in general.

The woman in the garden is next an object in the fruit episode. The serpent initiates conversation with the woman: "he says to her" (3:1). After the woman in the garden answers, the serpent speaks again to the woman.

6. Von Rad, *Genesis*, 82.
7. Ibid.
8. Speiser, *Genesis*, 17.
9. Ibid.
10. Meyers, "Eve," 80–81.
11. Ibid., 81.
12. Ibid.
13. Mary Phil Korsak, "Genesis: A New Look," in Brenner, *Feminist Companion to Genesis*, 48–49.
14. Brown, Driver, and Briggs, *Lexicon*, 854.
15. Ibid., 124.

The woman is singled out as the person with whom the serpent speaks, but his comments that "you" are not going to die and Elohim knows as soon as "you" eat of it "your" eyes will be opened and "you" will be like a divine being knowing good and bad (3:5) are directed to a masculine plural audience.

The reason for the serpent to address the woman and yet refer to a plural audience could be that he is speaking to the theoretical "you," meaning the man and the woman. Or the serpent may be speaking to both of them, though he directs his comments originally to the woman. The woman in the garden gives fruit to her man/husband. Because the man is not the focus of that unit there is no discussion that he too eats of the fruit, though it is included in the text (3:6). In that same verse when she gives the man/husband to eat, he is "with her" (3:6). According to the Hebrew Bible, the woman speaks with the serpent, takes the fruit, eats of the fruit, gives it to her man/husband who is with her, and he eats. There is no break in the sequence. Thus a logical reading of the text is that the man is with the woman when she converses with the serpent and eats when she does, or shortly thereafter.

The next person to make the woman the object in a sentence is the man. When the Deity discovers they have eaten from the tree, the Deity asks the man how he knows he is naked, followed by a somewhat rhetorical question about whether the man has eaten from the tree (3:11). The man's answer is to blame the woman, saying, "The woman you put at my side—she gave me of the tree." The man is explicit that he is referring to the woman in the garden, and most translate "woman" rather than "wife."

The next time the woman is an object is when the Deity addresses her specifically to learn what happened. The Deity says to the woman, "What is this you have done?" (3:13).

The Deity again speaks to the woman after cursing the serpent (3:16). Curse language is not used concerning the woman.[16] The word order is inverted, so the translation should read, "to the woman [the Deity] said" (3:16). In the body of the text revealing what will happen to her personally or to future women because of her, the term "your" refers to a feminine singular object, though no one is named.

If one separates the woman in the garden from Eve, then the list of what the Deity will do to future women is the last time the woman in the garden alone is an object. If the woman in the garden is Eve, then there are more places (discussed in chapter 15 on Eve) where she is an object. Nowhere in the discussion of Eve does she have pain in childbirth or any urges toward her husband/man. Meyers points out that the Hebrew Bible preserves a vocabulary associating the birth process with pain or suffering, but nowhere else in the Bible is the terminology used here associated with the description

16. Bledstein, "Are Women Cursed in Genesis 3.16?" 142.

of childbirth.[17] The woman is made by the Deity. She is taken to the man. He considers her a specially made object for and from him. She is spoken to and she is blamed by the Deity and the man for the fruit episode.

If both the man and the woman are contained in the first human created in 1:28, then Elohim creates them, male and female. The text uses different terminology to refer to the creation of the male/female human and the creation of the woman (2:22). If the woman in the garden is part of this first human, then Elohim blesses them and commands them to be fertile, increase, fill the earth, master it, rule the fish of the sea, birds of the sky, and all things on the earth (1:28). The references to "them" in the plural are the evidence suggesting that this is the case.

The man and the woman together are objects again after eating the fruit: the eyes of both of them are opened, leading them to discover they are naked (3:7). Following this verse they take actions based on their open eyes, leading to the Deity's discovery of what they have done. Once they are discovered they no longer work together.

Relationships of the Woman in the Garden

The woman in the garden has relationships with the man, the serpent, and the Deity. The man may originally include the woman. How that is expressed materially is unclear, but the text states, and the idea is reiterated in 5:2, that the Deity originally creates both male and female.

When the Deity realizes the man needs help, a partner or a companion, the woman in the garden appears as a separate entity. The man is pleased either that he now has a mate or that she is created from him. The man either trusts the woman so much that he ignores the specific command of the Deity that he not eat from the tree, or he is not listening while the woman has her conversation with the serpent. He listens to the woman in the garden. When the Deity realizes they have eaten from the tree, their relationship changes and they never again act together.

The woman in the garden has a relationship with the serpent before she has one with the Deity. The serpent speaks to her before either the man or the Deity is identified as doing so. What the serpent tells her is true: the fruit looks good, is good for eating, and she will not die from eating it. The serpent may be more honest with the woman than the man is since the woman does not appear to know there are two trees in the middle of the garden and only one has been denied them. The woman turns on the serpent as soon as the man turns on her. In the Deity's curse of the serpent, there is nothing positive about their relationship.

17. Meyers also argues for a slightly different understanding of the passage in general (Carol Meyers, "Gender Roles and Genesis 3.16 Revisited," in Brenner, *Feminist Companion to Genesis,* 118–41).

The Deity also has a relationship with the woman in the garden. The Deity builds her, though the motivation is for the man. The Deity does not speak with the woman until after the fruit episode. There the Deity reprimands the woman for eating the fruit, though this connection is never made directly. The woman in the garden never has pain in childbirth.

The question remains as to the relationship between the woman in the garden and Eve. By separating the characters their differences become apparent. Eve's concerns are the same as those of the other women in Genesis, creating children. The woman in the garden never mentions the topic, even after being told this will happen and it will be in pain. If Eve is the woman in the garden, and has children, she does not raise the issue when she bears her children.

Eve never refers to the garden. When she conceives, bears, and names her children, she uses language that differs from the two ways the woman in the garden may have been created. The woman in the garden has no positive relationship with the Deity. She is made by the Deity for the man. No speech between her and the man or the Deity is recorded before her encounter with the serpent. After the fruit episode there are no positive words between them. Such is not the case with Eve. Eve harbors no negative feelings toward the Deity and strives to connect herself to the Deity more than to her husband at the birth of her children. Treating the woman in the garden and Eve as separate characters is useful methodologically, to flesh out how the characters appear in the text and better reflect how the biblical text treats them.

Conclusion

The woman in the garden is difficult to assess because of the inconclusive starting point of her character and the possible ways she evolves. The woman in the garden, separate from Eve, carries out limited actions. Some are simple speech and sight. Her major action is that she eats and gives to her man/husband to eat. Those actions by themselves may not raise interest, but because of the location of the incident it becomes a significant theological issue.

The woman in the garden is never instructed by the Deity what she can and cannot do. The Deity, after building her, has no relationship with her until after discovering they have eaten fruit from the forbidden tree and the man blames her. Her relationship with the Deity ends with the Deity imposing pain in childbirth.

22

Deborah

Deborah, Rebekah's nurse, appears at key points in the story and may be instrumental in determining which of Rebekah's sons inherits. She is important enough to be included in the text. The location of her story may be more important than her actions.

Deborah's Description

Deborah is named and described in only one passage, Genesis 35:8. But there is good reason to consider another passage as obliquely referring to her. The first potential reference to Deborah appears when Rebekah is leaving her family to marry Isaac (24:59). The text notes that they send off their sister and her nurse, along with Abraham's servant and his men. The term used for "nurse" is *meneqet*. The noun used to describe this person comes from the verb *yanaq*, meaning "to suck," leading to the translation "wet nurse."[1]

Nowhere is Deborah depicted nursing a child, and it is highly unlikely that Deborah still nurses Rebekah, nor does Rebekah have children. It is not clear why she accompanies Rebekah. The reason to connect this woman to the Deborah who dies in 35:8 is that she is also labeled Rebekah's "nurse." This title is used infrequently in the biblical text and its use for both of these

---

1. See Brown, Driver, and Briggs, *Lexicon*, 413; for "wet nurse" see Carol Meyers, "Deborah 1," in Meyers, *Women in Scripture*, 65.

women connected with Rebekah strongly supports their identification.[2] The reference to her death is unusual.

To sum up, Deborah is likely referred to twice in the book of Genesis. First she is only described as a nurse; later she has a name and a title. She is known only by her job, thereby being unique in Genesis. The text does not discuss her relationships, and her background is not given.

Deborah as a Subject

Deborah is the subject of one verb: she "dies" (35:8). Deborah is described only by her occupation, but she is never depicted doing her job. Despite this, her death is recorded when Rebekah's is not. Her importance must lie in something other than her abilities as a nurse.

Deborah as an Object

Deborah is an object in only one place, and in that context she is not named. When Rebekah is sent off with Abraham's servant to marry Isaac, her nurse accompanies her (24:59). She is not named, but because she carries the same title later it is likely she is the same character. What her inclusion at this point in the story signifies is that she is with Rebekah from before she is married until Deborah's death. Relevant events in Rebekah's life concern the birth of Rebekah's twin sons and one of them leaving and going elsewhere to find wives. Her presence in Rebekah's life is likely the reason for her inclusion.

Deborah's Relationships

Deborah is one of the female characters in Genesis whose importance is best revealed by her relationships. The key relationship for Deborah is her connection to Rebekah, the only way she is described. Deborah's death may be decisive not because of where she dies but when.

There is no reason for Deborah to be with Jacob since Rebekah is not with them and there is no reference of Deborah joining Jacob on his journey. Immediately following Deborah's death, Elohim changes Jacob's name, for the second time, to Israel (35:10), and Israel is officially given the land that the Deity assigned to Abraham and Isaac (35:12).[3]

2. The other two "nurses" serve Moses (Exod. 2:7) and Joash (2 Kings 11:2 = 2 Chron. 22:11). There is a reference in Isaiah 49:23 but it is to theoretical future "nurses," not specific individuals.

3. Jacob's name is changed in 32:29, but he is not given the land at that time.

The next event in the text after Jacob/Israel receives the Deity's promise is Rachel's death (35:18). When Rachel dies only one person is with her, identified as a midwife, a different title than Deborah's but useful in understanding the birthing process: one woman is with the bearing mother. If so, the midwife is the person who knows what happens at the birth scene.

Deborah is labeled not a midwife but a wet nurse. The text does not suggest who is with Rebekah when she bears her twin boys. Could it be that Deborah is there when Rebekah bears Esau and Jacob? If so, Deborah is the only person who witnesses which child emerges first. Throughout the text the situation of the primogenitor is an issue and here it is particularly important: the Deity conveys to Rebekah that the older shall serve the younger. In this volume I have argued that this is a major concern of Rebekah, ensuring that the Deity's plan comes true. Deborah, Rebekah's nurse, would be the only person who knows which son of Rebekah should receive the promise.

The timing of the event suggests Deborah's importance. Her existence, with a name, is raised for the first time immediately before Jacob/Israel receives the promise, or the Deity gives him the promise as soon as she dies. The appearance of another midwife with a mother—this time Rachel—in labor, serving as a witness to the naming process, occurs as soon as Jacob receives the promise. The timing of these issues may not demand they be read in light of each other, but they are suggestive.

Conclusion

Deborah is the only female in Genesis defined by her occupation (wet nurse), though she is never the subject of any verbs related to that profession. She is a subject only when she dies. The placement of her death at a transitional point in the family's story highlights her role as a witness to the Deity's promise.

23

Mrs. Potiphar

Mrs. Potiphar's primary identification is as a wife, but not a good one. Her husband is never named in the verses where she appears. She is the subject of verbs but they cluster around a similar action. Her role in the text, especially compared to Joseph, is unusual in Genesis.

Mrs. Potiphar's Description

Mrs. Potiphar is first described after Joseph has been living in the house of an Egyptian, Potiphar, courtier of Pharaoh and his chief steward (39:1, 7). The Deity is with Joseph, who is successful (39:2), and his Egyptian master puts him in charge of his household (39:5). The last thing the narrator notes before introducing Mrs. Potiphar is that Joseph is in charge of everything, and the text includes reference to his looks. Joseph is "nice of appearance and figure" (39:6), described with the same terminology as his mother, Rachel (29:17).

Mrs. Potiphar's introduction is sudden and may be connected to Joseph's appearance. After some time, his master's wife casts her eyes upon Joseph, asking him to lie with her (30:7). The master's name is not used, though it appears at the beginning of the chapter (39:1). When Joseph responds to his master's wife (39:8) by noting that his master has withheld nothing from Joseph except her, he also refers to her as a wife (39:9). She is labeled a wife when Joseph's master hears the story she tells him (39:19).

Mrs. Potiphar is described only as a wife. The episode takes place in Egypt and her husband is an Egyptian, yet she is never so labeled. Mrs. Potiphar's physical appearance is never described, in contrast to Joseph. There is no evidence she has children.

Mrs. Potiphar as a Subject

Mrs. Potiphar is active for a woman in Genesis who appears only in one chapter. She is the subject of many verbs, and they are unusual ones for a female.

When Mrs. Potiphar is first introduced in the text she is the subject of two verbs. The first is "lifts up her eyes at Joseph" (39:7). Speiser points out that the sense of the Hebrew text is that she "fixed her eye on" Joseph.[1] Not only does the sense of the story reaffirm that understanding of the phrase, but Speiser also shows how an Akkadian parallel supports it: the identical idiom is used to describe Ishtar's designs on Gilgamesh.[2] Since the text has just described Joseph as attractive, it is not surprising that an idiom based on sight would be appropriate here.

After she "eyes" Joseph, she speaks to him (39:7). Many women "say" things in Genesis, but her words are unusual since she says, "Lie with me" (39:7). She too employs the term *shakab*, but she uses the preposition *'im*, "with," indicating that she would like the encounter to be mutual.

Mrs. Potiphar again is the subject of "says" after she grabs Joseph and he runs away, leaving his coat in her hand. Her speaking is not problematic but what she says is: "Look, he brought to us a Hebrew man to play with us! He came to me to lie with me and I called out in a big voice" (39:14). Mrs. Potiphar blames her husband for bringing a man, a Hebrew, into her house. She plays up her role as the almost raped woman and the woman whose husband has imposed this menace on her. The other issue is fairly obvious: she claims attempted rape. In this case the woman is in the position of power and the man is in the subservient role and has no one to protect him.

She is again the subject of a verb, after Joseph refuses her initial request, when she "speaks" to Joseph day after day (39:10). The verb is *dabar*, not an unusual verb, for women or men. She speaks to Joseph daily about lying with her.

Mrs. Potiphar is the subject of this verb when she speaks with her husband (39:17) after she grabs Joseph and he flees without his coat (39:12). She tells her husband the same story, which in this telling is that the Hebrew slave he brought into their house came to her daily (39:17). The more times the story

1. Speiser, *Genesis*, 303.
2. Gilgamesh, Tablet VI, line 6; see Speiser, *Genesis*, 303.

is told the more modifications there are to it as Potiphar's wife pitches the story to her audience.

Thus far Mrs. Potiphar's actions are primarily speech, but that changes when she grabs hold of Joseph by his garment and says, "Lie with me" (39:12). This gesture is forthright and physical, and not an action carried out by any other woman in Genesis. Joseph has issues with his clothing, having received a special coat from his father (37:3), which his brothers stripped off him (37:23) to use as proof that he was killed by wild beasts (37:31–34)—and now this. Though she is an independent character carrying out actions, she is working within the paradigm already established by the Joseph story.

Mrs. Potiphar "sees" that he left the garment in her hand (39:14). This verse and the images that flow from it play with images of sight. Mrs. Potiphar is drawn to Joseph because of his "looks," she gives him the "eye," and she "sees" what is left. What others "see" by her having his coat in her hand will further the story, highlighting how following one's eyes is not always correct.

After Joseph flees, Mrs. Potiphar "calls out" to her servants (39:14). Many female characters in Genesis use this verb since it is the same used for naming a child, but in this context it carries the connotation of "crying out," because she does it to her servants. Her comment that follows is that her husband brought in a Hebrew who tried to lay with her.

Mrs. Potiphar continues recounting her side of the situation: she claims that when he (Joseph) hears her screaming at the top of her voice, he leaves his garment with her and flees (39:15). Mrs. Potiphar's main action is to use her voice, in different ways, highlighting how important what someone says can be, especially when status is concerned.

The final verb for which Mrs. Potiphar is the subject is associated with speaking. The Hebrew construction is that Mrs. Potiphar claims, "I raised my voice and called out" (39:18).

Mrs. Potiphar is the subject of a number of verbs, but most are associated with speaking and conveying ideas, regardless of whether they are true. Mrs. Potiphar says, speaks, cries out, and raises her voice. The only other actions she carries out are to "raise her eyes" and "grab." This is a bit of role reversal for the book of Genesis and women in general. Most women in Genesis have had little to no role in choosing their sexual partners. Most of the women who carry out actions to gain sexual access to a man do so for procreative purposes. Here is a rare case where the man is in the servile category, the woman makes advances, and what she says is more powerful than the man's actions.[3]

---

3. Joseph's looks are described like his mother's. Mrs. Potiphar uses male language to set up a sexual encounter that he rejects. Joseph never "takes" a woman; Pharaoh "takes" her for him. Joseph expresses few male actions, especially regarding sexual encounters. The text hints that Joseph's sexual interests lie elsewhere.

Mrs. Potiphar as an Object

Mrs. Potiphar is not the object of many verbs or phrases, and some of the places where she appears as an object she is still in control of the situation. Mrs. Potiphar tells Joseph, "Lie with me" (39:7). Technically she is the object of that preposition, but it is in the context of her issuing a command to Joseph, and she does not use the particle of entreaty, *na'*.

Joseph's answer to Mrs. Potiphar places her as the object in the phrase "wife of his master" (39:8), and yet this does not place him in a position of power and objectify her, but the opposite. Joseph is in a delicate situation because she is the wife of Joseph's owner. The situation in the next verse is similar when Joseph notes that his master has withheld nothing from him, except her, because she is his wife (39:9). Mrs. Potiphar is also "his wife" when "his [Joseph's] master" hears the story his wife tells him (39:19).

As the initial scenario continues, Joseph does not yield to "her" requests to lie beside "her" to be with "her" (39:10). After she grabs his coat, the garment remains with "her" (39:16). In all these cases she is technically an object, but the story line makes it difficult to view her as a defenseless one.

In a few cases Mrs. Potiphar places herself as an object. When she recounts her story to the servants about what happened, she notes that he came to lie with "me" (39:14) and he left his garment with "me" (39:15). She even argues that he came to play with "me" when explaining the story to her husband (39:17). When the text summarizes what Potiphar's wife tells him, she recounts what his slave did to "me" (39:19). Here too, technically, she is the object in the sentence, but one with power.

Mrs. Potiphar appears as an object a number of times but in none is she objectified. In many of the situations she is the subject of verbs since she is the one who is telling the story.

Mrs. Potiphar's Relationships

Mrs. Potiphar is depicted primarily in relationships, though few are positive. She is first and primarily identified as a wife. Her relationship with her husband is not idyllic. She seeks to have a sexual liaison with her handsome servant. She tries repeatedly. She is regularly rejected.

Mrs. Potiphar has other servants. It is unclear how attractive they are, but she does turn to them after Joseph runs away and her husband is not home. The only people with whom she is in contact are her servants and her husband, who does not appear to be home often nor does he seem to care much about his household after putting it all in Joseph's charge (39:6).

Mrs. Potiphar's relationship with Potiphar is not impressive. She turns to a servant for sexual encounters, the only woman in Genesis to seek out sexual encounters for anything other than procreation. She complains to the servants and to her husband about how her husband brings this Hebrew into their house. Joseph and Potiphar have a better relationship than Potiphar and his wife because Potiphar trusts Joseph with everything and Joseph couches his reason for not lying with Mrs. Potiphar in terms of his relationship with Potiphar.

Mrs. Potiphar appears as an ancient depiction of a modern, lonely, bored, wealthy housewife. Her relationships are mostly with servants. Her limited relationship with her husband consists of complaining about him for bringing Joseph into the house.

Conclusion

Mrs. Potiphar is only a wife, and, if it were up to her, she would be the only unfaithful one in Genesis. She is never named a mother nor is any child ever ascribed to her. She is the subject of many verbs, yet most concern various ways of speaking. She appears as an object, and yet in none of those instances is she objectified; rather, she is in control. Role reversal appears to be at play, with the handsome Joseph the object of Mrs. Potiphar's attention.

Mrs. Potiphar is the cause of Joseph going to jail, and his imprisonment has significant consequences: he takes charge of Egypt, saves his family, and brings the Israelites to Egypt. This story ignores key elements about her. She lives in Egypt and has an Egyptian husband, but is not so labeled, similar to Asenath, who becomes Joseph's wife. Mrs. Potiphar is in charge, not Joseph, though Joseph is in charge of Potiphar's house and is about to be in charge of all of Egypt.

24

Review of Part 4

Women Who Do Not Bear

T he women who do not bear children appear in very different contexts, making synthesis difficult.

Descriptions of Women Who Do Not Bear

There are no descriptions common to all three women. The woman in the garden and Mrs. Potiphar are identified by the same term: "wife/woman." The difference is that translators refer to the woman in the garden with both senses of the term, while Mrs. Potiphar is only a wife. The fluidity of translation reveals the difficulty in labeling the relationship between the man and woman.

Women Who Do Not Bear as Subjects

There are no common verbs for these women, though some verbs that are common to other women in Genesis do not occur with these women as subjects, and there are correlations between the woman in the garden and Mrs. Potiphar. None of these women bears children. The woman least likely to bear, Deborah, does not appear in connection with any man, yet she is the most identified with childbearing through her occupation. Her presence in the text may concern what she witnesses: the birth of Esau and Jacob.

The woman in the garden and Mrs. Potiphar are the subject of similar verbs. Both "speak." Both "see" something appealing to them, though different terminology is used. Both act on what they see by taking it: Mrs. Potiphar grabs Joseph's coat, and the woman in the garden takes fruit.

Women Who Do Not Bear as Objects

Primarily because of the limited data about Deborah, all three do not overlap in any particular way, and most connections concern the woman in the garden and Mrs. Potiphar. The main connection between the latter two is that both are designated wives of their husbands.

Relationships of Women Who Do Not Bear

Deborah does not appear with anyone other than Rebekah. One assumes a positive relationship since Rebekah takes Deborah with her. How or if Deborah connects to Jacob is not clear.

Mrs. Potiphar and the woman in the garden have similarities regarding their relationships with their men/husbands. Neither one's relationship is ideal. The man blames the woman in the garden as soon as the Deity finds out that they ate the forbidden fruit, and they are never portrayed together in an amicable way. Mrs. Potiphar seeks a sexual relationship with her servant and blames her husband for bringing him into the house. The two women agree that neither is thrilled with their spouse and their spouse's treatment of them.

Conclusion

None of these women bears children, so their role lies elsewhere. Deborah is connected to the promise because she knows who should receive the promise.

It is not clear what the role of the woman in the garden is when she is not connected to Eve. Her role leads to the man being sent from the garden, though neither the woman nor Eve is kicked out. The woman is an example of what happens when men do not convey the Deity's rules to women.

Mrs. Potiphar does not recount the full story, but her actions result in placing Joseph so he can bring the Israelites to Egypt.

Conclusions

In these final pages I offer a summary of what can be said about the women in Genesis, what the process of "verbing the character" does and does not do, and where to go from here.

As the summaries of each section reveal, there are no consistent descriptions of all women in any category considered. The women do not cluster as subjects of one verb or verb type, nor as objects. Despite this, a number of consistencies emerge.

The main role and function of women in Genesis concern women's capacity to bear children. Only four women do not bear: the woman in the garden; Deborah, Rebekah's nurse; Dinah; and Mrs. Potiphar. If the woman in the garden is Eve, of course she bears. Because the woman in the garden eats the fruit, women bear children in pain. Deborah, while she does not bear, is probably in the text because she observes Esau and Jacob's births. Dinah does not bear, but that may be intended by her brothers, and thus her role as a nonmother reinforces the importance of women bearing.

There are few studies of how the women in Genesis function as a unified group. This study shows that with the exception of Mrs. Lot and Mrs. Potiphar, the role women play in Genesis as wives is almost insignificant.

The primary role of women in other biblical books is not as mother. Women do not play a major role in many biblical books, but in several books some women are prominent. In Exodus women play a number of different roles, from midwives to Miriam, who does not have children but is a prophet. In Judges prominent women abound but few are mothers. The same case can be made for the books of Samuel, where few women appear as mothers, though many women are active.

The women serve as more than just people who bear—who the mother is controls the destiny of the children. For some of the women, all we have is their background: Hagar, Esau's wives, Mrs. Judah, Dinah, Asenath, and Mrs. Potiphar. There is little to no background for women like Eve, Adah, Zillah, Sarah, Zilpah, Bilhah, and Tamar. For many women, the lack of background protects them or does not disqualify either them or their children. In other cases the women take action that controls their ability to have children, and therefore the destiny of their children. Thus one cannot simply label the primary role of the female characters as mothers.

Some issues cannot be resolved only with this study. Who ultimately is considered as inheriting is a question to which this study contributes but cannot answer conclusively. How clear-cut is the category of matriarchs? If there is such a category as matriarchs, what elements define it? Also at issue is what elements of a mother are most meaningful for the biblical text in terms of how her child will be accepted within the divine promise.

Despite these lingering questions, some answers emerge. Who a male's mother is clearly matters in the biblical text. The Deity plays an active role in helping the matriarchs become mothers of those who inherit the promise. The actions of some women reveal their loyalty to the Israelite Deity or to the family of the promise. The constant refrain in the cases of women in Genesis, except Mrs. Lot and Mrs. Potiphar, is that some characteristic of the female is significant in her becoming a mother and affects her male child's future.

The idea that women's primary role in Genesis is mother is not a positive or negative comment. I have offered little discussion here concerning what makes a good mother; that evaluation is delicate. The mothers in Genesis are rarely evaluated by what they do for their children, since for most there are few to no depictions of the woman acting as a mother. The focus in Genesis is whether they can bear, who provides their fertility, and what circumstances allow them to become pregnant. The physical act of bearing, not motherhood, is the issue.

The method used in this study, verbing the character, reveals some of the richness and complexity of the different situations presented for each female character. The main role and function can be isolated to something as simple as: the primary purpose of women in Genesis is to bear children. The variety of descriptions, verbs, and objects where these characters appear reveals the complex setting the narrator paints. Even the matriarchs, the most compact group, show fissures where they are not all treated the same, in life or in death.

One problem with the method here is that the focus is only on one group of characters: females. This focus places a spotlight on one group, who may or may not be the main character or point of the story. My goal has been to focus on a group not usually considered thoroughly to ascertain what highlighting them reveals. The other side of the process is that in one study one cannot fully flesh out the complete situation of any character because the same is not done for the male characters with whom they interact. As a by-product,

I have addressed aspects of some male characters, such as Abraham, Lot, Laban, Isaac, and Jacob. Those characters are considered only as they affect the female characters, the focus here.

What does this study contribute to the larger question of the place of women in the Hebrew Bible? What questions arise from this contribution and how does one proceed to address them? It is clear we are only beginning to understand the role of women in the text of the Hebrew Bible in general and in Genesis in particular. Focusing on each character separately reveals how connected the women are to one another and to the other characters. Many of the male characters must now be evaluated in light of how they are described by the text, where they are the subject of verbs, and how they appear as objects as well as how they interact with the females in their stories. Such an approach is necessary to better understand and compare the male characters to the female characters concerning matters ranging from how the patriarchs relate to the Israelite Deity to how Joseph is depicted. What might be truly beneficial for scholars in general is to evaluate all the characters as thoroughly as these female characters have been treated. Such a commentary could be feminist in approach but would provide a more evenhanded analysis of who the biblical characters are and what issues the text raises as significant. It would reveal the male characters to be more multidimensional than traditional presentations.

The female characters are complex, and while there is not much text devoted to each, often the information provided is significant to understand the character and the larger story. One goal of this study is to reveal how minor details contribute to and are necessary to understand how Genesis fits together. The intention is to ask new questions about the characters based on a fuller evaluation of the data. This is not the last word on the subject, but I hope other scholars will use this information and method as another analytical tool.

Contrary to initial assumptions, the following points are now clear. Eve, first mother and first woman to lose a child, does not differ from other women in Genesis. Sarah is chosen by the Deity and frees Hagar. Hagar is brave and is allowed to play a major role in her son's life. Lot does not provide his wife the instructions to protect herself; his daughters try to repopulate the world. Rebekah protects her sons and the Deity's promise. Leah learns to be happy with what she has and honors the Deity. Rachel is proof that being loved for one's looks is fraught with problems. Everyone brings their own issues into Dinah's rape, neglecting her. And Tamar goes to extremes to do the right thing when Judah does not. The book of Genesis is filled with impressive women.

Bibliography

Alter, Robert. *Genesis: Translation and Commentary*. New York: Norton, 1996.

Bach, Alice, ed. *Women in the Hebrew Bible: A Reader*. New York: Routledge, 1999.

Bal, Mieke. *Death and Dissymmetry: The Politics of Coherence in the Book of Judges*. Chicago: University of Chicago Press, 1988.

Bar-Efrat, Shimon. *Narrative Art in the Bible*. Journal for the Study of the Old Testament Supplement 70. Sheffield: Almond, 1989.

Bechtel, Lyn M. "Dinah." In *Women in Scripture: A Dictionary of Named and Unnamed Women in the Hebrew Bible, the Apocryphal/Deuterocanonical Books, and the New Testament*, edited by Carol Meyers, 69–70. Boston: Houghton Mifflin, 2000.

Beck, Astrid Billes. "Rachel." In *Anchor Bible Dictionary*, edited by D. N. Freedman, 5:605–8. New York: Doubleday, 1992.

Bellis, Alice Ogden. *Helpmates, Harlots, and Heroes: Women's Stories in the Hebrew Bible*. Louisville: Westminster John Knox, 1994.

Berlin, Adele. "Abigail 1." In *Women in Scripture: A Dictionary of Named and Unnamed Women in the Hebrew Bible, the Apocryphal/Deuterocanonical Books, and the New Testament*, edited by Carol Meyers, 43. Boston: Houghton Mifflin, 2000.

Bird, Phyllis. "'Male and Female He Created Them': Genesis 1:27b in the Context of the Priestly Account of Creation." *Harvard Theological Review* 74 (1981): 129–59.

Bledstein, Adrien Janis. "Are Women Cursed in Genesis 3.16?" In *A Feminist Companion to Genesis*, edited by Athalya Brenner, 142–45. The Feminist Companion to the Bible 1st ser., 2. Sheffield: Sheffield Academic Press, 1993.

———. "Binder, Trickster, Heel and Hairy-Man: Rereading Genesis 27 as a Trickster Tale Told by a Woman." In *A Feminist Companion to Genesis*, edited by Athalya Brenner, 282–95. The Feminist Companion to the Bible 1st ser., 2. Sheffield: Sheffield Academic Press, 1993.

Boling, Robert G. *Judges: Introduction, Translation, and Commentary*. Anchor Bible. Garden City, NY: Doubleday, 1975.

Bottéro, Jean. "The Code of Hammurabi." In *Mesopotamia: Writing, Reasoning, and the Gods*, translated by Zainab Bahrani and Marc Van De Mieroop, 156–84. Chicago: University of Chicago Press, 1992.

Brenner, Athalya. *The Israelite Woman: Social Role and Literary Type in Biblical Narrative*. Biblical Seminar 2. Sheffield: JSOT Press, 1985.

Briggs, Sheila. "Hagar in the New Testament." In *Women in Scripture: A Dictionary of Named and Unnamed Women in the Hebrew Bible, the Apocryphal/Deutero-canonical Books, and the New Testament*, edited by Carol Meyers, 88. Boston: Houghton Mifflin, 2000.

Brown, Francis, S. R. Driver, and Charles A. Briggs. *The Brown-Driver-Briggs Hebrew and English Lexicon*. Repr. Peabody, MA: Hendrickson, 2000.

Brueggemann, Walter. *Genesis*. Interpretation: A Bible Commentary for Teaching and Preaching. Atlanta: John Knox, 1982.

Callender, Dexter E. *Adam in Myth and History: Ancient Israelite Perspectives on the Primal Human*. Harvard Semitic Studies 48. Winona Lake, IN: Eisenbrauns, 2000.

Collins, Adela Yarbro, ed. *Feminist Perspectives on Biblical Scholarship*. Atlanta: Scholars Press, 1985.

Cotter, David W. *Genesis*. Berit Olam. Collegeville, MN: Liturgical Press, 2003.

Darr, Katheryn Pfisterer. *Far More Precious than Jewels: Perspectives on Biblical Women*. Gender and the Biblical Tradition 1. Louisville: Westminster John Knox, 1991.

Davison, Lisa W. "Leah." In *Eerdmans Dictionary of the Bible*, edited by David Noel Freedman, 797. Grand Rapids: Eerdmans, 2000.

Day, Peggy L. "Concubine." In *Eerdmans Dictionary of the Bible*, edited by David Noel Freedman, 273. Grand Rapids: Eerdmans, 2000.

Diakonoff, I. M. "Slave Labour vs. Non-Slave Labour: The Problem of Definition." In *Labor in the Ancient Near East*, edited by Marvin A. Powell, 1–3. American Oriental Series 68. New Haven: American Oriental Society, 1987.

Dijk-Hemmes, Fokkelien van. "Sarai's Exile: A Gender-Motivated Reading of Genesis 12.10–13.2." In *A Feminist Companion to Genesis*, edited by Athalya Brenner, 222–34. The Feminist Companion to the Bible 1st ser., 2. Sheffield: Sheffield Academic Press, 1993.

Douglas, Susan J., and Meredith W. Michaels. *The Mommy Myth: The Idealization of Motherhood and How It Has Undermined All Women*. New York: Free Press, 2004.

Edwards, Douglas R. "Dress and Ornamentation." In *Anchor Bible Dictionary*, edited by D. N. Freedman, 2:232–38. New York: Doubleday, 1992.

Eichler, Barry L. "Nuzi and the Bible: A Retrospective." In *DUMU-E2-DUB-BA-A: Studies in Honor of Ake W. Sjoberg*, edited by Erle Leichty, 107–20. Occasional Publications of the Samuel Noah Kramer Fund 11. Philadelphia: University Museum, 1989.

221

Exum, J. Cheryl. "Who's Afraid of 'The Endangered Ancestress'?" In *Women in the Hebrew Bible: A Reader*, edited by Alice Bach, 141–56. New York: Routledge, 1999.

Fewell, Dana Nolan, and David M. Gunn. *Gender, Power, and Promise: The Subject of the Bible's First Story*. Nashville: Abingdon, 1993.

Finlay, Timothy D. *The Birth Report Genre in the Hebrew Bible*. Forschungen zum Alten Testament 2/12. Tübingen: Mohr Siebeck, 2005.

Fox, Everett. "Stalking the Younger Brother: Some Models for Understanding a Biblical Motif." *Journal for the Study of the Old Testament* 60 (1993): 45–68.

Freedman, D. N., ed. *Anchor Bible Dictionary*. 6 vols. New York: Doubleday, 1992.

Freedman, David Noel, ed. *Eerdmans Dictionary of the Bible*. Grand Rapids: Eerdmans, 2000.

Frymer-Kensky, Tikva. "Bilhah." In *Women in Scripture: A Dictionary of Named and Unnamed Women in the Hebrew Bible, the Apocryphal/Deuterocanonical Books, and the New Testament*, edited by Carol Meyers, 62. Boston: Houghton Mifflin, 2000.

———. "Deborah 2." In *Women in Scripture: A Dictionary of Named and Unnamed Women in the Hebrew Bible, the Apocryphal/Deuterocanonical Books, and the New Testament*, edited by Carol Meyers, 66–67. Boston: Houghton Mifflin, 2000.

———. "Leah." In *Women in Scripture: A Dictionary of Named and Unnamed Women in the Hebrew Bible, the Apocryphal/Deuterocanonical Books, and the New Testament*, edited by Carol Meyers, 109. Boston: Houghton Mifflin, 2000.

———. "Rachel." In *Women in Scripture: A Dictionary of Named and Unnamed Women in the Hebrew Bible, the Apocryphal/Deuterocanonical Books, and the New Testament*, edited by Carol Meyers, 138–40. Boston: Houghton Mifflin, 2000.

———. *Reading the Women of the Bible*. New York: Schocken, 2002.

———. "Tamar 1." In *Women in Scripture: A Dictionary of Named and Unnamed Women in the Hebrew Bible, the Apocryphal/Deuterocanonical Books, and the New Testament*, edited by Carol Meyers, 162. Boston: Houghton Mifflin, 2000.

Fuchs, Esther. "'For I Have the Way of Women': Deception, Gender, and Ideology in Biblical Narrative." In *Reasoning with the Foxes: Female Wit in a World of Male Power*, edited by J. Cheryl Exum and Johanna W. H. Bos, 68–83. Semeia 42. Atlanta: Society of Biblical Literature, 1988.

———. "The Literary Characterization of Mothers and Sexual Politics in the Hebrew Bible." In *Feminist Perspectives on Biblical Scholarship*, edited by Adela Yarbro Collins, 117–36. Atlanta: Scholars Press, 1985.

Greengus, Samuel. "Legal and Social Institutions of Ancient Mesopotamia." In *Civilizations of the Ancient Near East*, edited by Jack M. Sasson, 1:469–84. New York: Charles Scribner's Sons, 1995.

Greenspahn, Frederick E. *When Brothers Dwell Together: The Preeminence of Younger Siblings in the Hebrew Bible*. New York: Oxford University Press, 1994.

Hamilton, Victor P. "Marriage (OT and ANE)." In *Anchor Bible Dictionary*, edited by D. N. Freedman, 4:559–69. New York: Doubleday, 1992.

Harrill, J. Albert. "Slave." In *Eerdmans Dictionary of the Bible*, edited by David Noel Freedman, 1232. Grand Rapids: Eerdmans, 2000.

Harrisville, Roy A. "Biblical Criticism." In *Eerdmans Dictionary of the Bible*, edited by David Noel Freedman, 183–86. Grand Rapids: Eerdmans, 2000.

Heard, R. Christopher. *Dynamics of Diselection: Ambiguity in Genesis 12–36 and Ethnic Boundaries in Post-Exilic Judah*. Semeia Studies. Atlanta: Society of Biblical Literature, 2001.

Hendel, Ronald S. "Genesis, Book of." In *Anchor Bible Dictionary*, edited by D. N. Freedman, 2:933–41. New York: Doubleday, 1992.

Hollyday, Joyce. *Clothed with the Sun: Biblical Women, Social Justice, and Us*. Louisville: Westminster John Knox, 1994.

Jacob, Irene, and Walter Jacob. "Flora." In *Anchor Bible Dictionary*, edited by D. N. Freedman, 2:803–17. New York: Doubleday, 1992.

Jeansonne, Sharon Pace. *The Women of Genesis: From Sarah to Potiphar's Wife*. Minneapolis: Fortress, 1990.

Jobling, David. *1 Samuel*. Berit Olam. Collegeville, MN: Liturgical Press, 1998.

Jonge, Marinus de. "Patriarchs, Testaments of the Twelve." In *Anchor Bible Dictionary*, edited by D. N. Freedman, 5:181–86. New York: Doubleday, 1992.

Korsak, Mary Phil. "Genesis: A New Look." In *A Feminist Companion to Genesis*, edited by Athalya Brenner, 39–52. The Feminist Companion to the Bible 1st ser., 2. Sheffield: Sheffield Academic Press, 1993.

Kramer, Phyllis Silverman. "The Dismissal of Hagar in Five Art Works of the Sixteenth and Seventeenth Centuries." In *Genesis*, edited by Athalya Brenner, 195–216. The Feminist Companion to the Bible 2nd ser., 1. Sheffield: Sheffield Academic Press, 1998.

Lapsley, J. E. "The Voice of Rachel: Resistance and Polyphony in Genesis 31.14–35." In *Genesis*, edited by Athalya Brenner, 233–48. The Feminist Companion to the Bible 2nd ser., 1. Sheffield: Sheffield Academic Press, 1998.

Leeb, Carolyn S. *Away from the Father's House: The Social Location of na'ar and na'arah in Ancient Israel*. Journal for the Study of the Old Testament Supplement 301. Sheffield: Sheffield Academic Press, 2000.

Levenson, Jon D. "Genesis." In *The Jewish Study Bible*, edited by Adele Berlin and Marc Zvi Brettler, 8–101. New York: Oxford University Press, 2004.

Levenson, Jon D., and Baruch Halpern. "The Political Import of David's Marriages." *Journal of Biblical Literature* 99 (1980): 507–18.

Mariottini, Claude F. "Laban." In *Anchor Bible Dictionary*, edited by D. N. Freedman, 4:113–14. New York: Doubleday, 1992.

Meyers, Carol. "Adah 1." In *Women in Scripture: A Dictionary of Named and Unnamed Women in the Hebrew Bible, the Apocryphal/Deuterocanonical Books, and the New Testament*, edited by Carol Meyers, 46. Boston: Houghton Mifflin, 2000.

———. "Deborah 1." In *Women in Scripture: A Dictionary of Named and Unnamed Women in the Hebrew Bible, the Apocryphal/Deuterocanonical Books, and the New Testament*, edited by Carol Meyers, 65–66. Boston: Houghton Mifflin, 2000.

———. "Eve." In *Women in Scripture: A Dictionary of Named and Unnamed Women in the Hebrew Bible, the Apocryphal/Deuterocanonical Books, and the New Testament*, edited by Carol Meyers, 79–80. Boston: Houghton Mifflin, 2000.

———. "Gender Roles and Genesis 3.16 Revisited." In *A Feminist Companion to Genesis*, edited by Athalya Brenner, 118–41. The Feminist Companion to the Bible 1st ser., 2. Sheffield: Sheffield Academic Press, 1993.

———. "Gen 12:16; 20:14; 24:35; 30:43; 32:5; Exod 11:5; 1 Sam 25:41; 2 Kgs 5:26; Esth 7:4: Female (and Male) Slaves." In *Women in Scripture: A Dictionary of Named and Unnamed Women in the Hebrew Bible, the Apocryphal/Deuterocanonical Books, and the New Testament*, edited by Carol Meyers, 178–79. Boston: Houghton Mifflin, 2000.

———. "Naamah 1." In *Women in Scripture: A Dictionary of Named and Unnamed Women in the Hebrew Bible, the Apocryphal/Deuterocanonical Books, and the New Testament*, edited by Carol Meyers, 129. Boston: Houghton Mifflin, 2000.

———. "Rebekah." In *Women in Scripture: A Dictionary of Named and Unnamed Women in the Hebrew Bible, the Apocryphal/Deuterocanonical Books, and the New Testament*, edited by Carol Meyers, 143–44. Boston: Houghton Mifflin, 2000.

———, ed. *Women in Scripture: A Dictionary of Named and Unnamed Women in the Hebrew Bible, the Apocryphal/Deuterocanonical Books, and the New Testament*. Boston: Houghton Mifflin, 2000.

———. "Zillah." In *Women in Scripture: A Dictionary of Named and Unnamed Women in the Hebrew Bible, the Apocryphal/Deuterocanonical Books, and the New Testament*, edited by Carol Meyers, 169. Boston: Houghton Mifflin, 2000.

Millard, A. R., and D. J. Wiseman, eds. *Essays on the Patriarchal Narratives*. Winona Lake, IN: Eisenbrauns, 1980.

Nash, Kathleen S. "Widow." In *Eerdmans Dictionary of the Bible*, edited by David Noel Freedman, 1377. Grand Rapids: Eerdmans, 2000.

Niditch, Susan. "Genesis." In *The Women's Bible Commentary*, edited by Carol A. Newsom and Sharon H. Ringe, 10–25. Rev. ed. Louisville: Westminster John Knox, 1998.

Rad, Gerhard von. *Genesis: A Commentary*. Rev. ed. Old Testament Library. Philadelphia: Westminster, 1972.

Roth, Martha T. *Law Collections from Mesopotamia and Asia Minor*. Society of Biblical Literature Writings from the Ancient World 6. Atlanta: Scholars Press, 1995.

Sakenfeld, Katharine Doob. *Just Wives? Stories of Power and Survival in the Old Testament and Today*. Louisville: Westminster John Knox, 2003.

Sanders, E. P. "Patriarchs, Testaments of the Three." In *Anchor Bible Dictionary*, edited by D. N. Freedman, 5:180–81. New York: Doubleday, 1992.

Schmitt, John J. "Virgin." In *Anchor Bible Dictionary*, edited by D. N. Freedman, 6:853–54. New York: Doubleday, 1992.

Schneider, Tammi J. *Judges*. Berit Olam. Collegeville, MN: Liturgical Press, 2000.

———. *Sarah: Mother of Nations*. New York: Continuum, 2004.

Scholz, Susanne, *Rape Plots: A Feminist Cultural Study of Genesis 34*. Studies in Biblical Literature 13. New York: P. Lang, 2001.

Solvang, Elna K. *A Woman's Place Is in the House: Royal Women of Judah and Their Involvement in the House of David.* Journal for the Study of the Old Testament Supplement 349. London: Sheffield Academic Press, 2003.

Speiser, E. A. *Genesis: A New Translation with Introduction and Commentary.* 3rd ed. Anchor Bible. Garden City, NY: Doubleday, 1985.

Steinberg, Naomi A. *Kinship and Marriage in Genesis: A Household Economics Perspective.* Minneapolis: Fortress, 1993.

———. "Zilpah." In *Women in Scripture: A Dictionary of Named and Unnamed Women in the Hebrew Bible, the Apocryphal/Deuterocanonical Books, and the New Testament,* edited by Carol Meyers, 170. Boston: Houghton Mifflin, 2000.

Stone, Ken. "Daughters of Lot." In *Women in Scripture: A Dictionary of Named and Unnamed Women in the Hebrew Bible, the Apocryphal/Deuterocanonical Books, and the New Testament,* edited by Carol Meyers, 179. Boston: Houghton Mifflin, 2000.

Thomas, Matthew A. *These Are the Generations: Identity, Promise, and the Toledot Formula.* Ann Arbor, MI: University Microfilms, 2006.

Thompson, Thomas L. *The Historicity of the Patriarchal Narratives: The Quest for the Historical Abraham.* Harrisburg, PA: Trinity Press International, 2002.

Trible, Phyllis. "Genesis 22: The Sacrifice of Sarah." In *Women in the Hebrew Bible: A Reader,* edited by Alice Bach, 271–92. New York: Routledge, 1999.

———. *Texts of Terror: Literary-Feminist Readings of Biblical Narratives.* Overtures to Biblical Theology. Philadelphia: Fortress, 1984.

Vancil, Jack W. "Sheep/Shepherd." In *Anchor Bible Dictionary,* edited by D. N. Freedman, 5:1189. New York: Doubleday, 1992.

Waltke, Bruce K., and M. O'Connor. *An Introduction to Biblical Hebrew Syntax.* Winona Lake, IN: Eisenbrauns, 1990.

Wolf, Naomi. *The Beauty Myth: How Images of Beauty Are Used Against Women.* New York: W. Morrow, 1991.

Yee, Gale A. "Leah." In *Anchor Bible Dictionary,* edited by D. N. Freedman, 4:268. New York: Doubleday, 1992.

Yoffee, Norman. "The Economy of Ancient Western Asia." In *Civilizations of the Ancient Near East,* edited by Jack M. Sasson, 3:1395–96. New York: Charles Scribner's Sons, 1995.

Index of Biblical References

Exodus

Leviticus

Numbers

Deuteronomy

Judges

Ruth

Index of Subjects